AAT

Level 3

Diploma in Accounting

Management Accounting Techniques

Course Book

For assessments from
September 2022

First edition 2021

ISBN 9781 5097 4388 9
ISBN (for internal use only) 9781 5097 4322 3
eISBN 9781 5097 4275 2

British Library Cataloguing-in-Publication Data
A catalogue record for this book is available from the British Library

Published by

BPP Learning Media Ltd
BPP House, Aldine Place
142-144 Uxbridge Road
London W12 8AA

www.bpp.com/learningmedia

Printed in the United Kingdom

Your learning materials, published by BPP Learning Media Ltd, are printed on paper obtained from traceable sustainable sources.

Contents

Introduction to the course

Syllabus overview

This unit teaches students the knowledge and skills needed to understand the role of management accounting. Students will be able to gather, analyse and report cost and revenue information to support managerial planning, control and decision making. They will also develop a further understanding of the fundamental principles that underpin management accounting methodology and techniques, how costs are handled in organisations, and why different organisations treat costs in different ways.

Students will learn techniques for dealing with direct costs and revenues, the treatment of short-term overhead costs. They will be required to use spreadsheets when making calculations, manipulating and analysing data, reporting and forecasting.

Test specification for this unit assessment

Assessment method	Marking type	Duration of assessment
Computer-based assessment	Computer marked	2.5 hours

Learning outcomes	
1	Understand the purpose and use of management accounting within organisations
2	Use techniques required for dealing with costs
3	Attribute costs according to organisational requirements
4	Investigate deviations from budgets
5	Use spreadsheet techniques to provide management accounting information
6	Use management accounting techniques to support short-term decision making
7	Understand principles of cash management

Assessment structure

2½ hours duration

Competency is 70%

Note that this is only a guideline as to what might come up. The format and content of each task may vary from what we have listed below.

Your assessment will consist of six tasks:

Task	Expected content	Max marks	Chapter ref	Study complete
1	**Costing techniques** Understanding budgeting and purposes of costing, appropriate costing methods. Calculations including cost card, EOQ, prime cost, marginal cost, absorption cost, production cost, cost per equivalent unit, closing WIP value, total revenue, unit profit. Journal entries.	24	1 Introduction to management accounting 3 Materials and labour costs 5 Absorption costing 6 Job, batch and service costing 9 Marginal costing	
2	**Attributing costs** Understanding ABC. OAR calculations (absorption and ABC), calculations of overheads absorbed, under/over-absorption calculation and its effect on profit, allocation and apportionment calculations.	24	4 Allocation and apportionment 5 Absorption costing	
3	**Short-term decision making** Understanding contribution and cost behaviour. Calculations such as: Cost forecasts (eg high–low method) Breakeven point Margin of safety Target profit sales volume Profit–volume ratio.	24	2 Cost classification and cost behaviour 9 Marginal costing 10 Short-term decision making	
4	**Budgeting and cash management** Understanding types of budgets, standard costs, operating statements, liquidity, reconciling profit with cash, improving cash flow. Calculation of working capital ratios/ working capital cycle.	16	7 Standard costing and budgeting 11 Cash management	

Task	Expected content	Max marks	Chapter ref	Study complete
5	**Preparation of budgets** Preparation of cash budget, inventory budget, other budget. Understanding of spreadsheet formulas and formatting.	16	7 Standard costing and budgeting 11 Cash management 12 Spreadsheets	
6	**Budgets and deviations** Flexing a budget and calculating the resulting variances. Understanding of spreadsheet formulas and formatting.	16	7 Standard costing and budgeting 8 Variance analysis 12 Spreadsheets	

Skills bank

Our experience of preparing students for this type of assessment suggests that to obtain competency, you will need to develop a number of key skills.

What do I need to know to do well in the assessment?

This unit is one of the mandatory Level 3 units. It takes you from Level 2 *Principles of Costing* and prepares you for the Level 4 unit *Applied Management Accounting*.

To be successful in the assessment you need to:

- Understand cost and management accounting principles.

- Apply relevant techniques. This will often be tested in numerical questions, and the use of spreadsheets, but you will also have to demonstrate your understanding of key data (such as reasons for variances) via a narrative multiple choice questions.

Assumed knowledge

Management Accounting Techniques builds on the fundamental concepts and techniques introduced in Level 2 *Principles of Costing*. The following topics were introduced there and are also relevant to this assessment:

- Cost behaviour
- Absorption costing and marginal costing
- Variance calculation
- Inventory and labour costs

Assessment style

In the assessment you will complete tasks by:

1   Entering narrative by selecting from drop down menus of narrative options known as **picklists**

2   Using **drag and drop** menus to enter narrative

3   Typing in numbers, known as **gapfill** entry

4   Entering **ticks**

5   Entering **dates** by selecting from a calendar

6   Entering **formulas** and using **spreadsheet techniques**

You must familiarise yourself with the style of the online questions and the AAT software before taking the assessment. As part of your revision, log in to the **AAT website** and attempt their **online practice assessments**.

Introduction to the assessment

The question practice you do will prepare you for the format of tasks you will see in the *Management Accounting Techniques* assessment. It is also useful to familiarise yourself with the introductory information you **may** be given at the start of the assessment. For example:

You have **2 hours and 30 minutes** to compete this sample assessment.

This assessment contains **six tasks** and you should attempt to complete every task.

Each task is independent. You will not need to refer to your answers to previous tasks.

The total number of marks for this assessment in 120.

Read every task carefully to make sure you understand what is required.

Where the date is relevant, it is given in the task data.

Both minus signs and brackets can be used to indicate negative numbers **unless** task instructions state otherwise.

You must use a full stop to indicate a decimal point. For example, write 105.57 not 100,57 or 10057

You may use a comma to indicate a number in the thousands, but you don't have to. For example 10000 and 10,000 are both acceptable.

1   As you revise, use the **BPP Passcards** to consolidate your knowledge. They are a pocket-sized revision tool, perfect for packing in that last-minute revision.

2   Attempt as many tasks as possible in the **Question Bank**. There are plenty of assessment-style tasks which are excellent preparation for the real assessment.

3   Always **check** through your own answers as you will in the real assessment, before looking at the solutions in the back of the Question Bank.

Key to icons

 Key term

A key definition which is important to be aware of for the assessment

 Formula to learn

A formula you will need to learn as it will not be provided in the assessment

 Formula provided

A formula which is provided within the assessment and generally available as a pop-up on screen

 Activity

An example which allows you to apply your knowledge to the technique covered in the Course Book. The solution is provided at the end of the chapter

 Illustration

A worked example which can be used to review and see how an assessment question could be answered

 Assessment focus point

A high-priority point for the assessment

 Open book reference

Where use of an open book will be allowed for the assessment

 Real-life examples

A practical real-life scenario

AAT qualifications

The material in this book may support the following AAT qualifications:

AAT Level 3 Diploma in Accounting
AAT Diploma in Accounting at SCQF Level 7

Supplements

From time to time we may need to publish supplementary materials to one of our titles. This can be for a variety of reasons, from a small change in the AAT unit guidance to new legislation coming into effect between editions.

You should check our supplements page regularly for anything that may affect your learning materials. All supplements are available free of charge on our supplements page on our website at:

www.bpp.com/learning-media/about/students

Improving material and removing errors

There is a constant need to update and enhance our study materials in line with both regulatory changes and new insights into the assessments.

From our team of authors BPP appoints a subject expert to update and improve these materials for each new edition.

Their updated draft is subsequently technically checked by another author and from time to time, non-technically checked by a proof reader.

We are very keen to remove as many numerical errors and narrative typos as we can but given the volume of detailed information being changed in a short space of time we know that a few errors will sometimes get through our net.

We apologise in advance for any inconvenience that an error might cause. We continue to look for new ways to improve these study materials and would welcome your suggestions. Please feel free to contact our AAT Head of Programme at nisarahmed@bpp.com if you have any suggestions for us.

Introduction to management accounting

Learning outcomes

Having studied this chapter you will be able to:

1	Understand the purpose and use of management accounting within organisations

1.1	Internal reporting calculations
	• The purpose of costing, budgeting and internal reporting
	• The importance of providing accurate information to management for the purposes of planning, control and decision-making
	• Calculate revenue, costs, contribution and reported profits for an organisation
	• Calculate segmented revenue, costs, contribution and reported profits by product

Assessment context

The contents of this chapter mainly serve as an introduction to AAT's *Management Accounting Techniques* paper. However, this chapter is examinable and you can expect questions on it.

Qualification context

This chapter includes terminology that will be used throughout this paper and in Level 4 *Applied Management Accounting*.

Business context

Every business needs to understand and control its costs. This can be done by producing accurate information for the purposes of planning, control and decision making.

Chapter overview

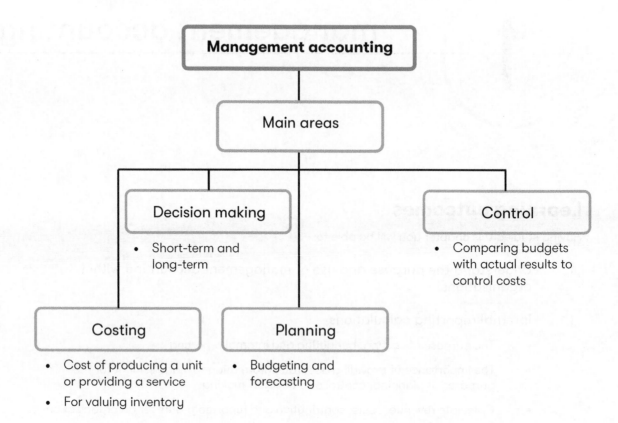

Introduction

In this opening chapter we will consider the overall purposes of cost or **management accounting** together with an introduction to the key concepts and terms that will be used throughout this book.

1 Internal reporting information

The accounting function of a business deals with providing information for both management accounting purposes and financial accounting purposes. However, the type of information required, the timing of the information and the format of the information will be different for each.

Financial accounting is mainly concerned with the collection and classification of historic data in order to prepare the financial statements of the business. These financial statements are prepared for users outside of the business such as shareholders and prospective investors.

Management accounting, by contrast, is about providing the management of an organisation with the information that it needs to carry out its functions properly. Although management accounts are mainly used by internal management, sometimes third parties such as banks may wish to view management accounts.

1.1 Cost accounting and management accounting

Originally, cost accounting (sometimes known as costing) dealt with ways of accumulating historic costs and charging these costs to units of output or departments, in order to value inventory and establish profits. Costing has since been extended into planning, control and decision making. The terms costing, cost accounting and management accounting are now used interchangeably.

The purpose of **management accounting** is to assist management in running the business to achieve an overall objective. (For a profit-seeking business, this is to maximise shareholder wealth by maximising profits.) Management accounting can be broken down into three main areas:

- Planning
- Control
- Decision making

Therefore the purpose of management accounting information is to be relevant to these functions. This will require the provision of both historic information and estimates of future figures in a format that is useful to the relevant members of the management team. Most importantly, the information must be provided regularly and on a timely basis, particularly for the purposes of control, and can be one-off reports or information for decision-making purposes.

1.1.1 Planning

Planning involves defining objectives and assessing future costs and revenues to set up a budget.

A **budget** is a formalised, numerical plan of action for a business. It represents what the business wants to achieve in the forthcoming period, usually (although not always) a year. It is both a plan and a performance measure.

Planning is essential to help assess the purchasing/production requirements of the business.

1.1.2 Control

Once plans have been made, the company must ensure they are being followed and assess any inefficiencies in the business.

1.1.3 Decision making

There are many decisions managers may have to make such as:

- What should we produce?
- How should we finance the business?
- Is a project worthwhile?

Activity 1: Information for management

Management accountants may provide information for management on which of the following?

	✓
Cost of goods and services	
Actual costs compared to expected costs	
Expected profits and production plans	

1.2 Calculating costs and revenue, and segmented costs and revenue

One of the key concerns that management will have, will be how much the products that it produces, or the services that it provides, cost.

Management need to know this for the statement of profit or loss, to help set prices and to value inventory in the statement of financial position.

Costs can be presented in different ways in order to give management different types of information.

Costs in both manufacturing industries and service industries are traditionally split between:

- Material costs
- Labour costs
- Overheads (or expenses)

There are a few important terms that you need to understand:

- Cost unit
- Cost card
- Segmented cost

1.2.1 Cost unit and cost card

KEY TERM

A **cost unit** is a unit of product or service to which costs can be attached.

A **cost card** is a document which groups the costs of a product or service in order to arrive at a total cost.

A cost unit could be a single item such as a table, or a batch of items such as 200 loaves of bread. A batch is a more useful cost unit if the items are made in a batch and/or the individual cost of an item is very small: fractions of a penny, for example. For a restaurant, a cost unit could be a meal served.

The cost of a cost unit is an important piece of costing information that will be used in many different ways. The total cost is built up on a **cost card**, which groups the costs using the categories of materials, labour and overheads.

Cost card	£
Direct materials	X
Direct labour	X
Direct expenses	X
Prime cost	X

Production overheads	X
Production cost	X
Non-production overheads	
Selling and distribution	X
Administration	X
Finance	X
Total cost	X

A **direct cost** is a cost that can be directly attributed to a cost unit. **Indirect costs** cannot be attributed directly to a cost unit. The **prime cost** is the total of the direct costs. The production cost is the total of the manufacturing costs.

At this stage, don't worry too much about what each of the lines in the cost card mean. We will explain these in further detail in the next chapter.

1.2.2 Revenue

Once management understands its costs, it can then decide on suitable selling prices for its products or services. Sometimes sales prices are determined by the profit that a business wants to make; for example, a profit of 20% of cost. Other times the business will be forced to choose a selling price based on what the competition is charging.

The selling price multiplied by the sales volume gives the total sales revenue.

The sales revenue minus the costs gives the profit.

1.2.3 Segmented costs and revenue

Presenting information using a segmental approach means showing how particular components or sections of a business generate sales revenue, costs and profits.

Illustration 1: Segmented costs and revenue

HF Co manufactures two products, CT1 and CT2. The profit for the business last year was as follows:

			£	£
Sales revenue		CT1		150,000
		CT2		120,000
				270,000
Less costs:	Materials	CT1	60,000	
		CT2	50,000	
	Labour	CT1	30,000	
		CT2	35,000	
	Overheads	CT1	40,000	
		CT2	45,000	
				260,000
Profit				10,000

This shows that the business made a profit of £10,000 for the year. It doesn't show which of the two products made the biggest profit. For this, we need a segmented approach as follows:

		CT1 £	CT2 £	Total £
Sales revenue		150,000	120,000	270,000
Less costs:	Materials	60,000	50,000	110,000
	Labour	30,000	35,000	65,000
	Overheads	40,000	45,000	85,000
		130,000	130,000	260,000
Profit/(loss)		20,000	(10,000)	10,000

Now we can see that product CT2 actually made a loss. This information is useful to management. They may now decide to discontinue making CT2. However, there may be other factors to consider when making this decision. For example, sales of CT1 may be linked to sales of CT2.

Assessment focus point

Assessment questions may present information to you using a segmented approach. Alternatively, questions may ask you to fill in a segmented table to show the individual segments and the company's total profit or loss.

2 The purpose of budgets

We will cover budgeting in more detail later in this Course Book but it's worth explaining at this point, how budgets relate to planning and control.

2.1 Budgets for planning

A **budget** is a financial plan of resources (eg materials and labour) and sales, and is used as part of the organisation's **planning process** in order for it to achieve its strategic aims. A starting point when setting a budget is to prepare forecasts of sales, production costs and other costs. A budget sets a target, whereas a forecast is an estimate of what is likely to happen in the future.

A **forecast** is an estimate of what may happen in the future based upon historical data and various assumptions. The forecast will make extensive use of internal data to establish past patterns of costs and sales in order to estimate what future values may be.

However, a forecast cannot rely on internal data alone. External factors, including economic and political conditions, the actions of competitors and technological advances, all affect sales and costs. The implications of these external factors on revenue and costs must be forecast, and these assumptions must be incorporated into the budget figures.

An organisation will use a range of internal and external data and information sources in order to establish as strong a forecast, and therefore as accurate a budget, as possible.

2.2 Budgets for cost control

The existence of a budget will ensure managers try to limit the expenditure to that contained within the budget.

Control over actual performance is provided by the comparisons of actual results against the budget plan.

Departures from budget can then be investigated and the reasons for any departures can be divided into controllable and uncontrollable factors; and action taken to improve performance.

3 Ethics

3.1 What do we mean by ethics?

Ethics is a set of moral principles to guide behaviour.

A professional accountant has a responsibility to act in the public interest, not just to satisfy the needs of a particular client or employer. Third parties, for example investors, governments and employees, rely on accountants and their expertise. Although management accounts are generally prepared for internal use, occasionally they are used by third parties, such as banks. Ethics are therefore important for all areas of accounting.

Professional accountants must be qualified but they also have an additional obligation to act ethically by following an ethical code. An ethical code helps maintain the reputation of the accounting profession.

Ethics and ethical codes are constantly changing to adapt with changes in business and society. High-profile cases of fraud in the US resulted in the perceived **integrity** of accountants becoming increasingly important.

3.2 Fundamental principles

The AAT publish the *AAT Code of Professional Ethics* (2014) which sets out a code of fundamental ethical principles with which students and members should comply. The code aims to:

- Give the required standards of professional behaviour
- Help protect the public interest
- Help maintain the AAT's reputation (AAT, 2014: p. 4)

The five fundamental principles are summarised in the table.

Fundamental principles	
Professional behaviour	A professional accountant should 'comply with relevant laws and regulations' (AAT, 2014: p. 9) and should avoid any action that discredits the profession.
Integrity	A professional accountant should be 'straightforward and honest in all professional and business relationships' (AAT, 2014: p. 9).
Professional competence and due care	A professional accountant has a continuing duty 'to maintain professional knowledge and skill at the level required to ensure that a client or employer receives competent professional service based on current developments in practice, legislation and techniques ... [A professional accountant should] act diligently and in accordance with applicable technical and professional standards when providing professional services' (AAT, 2014: p. 9).
Confidentiality	A professional accountant should 'respect the confidentiality of information acquired as a result of professional and business relationships and [should] not disclose any such information to third parties without proper and specific authority unless there is a legal or professional right or duty to disclose. Confidential information acquired as a result of professional and business relationships should not be used for the personal advantage of the professional accountant or third parties' (AAT, 2014: p. 9).
Objectivity	A professional accountant should 'not allow bias, conflict of interest or undue influence of others to override professional or business judgements' (AAT, 2014: p. 9).

Assessment focus point

Ethics are not specifically mentioned in the learning outcomes for Management Accounting Techniques. However, AAT has stated that the application of ethical principles is threaded throughout the unit and that all work must be carried out with integrity, objectivity and a high degree of professional competence.

Chapter summary

- Financial accounting is concerned with providing historic information to parties external to the organisation in the form of annual financial statements.

- Costing and management accounting are concerned with providing relevant, useful and timely information to management based upon actual costs and revenues and forecast figures in order that management can carry out its main functions of planning, control and decision making. Presenting information using a segmental approach means showing how particular components or sections of a business generate sales revenue, costs and profits

- Ethics is a set of moral principles to guide behaviour.

- Preparing management accounts requires integrity, the principle of honesty.

- Budgets can help management in their planning and control functions.

Keywords

- **Budget:** A formalised, numerical, often financial, plan of action

- **Cost card:** A document which groups the costs of a product or service in order to arrive at a total cost

- **Cost unit:** The individual product or service for which costs are ascertained

- **Financial accounting:** The provision of financial statements for parties external to the organisation based upon historical data

- **Management (cost) accounting:** The provision of both actual figures and forecast figures to enable management to carry out their prime functions of planning, control and decision making

Test your learning

1   Which of the following is the correct definition of a cost unit?

☐   The cost per hour of operating a machine

☐   The cost per unit of electricity consumed

☐   A unit of product or service in relation to which costs are ascertained

☐   A measure of work output in a standard hour

2   Identify which TWO of the following statements describe the purposes of budgeting.

☐   It is used as part of the planning process and represents what the organisation wants to achieve.

☐   It is used to produce financial statements for shareholders.

☐   It is used to confirm the level of an organisation's assets.

☐   It is used as a control mechanism by highlighting departures from budgeted figures.

3   The three main functions of management are

| | and
|---|

Cost classification and cost behaviour

Learning outcomes

Having studied this chapter you will be able to:

2	Use techniques required for dealing with costs

2.4 Cost behaviours

- The implications of different cost behaviours for cost analysis, decision making and reporting:
    - Fixed
    - Variable
    - Semi-variable
    - Stepped
- Use the high–low method to separate fixed and variable cost elements of semi-variable costs

6.2 Examine the effects of changing activity levels

- The effect of changing activity levels on unit revenue, costs and profits
- Calculate changes in forecast unit revenue, costs and profits

Assessment context

Assessment questions will test your understanding of cost classification and cost behaviour, including calculations that require the use of the high–low method. You need to understand cost behaviour to answer questions on budgets and variance analysis.

Qualification context

This chapter introduces concepts and terms that are fundamental to understanding *Applied Management Accounting* at Level 4.

Business context

Grouping costs together is essential for a business to be able to analyse costs, prepare budgets and plan effectively.

Chapter overview

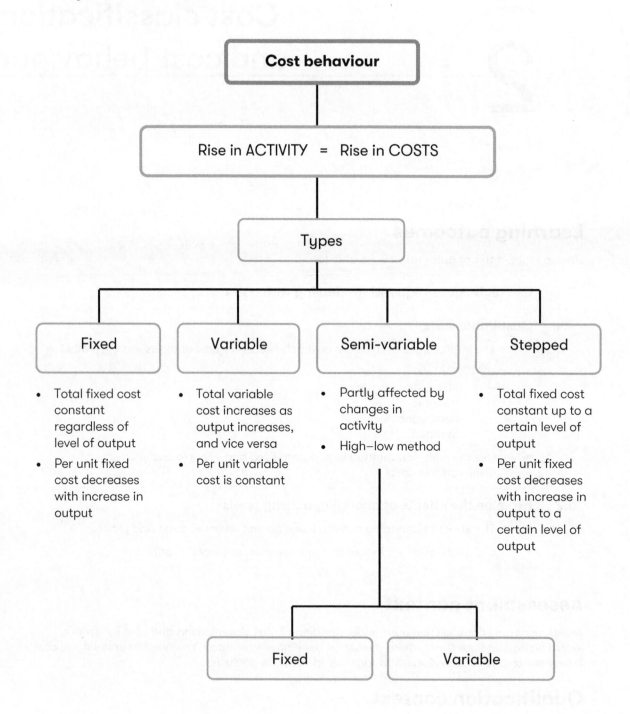

Cost behaviour

Rise in ACTIVITY = Rise in COSTS

Types

Fixed
- Total fixed cost constant regardless of level of output
- Per unit fixed cost decreases with increase in output

Variable
- Total variable cost increases as output increases, and vice versa
- Per unit variable cost is constant

Semi-variable
- Partly affected by changes in activity
- High–low method

Stepped
- Total fixed cost constant up to a certain level of output
- Per unit fixed cost decreases with increase in output to a certain level of output

Fixed

Variable

Cost classification by function

Arrange costs into logical groups for analysis

Production costs

- Associated with the production of goods and services

Non-production costs

- All other costs in a business eg
  selling and distribution
  administration
  financing

Materials

- Cost of material used in production

Labour

- Cost of workforce used in production

Overheads

- Cost of overhead required to support production

Direct cost

- Directly traced to product

Indirect cost

- Incurred as a result of making a product but not directly traceable

Introduction

A business will incur many different types of cost from day to day. For cost accounting purposes it is useful to group or classify these costs. There are, however, a number of different ways of doing this.

1 Classification

Cost classification is the arrangement of cost items into logical groups, for example by their **function** (such as administration or production) or by their **nature** (such as materials or wages).

The eventual aim of costing is to determine the cost of producing a product/providing a service.

1.1 Capital and revenue expenditure

The expenses of a business can be categorised as either capital expenses or revenue expenses.

Capital expenditure includes:

- The purchase of non-current assets (for example, machinery)
- The improvement of the earning capability of non-current assets

Non-current assets are assets that are used in the business for more than one accounting period to provide benefits. These benefits are (we hope!) the profits earned from using the non-current assets in the business. Plant and machinery, land and buildings, office equipment and motor vehicles are all examples of non-current assets that play their part in earning profits by being used within the business rather than being bought to make profit on their resale.

Revenue expenditure includes:

- The purchase of goods for resale
- The maintenance of the existing earning capacity of non-current assets
- Expenditure incurred in conducting the business

Capital expenditure is shown as a non-current asset in the statement of financial position, while revenue expenditure is charged as a cost in the statement of profit or loss. In costing terms, capital expenditure is not included in the cost of a product, only revenue expenses are included. It is therefore important to distinguish correctly between capital and revenue items, as this could hit profit quite hard given the relatively large figures involved where non-current assets are concerned. It would also mean that the statement of financial position would not show the correct cost of assets used by the business. For costing purposes it would mean that the amounts included in the calculations of **product costs** (costs of a finished product built up from its cost elements) would be inaccurate.

Some tricky items you might come across when deciding between capital and revenue categories often involve changes to non-current assets:

	Capital	Revenue
Extension to a building	✓	
Repairs to a building or machine		✓
Legal costs of buying a new factory	✓	
Installation of new machinery	✓	
Redecorating offices		✓

1.2 Classification by function

Revenue expenditure can be classified according to the function that causes the cost. The main functions within a manufacturing business will give rise to the following cost categories:

- **Production costs.** Materials and labour used to make the products, maintenance costs of the machinery and supervision of the workforce are examples of costs caused by the production function of a business.

- **Non-production costs – selling and distribution costs.** Advertising, delivery costs and sales staff salaries would be caused by the selling and distribution function.

- **Non-production costs – administration costs.** The administration function gives rise to management, secretarial and accounting costs in coordinating the other functions of the business.

- **Non-production costs – financing costs.** The financing function gives rise to all the expenses associated with raising money to finance the business, such as a loan or overdraft.

The distinction between these categories is not always clear, particularly when we are talking about administration costs, as there are no rules or regulations to follow, just common sense. What's more, these are not the only possible functions within a business. Large companies often have a research and development function, or a training function. It depends on the type of business.

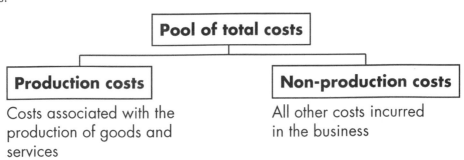

1.3 Direct and indirect cost elements

A different way of classifying production costs looks at the three major cost elements:

- Materials
- Labour
- Expenses

Each category is then sub-divided into either:

- Direct costs; or
- Indirect costs.

> **Direct costs** are costs that can be directly identified with a particular unit of production or service provided.
>
> **Indirect costs** are costs that cannot be directly identified with a unit of production or service.

It is usually easy to identify the amount of a direct expense that is spent on one unit, but it is more difficult to do so with indirect costs as they are not spent directly on one unit. They are usually spent in relation to a number of units.

Here are some examples:

Direct materials	Materials that are incorporated into the finished product (eg wood used in the construction of a table).
Indirect materials	Materials that are used in the production process but not incorporated into the product (eg machine lubricants and spare parts). Insignificant costs that are attributable to each unit are sometimes included in indirect materials for convenience (eg nails and glue).
Direct labour	Wages paid to those workers who make products in a manufacturing business (eg machine operators) or perform the service in a service business (eg hairdressers in a hair salon).
Indirect labour	Wages and salaries of the other staff, such as supervisors, storekeepers and maintenance workers.
Direct expenses	Expenses that are identifiable with each unit of production, such as patent royalties payable to the inventor of a new product or process.
Indirect expenses	Expenses that are not spent on individual units of production (eg rent and rates, electricity and telephone).

In costing, the three types of direct cost are often lumped together and called **prime cost**.

Prime cost = Direct materials + Direct labour + Direct expenses

The three types of indirect cost are often lumped together and called **overheads**.

Overheads = Indirect materials + Indirect labour + Indirect expenses

2 Cost behaviour

Costs can also be classified by their behaviour, that is, how the total cost is affected by a change in output or activity level (ie the number of units produced). Costs behave in different ways when the levels of activity in the organisation change. The main classifications are:

- Fixed costs
- Variable costs
- Semi-variable costs
- Stepped costs

KEY TERM

Fixed costs are total cost remains the same as output increases.

Variable costs are total cost increases as output increases.

Semi-variable costs are costs that contain elements of both fixed and variable costs. Also known as mixed costs.

Stepped costs are costs that remain the same up to a certain level of activity and then jump. Fixed costs often behave like this in practice.

These classifications only apply in the short term, as in the long term all costs are variable. Each of these will be illustrated in this chapter, and the concepts will then be used in later chapters in order to produce relevant management information.

2.1 Fixed costs

Fixed costs are not affected by changes in production level. They remain the same in total whether no units or many units are produced. They are incurred in relation to a period of time rather than production level, and are often referred to as **period costs**. This is the case with the salary of a supervisor, the rent of a factory or straight-line depreciation of plant and machinery.

A graph of fixed costs against output level would produce a horizontal line.

Graph of total fixed costs

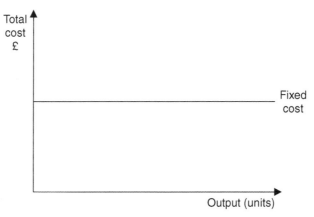

In practical terms fixed costs are only truly fixed over the **relevant range**. For example, the rent of the factory will only remain constant provided that the level of activity is within the production capacity of the factory. If production levels increase above the capacity of the current factory then more factory space must be rented thus increasing the rent cost for this level of production.

As the activity level increases the fixed cost remains fixed in total, but the fixed cost **per unit** will fall as the total cost is split over more units. This gives management an incentive to increase production as it will mean that each unit is cheaper to produce. This is demonstrated in the graph below.

Graph of fixed cost per unit

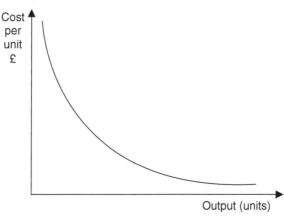

Activity 1: Fixed cost per unit

Sleet Ltd makes garden benches and incurs fixed costs of £20,000 per year.

Required

Calculate the fixed cost per garden bench at the following output levels:

(a)   1,000 units

(b)   10,000 units

(c)   20,000 units

(d)   100,000 units

The fixed cost per garden bench is:

(a)   £ [   ]

(b)   £ [   ]

(c) £ [   ]

(d) £ [   ]

2.2 Variable costs

Variable costs are costs that vary directly in line with changes in the level of activity. Direct materials are often viewed as variable costs. For example, if 1 kg of a material is needed for each cost unit then 100,000 kg will be required for 100,000 units of production and 500,000 kg for 500,000 units of production.

The total variable cost can be expressed as:

Total variable cost = Variable cost per unit × Number of units

A graph can be used to illustrate the total variable cost as activity levels change:

Graph of total variable costs

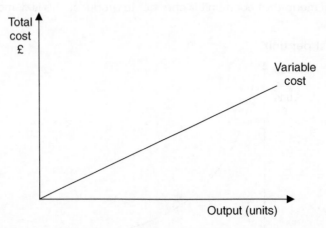

As a general rule, as the variable cost is spent directly on each unit of production, this will be the same amount for each unit, so a graph of **unit cost** against level of output will be horizontal.

Graph of variable cost per unit

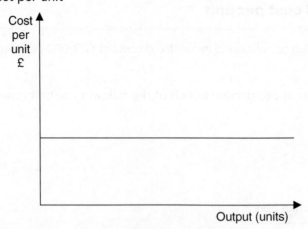

Assessment focus point

Assessment questions may ask you to calculate budgeted cost per unit using total budgeted costs and the number of units. You need to understand that

Total variable cost = Variable cost per unit × Number of units

and

Variable cost per unit = Total variable costs ÷ Number of units

2.3 Stepped costs (sometimes called step-fixed costs)

Stepped costs are costs that are fixed over a relatively small range of activity levels but then increase in steps when certain levels of activity are reached. For example, if one production supervisor is required for each 30,000 units of a product that is made then three supervisors are required for the production of 90,000 units, four for the production of 120,000 units, five for the production of up to 150,000 units and so on.

Stepped costs can be illustrated on a graph:

Graph of total stepped costs

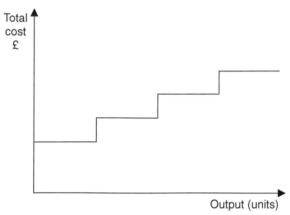

Stepped costs are really a fixed cost with a relatively short relevant range.

2.4 Semi-variable costs

Semi-variable costs are costs that have a fixed element and also a variable element. For example, the telephone bill includes a fixed element being the fixed line rental for the period and a variable element that will increase as the number of calls increases.

The total of a semi-variable cost can be expressed as:

Total cost = Fixed element + (Variable cost per unit × Number of units)

A semi-variable cost can be illustrated on a graph as follows:

Graph of total semi-variable costs

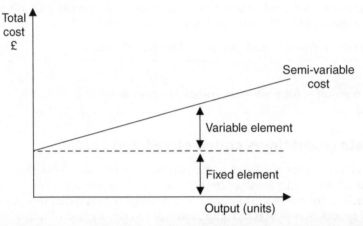

As activity levels increase, the total semi-variable cost increases. As activity levels increase, the semi-variable cost **per unit** decreases. This is because the cost is made up of a fixed element and a variable element. As the activity level increases the fixed element remains fixed in total, but the fixed cost **per unit** will fall as the total cost is split over more units. The variable element per unit remains the same.

Illustration 1: Changing activity levels

Let's look at an example using numbers. Let's say that a semi-variable cost is made up of a fixed element of £100 and a variable element of £5 per unit. The costs for various activity levels would be as follows:

Activity level (units)	Total cost £	Cost per unit £
100	(100 + (5 × 100)) = 600	600 / 100 = 6.00
200	(100 + (5 × 200)) = 1,100	1,100 / 200 = 5.50
300	(100 + (5 × 300)) = 1,600	1,600 / 300 = 5.33
400	(100 + (5 × 400)) = 2,100	2,100 / 400 = 5.25
500	(100 + (5 × 500)) = 2,600	2,600 / 500 = 5.20

As you can see, as activity levels increase, the total semi-variable cost increases but the semi-variable cost **per unit** decreases.

There are several ways of calculating the fixed and variable elements of a semi-variable cost. You could be given a percentage to use or you might have to use the **high–low method** (covered later in this chapter).

3 Calculating the fixed and variable elements of semi-variable costs

Assessment focus point

Assessment questions could ask you to calculate the fixed and variable elements of costs based on a particular percentage.

Activity 2: Fixed and variable elements of cost

An overhead cost of £580,000 is made up of a fixed and variable element. The fixed element is 55% of the total cost and the rest is variable.

The fixed element of the overhead cost is   £ [   ]

The variable element of the overhead cost is   £ [   ]

Another way of calculating the fixed and variable elements of a cost is to use the high–low method. The high–low method requires several observations of the costs incurred at different output levels. This data can then be used to predict costs that would be incurred at other output levels.

Illustration 2: High–low method

Over the last five years, Stormbreak Ltd has recorded the following costs:

Year	Output Units	Total cost £
20X1	32,000	505,000
20X2	37,000	580,000
20X3	48,000	745,000
20X4	53,000	820,000
20X5	51,000	790,000

Stormbreak Ltd wants to estimate the cost for 20X6, when they expect to produce 52,000 units.

This problem can be tackled by following four steps.

Step 1   Identify the high and low output and associated costs.

Look carefully at the information given and identify the highest and lowest output levels. Write these down, along with the total costs at those levels. (Don't be put off by any other information, such as the year, or the order in which the data is given, even if the cost column is given first – it is the highest and lowest outputs that matter.)

	Output Units	Total cost £
Highest	53,000	820,000
Lowest	32,000	505,000

Step 2   Deduct the lowest output/costs from the highest output/costs.

	Output Units	Total cost £
Highest	53,000	820,000
Lowest	32,000	505,000
Increase	21,000	315,000

This tells us that an increase of 21,000 units has led to an increase in costs of £315,000. This is due to the variable costs only, and gives us the figures we need for the next step.

Step 3   Calculate the variable cost per unit.

$$\text{Variable cost per unit} = \frac{\text{High cost} - \text{Low cost}}{\text{High output} - \text{Low output}}$$

$$= \frac{£315,000}{21,000}$$

$$= £15$$

Step 4   Find the fixed costs at one of the output levels used in the above calculations.

Choose either the highest or the lowest output level. Both will give the same result. Calculate the variable cost by taking the cost per unit from Step 3 multiplied by the number of units of output. Deduct this from the total cost at the same level of output and you will be left with the fixed cost.

At 53,000 units:

	£
Total cost	820,000
Less: Variable cost (53,000 × £15)	795,000
= Fixed cost	25,000

At 32,000 units (as a check):

	£
Total cost	505,000
Less: Variable cost (32,000 × £15)	480,000
= Fixed cost	25,000

Now we are in a position to answer the actual question asked, which is 'What are the expected costs when output is 52,000 units?' All we need to do is build up the total cost from the fixed and variable elements at this level of output.

	£
Fixed cost	25,000
Add: Variable cost (52,000 × £15)	780,000
= Total cost	805,000

Activity 3: High–low method – manufacturing business

S and N recorded the following costs for the last four months.

Month	Cost £	Production volume Units
1	106,000	7,000
2	115,000	8,000
3	112,300	7,700
4	97,000	6,000

Required

Calculate the costs that should be expected in month 5 when output is expected to be 7,500 units.

The total cost in month 5 when output is expected to be 7,500 units is

£ |_____| .

Activity 4: High–low method – service business

P and Q recorded the following information over the last five months.

Month	Cost £	Electricity consumed Units
January	204	2,600
February	212	2,800
March	200	2,500
April	220	3,000
May	184	2,100

Required

Using the high–low method, determine the cost of electricity in June if 2,750 units of electricity are consumed.

The cost of electricity in June if 2,750 units are consumed is £ |_____| .

Tutor's note

It is important to note that when we talk about different types of **cost behaviour**, we are usually referring to the short term. Over longer periods of time, however, say a number of years, all costs will tend to vary in response to large changes in activity level. Costs traditionally classified as fixed will become step costs as no cost can remain unchanged forever. And so as the time span increases, step costs become variable costs, varying with the passing of time. For example, when considered over many years, rent will appear as a variable cost, varying in the long term with large changes in the level of activity. So, in the long run, all costs are variable.

4 Effects of changing activity levels on revenue and profit

So far we have discussed the effects of changing activity levels on different types of cost. For example, we said that as activity levels increase, the fixed cost remains fixed in total, but the fixed cost **per unit** will fall, because the total cost is split over more units. As activity levels increase, the variable cost increases in total, but the variable cost **per unit** will stay the same.

Now we will briefly look at the impact of changing activity levels on unit revenue and profits.

4.1 Revenue

Sales revenue is determined by the number of units sold and the selling price per unit. (The selling price per unit is also known as the revenue per unit.)

Total revenue = Number of units sold × Revenue per unit

Notice that the total revenue is not affected by the activity level (production level) because it is based on the number of units sold, not the number of units produced. It doesn't matter whether activity levels increase or decrease, the revenue per unit will remain the same. The total revenue will only increase or decrease if the number of units sold increases or decreases.

4.2 Profit

We know that different types of costs are affected by the activity level and we know that revenue is not affected by the activity level (only the number of units sold). Now we consider the impact on profit of changing activity levels.

Profit per unit = Revenue per unit − Total cost per unit

Remember that total costs include all types of costs. Let's remind ourselves of the impact of an increase in activity levels on the different types of cost.

Activity 5: Changing activity levels – costs

Required

If activity levels increase, what will be the impact on the following costs per unit?

Cost	Stay the same	Increase	Decrease
Variable cost per unit			
Fixed cost per unit			
Semi-variable cost per unit			
Total cost per unit			

Now we know that the revenue per unit is unaffected by changing activity levels and the total cost per unit decreases as activity levels increase. A lower cost will mean a higher profit.

Therefore profit per unit will increase as activity levels increase.

> ### Assessment focus point
>
> Assessment questions could ask you to decide on the impact of changing activity levels on total cost per unit, revenue per unit or profit per unit.

Activity 6: Changing activity levels – revenue, cost and profit

Required

Identify whether the following statements are true or false.

Statement	True	False
As levels of output decrease, the amount of revenue per unit will decrease.		
As levels of output decrease, the amount of fixed cost per unit will stay the same.		
As levels of output increase, the amount of total cost per unit will increase.		
As levels of output increase, the amount of profit per unit will increase.		

Chapter summary

- Costs are either capital or revenue in nature. Revenue expenditure is included in the cost of a product, but capital expenditure is not.

- Costs can be classified by several methods:

  - By function: production, selling and distribution, administration and finance

  - By element

	Materials
Direct	Labour
	Expenses
	Materials
Indirect	Labour
	Expenses

  - By nature or cost behaviour: fixed, variable, stepped, semi-variable

  But in the long run, all costs are variable.

- Direct costs are costs that can be related directly to a cost unit whereas indirect costs are initially allocated or apportioned to a cost centre.

- At different production levels:

  - Total variable costs will change in line with the quantity produced, but total fixed costs will remain the same.

  - The variable cost per unit will be the same, but the fixed cost per unit will fall as the quantity produced increases.

  - The revenue per unit will be the same, and the profit per unit will increase as the quantity produced increases.

- The high–low technique can be used to find the variable and fixed elements of a semi-variable cost by identifying the costs at the highest and lowest levels of output.

Keywords

- **Activity level:** The number of units produced (also known as the level of output)
- **Cost behaviour:** The way a cost changes as production quantity or activity level changes
- **Direct costs:** Can be directly identified with a unit of production or service
- **Fixed costs:** Costs that do not vary with changes in production level
- **High–low method:** A method for estimating the fixed and variable parts of a semi-variable cost
- **Indirect costs:** Cannot be directly identified with a unit of production or service
- **Overheads:** Indirect costs (ie indirect materials, labour and expenses)
- **Period costs:** Costs which relate to a time period rather than the output of products or services
- **Prime cost:** The total of direct costs
- **Product cost:** A cost of a finished product made up from its cost elements
- **Production cost:** The total of manufacturing costs
- **Relevant range:** The relevant range of a fixed cost is the range of activity within which the cost does not change
- **Semi-variable (or semi-fixed, or mixed) costs:** Costs that have both a fixed element and a variable element
- **Stepped costs:** Costs that are fixed over a certain range, but when output increases beyond a certain level, there will be a sudden jump in cost to a higher fixed amount
- **Variable costs:** Vary according to the level of production

Test your learning

1   Study the list below and decide which items are capital and which are revenue. Tick the appropriate box.

	Capital ✓	Revenue ✓
A new telephone system		
Depreciation of vehicles		
Salesperson's car		
Road fund licence for delivery van		
Telephone bill		
Computer software costing £10,000		
Repairs to the Managing Director's company car after an accident		

2   Look at the following sketch graph and then decide which of the suggested costs could account for that shape of graph. (Tick the correct answers.)

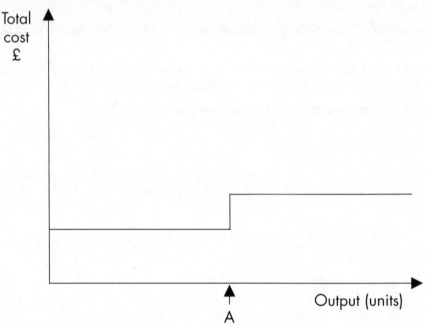

BPP
LEARNING
MEDIA

		Cost behaviour	
		Does fit the graph shape	**Does NOT fit the graph shape**
(a)	Plastic used in the manufacture of moulded plastic furniture. A bulk-buying discount is given at point A on the graph.		
(b)	Straight-line depreciation of a freehold factory. A new factory is bought at point A.		
(c)	Rent of a warehouse. A further warehouse is rented at point A.		
(d)	Electricity costs that have a standing charge and a cost per unit of power used. At point A the level of production reaches the point where a night shift is required, which uses electricity at a cheaper rate.		

3   **Use the high–low technique to predict the costs at a production level of 12,000 units, given the observed data in the table below.**

Year	Production level Units	Total cost £
20X2	9,000	22,500
20X3	6,500	17,500
20X4	13,500	31,500
20X5	10,300	25,100
20X6	12,600	29,700

Total cost at 12,000 units   £ [   ]

4   **Draw up a cost card using the following information. All costs given are per cabinet.**

To make a filing cabinet, metal sheeting to the value of £3.80 is cut, formed, welded and painted by machine. A group of machines are monitored, the production overhead cost of which has been worked out at £0.30. Metal fixtures costing £1.80 are attached manually, and the cabinets are then assembled and packaged. The labour cost of assembly and packaging is £6.70, and the packaging materials cost £0.90. The power used by the factory gives a cost of £0.20, and delivery costs and advertising works out at £3.00.

Cost card: Filing cabinet	£
Direct materials	
Direct labour	
Prime cost	
Production overheads	
Production cost	
Non-production overheads	
Selling and distribution	
Total cost	

5   **Variable costs are conventionally deemed to:**

☐   Be constant per unit of output

☐   Vary per unit of output as production volume changes

☐   Be constant in total when production volume changes

☐   Vary, in total, from period to period when production is constant

6   The following is a graph of cost against level of activity:

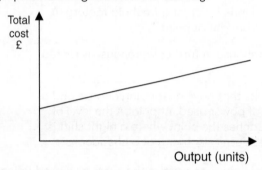

To which one of the following costs does the graph correspond?

☐   A   Electricity bills made up of a standing charge and a variable charge

☐   B   Bonus payment to employees when production reaches a certain level

☐   C   Salesperson's commissions payable per unit up to a maximum amount of commission

☐   D   Bulk discounts on purchases, the discount being given on all units purchased

The following information relates to questions 7, 8 and 9.

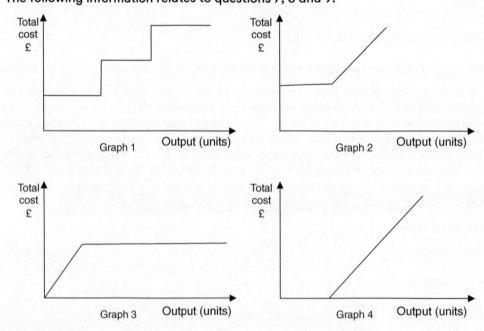

Which one of the graphs depicts the costs described in questions 7, 8 and 9?

7   Photocopier rental costs, where a fixed rental is payable up to a certain number of copies each period. If the number of copies exceeds this amount, a constant charge per copy is made for all subsequent copies during that period.

☐   Graph 1

☐   Graph 2

☐   Graph 3

☐   Graph 4

8   Supervisor salary costs, where one supervisor is needed for every five employees added to the staff.

☐   Graph 1

☐   Graph 2

☐   Graph 3

☐   Graph 4

9   Vehicle hire costs, where a constant rate is charged per mile travelled, up to a maximum monthly payment regardless of the miles travelled.

☐   Graph 1

☐   Graph 2

☐   Graph 3

☐   Graph 4

10   A production worker is paid a salary of £650 per month, plus an extra 5 pence for each unit produced during the month.

This labour cost is best described as:

☐   A variable cost

☐   A fixed cost

☐   A stepped cost

☐   A semi-variable cost

11   Prime cost is

☐   All costs incurred in manufacturing a product

☐   The total of direct costs

☐   The material cost of a product

☐   The cost of operating a department

12   Which of the following costs are part of the prime cost for a manufacturing company?

☐   Cost of transporting raw materials from the supplier's premises

☐   Wages of factory workers engaged in machine maintenance

☐   Depreciation of lorries used for deliveries to customers

☐   Cost of indirect production materials

13   Which of the following are direct expenses?

☐ The cost of special designs, drawing or layouts

☐ The hire of tools or equipment for a particular job

☐ Salesperson's wages

☐ Rent, rates and insurance of a factory

3 Materials and labour costs

Learning outcomes

Having studied this chapter you will be able to:

| 2 | Use techniques required for dealing with costs |

| 2.1 | Record and calculate materials, labour and overhead costs |

- Prepare and interpret inventory records for materials, work-in-progress and finished goods
- Calculate materials and labour costs

| 2.2 | Prepare cost accounting journals |

- Principles of cost accounting journal entries for

  - Direct materials or indirect materials
  - Direct or indirect labour
  - Overhead costs.

- Prepare cost accounting journals for

  - Materials
  - Labour
  - Overheads

| 2.3 | Apply inventory control methods |

- Calculate inventory control and valuation measures:

  - Inventory buffers, lead times, minimum/maximum order quantities

    1. Buffer inventory = re-order level − (average usage × average lead time)

    2. Re-order level = (average usage × average lead time) + buffer inventory

    Note. Students will be provided with either buffer inventory or re-order level values when completing calculations

    3. Maximum inventory level = buffer inventory + maximum re-order quantity

    4. Maximum re-order quantity = maximum inventory level − buffer inventory

    Note. Students will be provided with maximum inventory level or maximum re-order quantity values when completing calculations

    5. Minimum re-order quantity = average usage × average lead time

- Economic order quantity

    6. $=\sqrt{((2 \times \text{annual usage} \times \text{ordering cost}) \div \text{inventory holding cost})}$

- Compliance with inventory control policies

- The effect on reported profits of choice of method

- Account for inventories using first-in-first-out (FIFO) and average cost (AVCO) methods

- Analyse closing inventory balances

Assessment context

Materials cost is a key cost within a manufacturing environment. This is an important part of the syllabus and you need to be happy with all relevant calculations. Tasks in the assessment could ask you to calculate the economic order quantity or use first in, first out (FIFO) or average cost (AVCO) calculations or to calculate labour costs.

Qualification context

This unit gives you a good grounding in the inventory control process and labour costs and introduces some theoretical techniques to help with inventory ordering and valuation. Some of the basics were covered in Level 2 Principles of Costing, so may be familiar to you.

Business context

Many businesses use materials, hold inventory and employ labour. Management accountants need to understand the costs involved with holding and ordering materials and employing labour. In order to control the inventory that is held, businesses will regularly count their inventories and compare the physical quantity with the inventory records; any discrepancies should be investigated and corrected.

Chapter overview

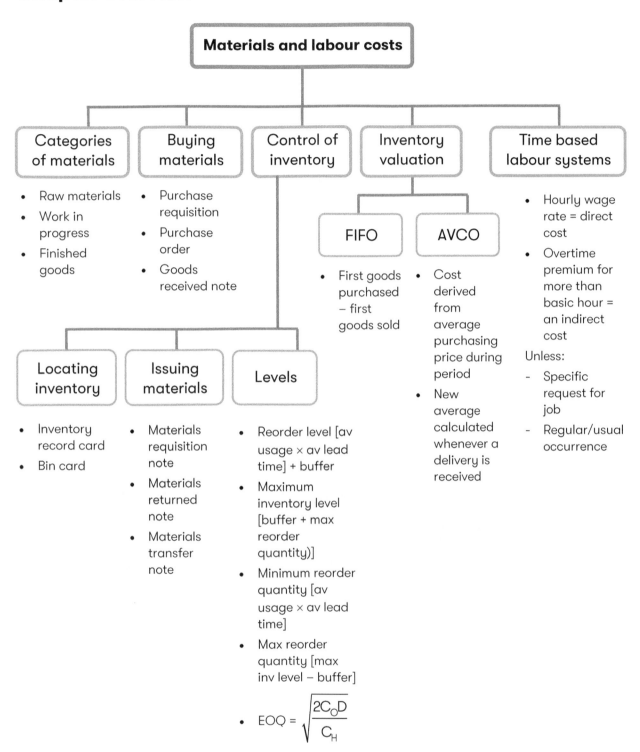

Materials and labour costs

Categories of materials
- Raw materials
- Work in progress
- Finished goods

Buying materials
- Purchase requisition
- Purchase order
- Goods received note

Control of inventory

Inventory valuation

FIFO
- First goods purchased – first goods sold

AVCO
- Cost derived from average purchasing price during period
- New average calculated whenever a delivery is received

Time based labour systems
- Hourly wage rate = direct cost
- Overtime premium for more than basic hour = an indirect cost

Unless:
- Specific request for job
- Regular/usual occurrence

Locating inventory
- Inventory record card
- Bin card

Issuing materials
- Materials requisition note
- Materials returned note
- Materials transfer note

Levels
- Reorder level [av usage × av lead time] + buffer
- Maximum inventory level [buffer + max reorder quantity)]
- Minimum reorder quantity [av usage × av lead time]
- Max reorder quantity [max inv level – buffer]
- $EOQ = \sqrt{\dfrac{2C_O D}{C_H}}$

Introduction – materials

Materials are an important component of any production process and often make up a significant proportion of the costs in manufacturing accounts. Having enough materials available for production when needed is crucial. However, storing materials is expensive. Businesses therefore need to strike a balance between holding enough materials and holding too many.

1 Types of material

Materials are broken down into three major categories for costing purposes:

Raw materials. Goods purchased for making into products for sale.

Work in progress (WIP). The stages in between raw materials and finished goods at which the purchased goods are being made ready for sale.

Finished goods. Manufactured goods ready for sale or despatch.

When these are stored before use or sale, materials are known as **inventory**.

Raw materials and components used by a manufacturer are classified as direct costs for costing purposes. Examples are fabric in a tailoring company, paper in a printing company and electrical components in a manufacturer of electrical goods.

A retailer, such as a shop, and a wholesaler, which acts as a 'middle man' between the manufacturer and the retailer, would buy the products of the manufacturing companies. So, the clothing, printed matter and electrical goods produced by the manufacturers would be the materials of the retailer and wholesaler.

All businesses will buy some sort of goods for consumption, which are generally classified as indirect materials and included in overheads. In a manufacturing business, machine spares and lubricants would be production overheads, while office stationery would be a non-production overhead.

2 Ordering and receiving raw materials

2.1 Purchase requisitions, purchase orders and goods received notes

Every movement of material should be documented in order that a proper physical record is kept and the correct entries can be entered in the 'books' of the company. Purchase requisitions are sometimes called materials requisitions.

Inventory control process:

Purchase requisition

- When the stores department need more materials they issue a purchase requisition, which is sent to the purchasing department.

Purchase requisition			
Job No.			
Supplier Date			
Requested by			
Quantity	Code	Description	Cost
Authorised:			

<table>
<tr><td>Purchase order (PO)</td></tr>
</table>

- The purchasing department raise a PO, which is sent to:
    - The supplier
    - The accounts department
    - Stores

Purchase order		No.	
To		Date	
Order ref			
Address			
Quantity	Code	Description	Cost
		Subtotal	
		VAT @ 20%	
		Total	

When the goods arrive at stores:

Delivery note/goods received note (GRN)

- Received with the goods into the stores department
- Signed off to confirm quantity and quality
- Sent to:
    - Purchasing department
    - Accounts department

Goods received note		
Date		No.
Time		
Out order no.		
Supplier no.		
Quantity	No./Code	Description
Received in good condition........................		

The accounts department should match the purchase order to the GRN and then to the invoice when it arrives from the supplier.

2.2 Cost bookkeeping for materials

The materials movements are recorded in the inventory control account. We will start with the opening balance, a debit entry in the account, as it is an asset, the opening inventory.

Inventory control account

		£			£
1 May	Opening balance	400			

Next, each of the purchases in the period are entered as debits in the inventory control account with the credit entry being to payables or cash depending upon whether the purchase was on credit or not.

Inventory control account

		£			£
1 May	Opening balance	400			
5 May	Bank/payables	840			
21 May	Bank/payables	1,350			

Then the issues to production should be recorded. They are entered as a credit entry in the inventory control account and a debit entry in the **production control account**. The production control account is the account in which we are going to gather together all of the direct costs of production during the period, starting here with the materials cost.

Inventory control account

		£			£
1 May	Opening balance	400	10 May	Production	568
5 May	Bank/payables	840	15 May	Production	420
21 May	Bank/payables	1,350	28 May	Production	252

Production control account

		£			£
10 May	Inventory control	568			
15 May	Inventory control	420			
28 May	Inventory control	252			

Finally, the inventory control account can be balanced to show the closing balance at 31 May.

Inventory control account

		£			£
1 May	Opening balance	400	10 May	Production	568
5 May	Bank/payables	840	15 May	Production	420
21 May	Bank/payables	1,350	28 May	Production	252
			31 May	Closing balance	1,350
		2,590			2,590

Inventory double entry – summary

The relevant double entries for a single purchase of materials working its way through into the final accounts are as follows:

(a)	DEBIT	Inventory	£X	
	CREDIT	Cash (or payables)		£X

Being the purchase of materials which are put into raw materials inventory.

(b)	DEBIT	Direct costs or Production	£X	
	CREDIT	Inventory		£X

Being the **issue** of materials to production for use in production.

(c)	DEBIT	Finished goods	£X	
	CREDIT	Direct costs or Production		£X

Being the transfer of units that are now finished to finished goods inventory.

(d)	DEBIT	Cost of sales	£X	
	CREDIT	Finished goods		£X

Being the taking of units out of finished goods inventory and selling them.

(e)	DEBIT	Statement of profit or loss	£X	
	CREDIT	Cost of sales		£X

Being the closing off of ledger accounts and the drawing up of financial statements.

This entry would be made at the end of a period.

Sometimes the materials which are issued to production for use in work in progress are not actually used. They are therefore returned to inventory. The double entry for this is:

DEBIT Inventory £X

CREDIT Direct costs or Production £X

Being the return of materials to stores.

2.3 Direct and indirect costs

We saw earlier in this Course Book that materials, labour and expenses can be classified as either direct or indirect depending upon whether or not they relate to a specific unit of product or service. The importance of this distinction is that the direct materials are part of the cost of the units produced which is being gathered together in the production control account, whereas the indirect materials are overheads which must be recorded separately in a **production overhead control account**.

Illustration 1: Cost bookkeeping for materials

During the month of June Gilchrist Chemicals made total purchases of materials of £71,400. Direct materials valued at £69,200 were issued to the factory for production and indirect materials for machine maintenance during the month were £3,600. At the beginning of June the total inventory valuation was £7,300.

The materials control account is initially debited with the opening inventory valuation and the purchases for the month.

Inventory control account

		£			£
1 Jun	Opening balance	7,300			
30 Jun	Purchases	71,400			

The issues from stores must now be entered on the credit side of the inventory control account. The direct materials are debited to the production control account while the indirect materials are debited to the production overhead control account.

Inventory control account

		£			£
1 June	Opening balance	7,300	30 June	Direct materials – Production	69,200
30 June	Purchases	71,400	30 June	Indirect materials – Production o/h control	3,600

Production control account

		£			£
30 June	Inventory control	69,200			

Production overhead control

		£			£
30 June	Inventory control	3,600			

Finally, the inventory control account can be balanced to find the closing inventory value. However, we will not balance the other two accounts yet as there are more entries to be made to them later in the chapter and in the next chapter.

Inventory control account

		£			£
1 June	Opening balance	7,300	30 June	Direct materials – Production	69,200
30 June	Purchases	71,400	30 June	Indirect materials – Production o/h control	3,600
			30 June	Closing balance	5,900
		78,700			78,700

Activity 1: Control accounts – Bodger & Co

Bodger & Co spends the following in 20X2:

	£
Inventory materials bought on credit	5,000

Required

Show how this cost would be initially recorded in the following accounts.

Payables control account
Inventory control account

Payables control account

	£		£

Inventory control account

	£		£

Activity 2: Issuing materials – Bodger & Co

Bodger & Co issues all the materials to production for use in production.

Required

Show how the issue of materials would be recorded in the following accounts.

Inventory control account
Production control account

Inventory control account

	£		£
Payables	5,000		

Production control account

	£		£

3 Inventory costs and control

There are many different costs that can occur if a business keeps inventory. These need to be controlled and kept to a minimum.

(a)   **Holding costs.** For example, warehouse rent, insurance, security, obsolescence and deterioration.

(b)   **Ordering costs.** For example, admin costs associated with placing an order, transport inwards costs.

Activity 3: Holding inventory

Required

Which of the following are reasons for holding inventory? Tick all those that are valid reasons.

	✓
To avoid production stoppages due to a shortage of materials	
To take advantage of quantity discounts	
To avoid the detrimental effect of price fluctuations	
To provide a buffer or fail-safe in times of general shortage or heavy demand	

3.1 Minimum inventory level or buffer inventory

The minimum level (also called inventory buffer) is an inventory level below which inventory should not normally fall.

It acts as a warning sign to management that inventory is very low and that there is an increased risk of running out of inventory.

Lead time is the time between placing an order for inventory and receiving the inventory.

Formula to learn

Minimum inventory level (or inventory buffer) = Reorder level − (Average usage × Average lead time)

3.2 Maximum inventory level

The maximum level is an inventory level above which inventory should not normally rise.

It acts as a warning sign to management that too much inventory is held, which may be uneconomical.

Formula to learn

Maximum inventory level = Inventory buffer + Maximum reorder quantity

3.3 Reorder level

When the level of inventory falls to the **'reorder level'**, more inventory should be ordered.

It is set so that, in theory, replacement inventory will be delivered just as the level reaches the buffer inventory level.

Formula to learn

Reorder level = (Average usage × Average lead time) + Inventory buffer

3.4 Reorder quantity

At the reorder level, more inventory is ordered. The quantity ordered depends on whether management want to order enough to restore inventory to the maximum level or the minimum level.

Formula to learn

Minimum reorder quantity = Average usage × Average lead time
Maximum reorder quantity = Maximum inventory level – Inventory buffer

Activity 4: Inventory control levels

A large retailer with multiple outlets maintains a central warehouse from which the outlets are supplied.

The following information is available for part number CB 2005:

Average usage	350 parts per day
Minimum usage	180 parts per day
Maximum usage	420 parts per day
Maximum inventory level	10,820 parts
Lead time for replenishment	11 days–15 days
Inventory buffer	1,750 parts

Required

(a) **What is the reorder level?**

Reorder level is [　　　　] parts.

(b) **What is the minimum inventory reorder quantity?**

Minimum inventory quantity is [　　　　] parts.

(c) **What is the maximum inventory reorder quantity?**

Maximum inventory quantity is [　　　　] parts.

3.5 The economic order quantity (EOQ)

Economic order quantity (EOQ) is a mathematical tool to calculate the amount of inventory to order in each order and minimise the holding costs, ordering costs and purchase costs.

Formula to learn

Total inventory costs = Ordering costs + Purchase costs + Holding costs

The total cost is minimised when:

Formula to learn

$$Q = EOQ = \sqrt{\frac{2C_oD}{C_H}}$$ **(Formula will NOT be given in the assessment.)**

Terms

D = annual demand in units

Co = fixed cost per order

C_H = cost of holding one unit for one year

Q = number of units ordered

The EOQ formula assumes that:

(a) Demand is constant
(b) Delivery is instantaneous or lead time is constant
(c) Purchase costs are constant (no discounts)

Activity 5: EOQ

The demand for a product is 150 units per month.

It costs £25 per unit to purchase the product.

The fixed cost per order is £32.

The holding cost is 18% pa of the purchase price.

Required

What is the EOQ (in units)? [   ]

4 FIFO and AVCO valuation

The **stores ledger accounts** or inventory record cards record the value of materials purchased, and this information can be obtained from the purchase order and invoice. When goods are issued to the production department from stores or a warehouse, a value will need to be recorded on the stores ledger accounts and on the costing details for the job or department that is going to bear that cost. The question is how do we value these issues if prices are changing regularly? How should the remaining inventories on hand be valued? This is not just a costing problem; it is also something that is needed for the preparation of the financial accounts.

Some items can be specifically priced from an invoice as they are individual items. However, most materials are bought in quantity and added to existing inventory where it is difficult to track the individual costs. Here, one of the following methods can be used to estimate the cost.

4.1 First in, first out (FIFO)

First in, first out (FIFO) assumes that the first items bought are the first items issued. So:

* Items issued are costed at the earliest invoice prices related to the inventory held, working forwards through to the later prices; and

* Inventory on hand is valued at the latest prices, working back.

FIFO is most appropriate in businesses where the oldest items are actually issued first, which is the case with perishable goods such as food, but actually this is a very popular method in many types of business.

Note that in a time of rising prices generally, FIFO values inventory at the highest amounts. This leads to a high value of closing inventory at the end of an accounting period, which can make that period's profit look better.

Say, for example, ABC Ltd's inventory consisted of four deliveries of raw material in the last month:

	Units		
1 September	1,000 at	£2.00
8 September	500 at	£2.50
15 September	500 at	£3.00
22 September	1,000 at	£3.50

If on 23 September 1,500 units were issued to production, 1,000 of these units would be priced at £2.00 (the cost of the 1,000 oldest units in inventory) and 500 at £2.50 (the cost of the next oldest 500). 1,000 units of closing inventory would be valued at £3.50 (the cost of the 1,000 most recent units received) and 500 units at £3.00 (the cost of the next most recent 500).

Note that FIFO (and **AVCO**) are just methods for **accounting** for inventory. They are not used for **physically issuing** inventory. For example, the inventory is not issued on a FIFO basis, it is just valued on a FIFO basis.

Advantages and disadvantages of the FIFO method

Advantages	Disadvantages
• It is a logical pricing method which probably represents what is physically happening: in practice the oldest inventory is likely to be used first	• FIFO can be cumbersome to operate because of the need to identify each batch of material separately
• It is easy to understand and explain to managers. FIFO also complies with the IAS 2 accounting standard so can be used for inventory valuation in financial accounting	• Managers may find it difficult to compare costs and make decisions when they are charged with continually varying prices for the same materials
• The closing inventory value will probably be similar to its replacement cost	

Note that there is another method for accounting for inventory, called LIFO (last in, first out) that you covered in *Principles of Costing*, but this method will not be in your *Management Accounting Techniques* assessment.

4.2 Average cost (AVCO)

With the **average cost (AVCO)** method, a weighted average cost is calculated each time a new delivery is received. The weighting is provided by the number of units at each price brought into the calculation. The general formula is

Formula to learn

$$\text{Average price per unit} = \frac{\text{Total value of opening inventory} + \text{Total value of units added to inventory}}{\text{Units of opening inventory} + \text{Units added to inventory}}$$

AVCO would be most appropriate if the inventories were to be mixed when they are stored, for example chemicals stored in a vat.

When prices are generally rising, AVCO distorts period profits less than FIFO, since it uses an average of the prices at which the actual inventory was purchased.

Advantages and disadvantages of the AVCO method

Advantages	Disadvantages
• Fluctuations in prices are smoothed out, making it easier to use the data for decision making	• The resulting issue price is rarely an actual price that has been paid and can run to several decimal places
• It is easier to administer than FIFO, because there is no need to identify each batch separately	• Prices tend to lag a little behind current market values when there is rapid inflation

Illustration 2: FIFO and AVCO

ABC Ltd recorded the following transactions during May:

Transactions during May 20X3

	Quantity Units	Unit cost £	Total cost £	Sales price per unit on date of transaction £
Opening balance, 1 May	100	2.00	200	
Receipts, 3 May	400	2.10	840	2.11
Issues, 4 May	200			2.11
Receipts, 9 May	300	2.12	636	2.15
Issues, 11 May	400			2.20
Receipts, 18 May	100	2.40	240	2.35
Issues, 20 May	100			2.80
Closing balance, 31 May	200			2.83
			1,916	

FIFO

Using FIFO, the cost of issues and the closing inventory value in the example would be as follows.

Date of issue	Quantity issued Units	Value	£	£
4 May	200	100 o/s at £2.00	200	
		100 at £2.10	210	
				410
11 May	400	300 at £2.10	630	
		100 at £2.12	212	
				842
20 May	100	100 at £2.12		212
Cost of issues				1,464
Closing inventory value	200	100 at £2.12	212	
		100 at £2.40	240	
				452
				1,916

The cost of materials issued plus the value of closing inventory equals the cost of purchases plus the value of opening inventory (£1,916).

The value of closing inventory represents the latest items to be bought,
100 @ £2.12 + 100 @ £2.40.

The market price of purchased materials is rising dramatically. In a period of inflation, there is a tendency with FIFO for materials to be issued at a cost lower than the current market value, although closing inventories tend to be valued at a cost approximating to current market value.

The format for the FIFO Inventory record card is as follows:

	Inventory record card							
	Purchases			**Sales**			**Balance**	
Date	Quantity Units	Cost £	Total cost £	Quantity Units	Cost £	Total cost £	Quantity Units	Total cost £
Balance at 1 May							100	200
3 May	400	2.10	840				500	1,040
4 May				100 100	2.00 2.10	200 210	300	630
9 May	300	2.12	636				600	1,266
11 May				300 100	2.10 2.12	630 212	200	424

Inventory record card								
	Purchases			**Sales**			**Balance**	
Date	**Quantity** **Units**	**Cost** **£**	**Total cost** **£**	**Quantity** **Units**	**Cost** **£**	**Total cost** **£**	**Quantity** **Units**	**Total cost** **£**
18 May	100	2.40	240				300	664
20 May				100	2.12	212	200	452

AVCO

The average costing method or cumulative weighted average pricing method calculates a **weighted average price** for all units in inventory. Issues are priced at this average cost, and the balance of inventory remaining would have the same unit valuation. The average price is determined by dividing the total cost by the total number of units.

A new weighted average price is calculated whenever a new delivery of materials into store is received. This is the key feature of cumulative weighted average pricing.

In our example, issue costs and closing inventory values would be as follows:

Date	Received Units	Issued Units	Balance Units	Total inventory value £	Unit cost £	£
Opening inventory			100	200	2.00	
3 May	400			840	2.10	
			* 500	1,040	2.08	
4 May		200		(416)	2.08	416
			300	624	2.08	
9 May	300			636	2.12	
			* 600	1,260	2.10	
11 May		400		(840)	2.10	840
			200	420	2.10	
18 May	100			240	2.40	
			* 300	660	2.20	
20 May		100		(220)	2.20	220
						1,476
Closing inventory value			200	440	2.20	440
						1,916

* A new inventory value per unit is calculated whenever a new receipt of materials occurs.

Notes

(a)   The cost of materials issued plus the value of closing inventory equals the cost of purchases plus the value of opening inventory (£1,916).

(b)   In a period of inflation, using the cumulative weighted average pricing system, the value of material issues will rise gradually, but will tend to lag a little behind the current market value at the date of issue. Closing inventory values will also be a little below current market value. The value of closing inventory is calculated using the latest average inventory value per unit.

The format of the AVCO Inventory record card is as follows:

Inventory record card								
	Purchases			**Sales**			**Balance**	
Date	**Quantity** **Units**	**Cost** **£**	**Total cost** **£**	**Quantity** **Units**	**Cost** **£**	**Total cost** **£**	**Quantity** **Units**	**Total cost** **£**
Balance at 1 May							100	200
3 May	400	2.10	840				500	1,040
4 May				200	2.08	416	300	624
9 May	300	2.12	636				600	1,260
11 May				400	2.10	840	200	420
18 May	100	2.40	240				300	660
20 May				100	2.20	220	200	440

Activity 6: CCS Ltd

The demand for a product is 150 units per month.

Charlotte's Country Soups Ltd (CCS) is a new business that has only been established since March 2009. The company makes a small range of specialist organic soups that it sells to supermarkets and independent retailers.

Prices of all the ingredients that the company has to buy are increasing. Bearing this in mind, CCS would like to use the inventory issue and valuation method that would give it the highest reported profit in its first year of trading.

Required

(a)   **Identify the method that would achieve this.**

[   ]

(b) Use the method identified in (a) to complete the inventory record card below.

Inventory record card for potatoes

| Date | Receipts | | | Issues | | | Balance | |
	Quantity tonnes	Cost per tonne £	Total cost £	Quantity tonnes	Cost per tonne £	Total cost £	Quantity tonnes	Total cost £
Balance as at: 1 June							72	10,512
2 June	70	150.00	10,500				142	21,012
3 June				90				
4 June	50	152.00						
5 June				70				

A business may choose to use FIFO or AVCO but it is important that it uses a consistent inventory valuation policy and doesn't change it without good reason.

5 Inventory counting (stocktaking)

Another aspect of inventory control is the minimisation of inventory discrepancies. A major part of this is inventory counting: the counting of physical quantities of inventory. It is sometimes called an 'inventory count'. If the inventory count list does not match the stores ledger accounts then the differences should be investigated and the system tightened up where necessary.

Periodic inventory counting is usually carried out once per year with all inventory being counted on a particular day. Many businesses will use this method to actually establish an inventory figure for their annual accounts as they do not keep a perpetual (continuously updated) inventory.

Continuous inventory counting occurs on a year-round basis. A number of items are checked each week so that each inventory line will have been checked over the period of one year, while valuable or high-turnover items are checked more often. This method is run alongside a perpetual inventory system as updated inventory records are needed for checking. It also means that the inventory value shown in the records can be used in the financial accounts without the disruption that is often caused by a periodic inventory count.

6 Work in progess (WIP)

At the end of the accounting period we may have two types of units or output:

(a) Fully completed good output
(b) Output that is incomplete

This partially completed output is known as work in progress (WIP).

To spread the cost fairly between units we use a measure called **equivalent units (EU).**

KEY TERM

Equivalent units (EU) are the number of complete units to which the work in progress is equivalent.

To calculate an equivalent unit, we calculate how many finished units the WIP equates to. For example, two shirts each 50% complete have had the same amount of fabric and labour input as one finished shirt, so in this case the two work in progress units are one equivalent unit.

The number of equivalent units is then used to calculate the cost per equivalent unit. This then allows a value to be given to the finished goods and the closing WIP.

Illustration 3: EU and closing WIP

During the month of May the costs of production were £21,000 and the output was 10,000 completed units and 1,000 units that were half completed. How do we value each of the units of completed output and work in progress? We use equivalent units.

	Equivalent units
Completed production	10,000
Work in progress (1,000 × ½)	500
	10,500

Therefore during the period the equivalent of 10,500 completed units have passed through production. The cost per equivalent unit (EU) can now be found.

$$\text{Cost per equivalent unit} = \frac{£21,000}{10,500\,\text{EU}}$$

$$= £2 \text{ per equivalent unit}$$

The completed production will be valued at:

Completed production 10,000 × £2 = £20,000

The closing work in progress will be valued at £2 for each equivalent unit:

Closing work in progress 500 × £2 = £1,000

Activity 7: Closing work in progress

Production costs for June included direct materials of £30,000, direct labour of £20,000 and production overhead of £10,000. At the end of the month, 3,460 units were complete and 900 units were 60% complete.

Required

Calculate the cost per equivalent unit. Enter your answer to the nearest whole number.

£

Calculate the closing value of work in progress. Enter your answer to the nearest whole number.

£

7 Labour

The principle of recording and controlling costs incurred by a business, already demonstrated in respect of materials, also applies to labour costs. Businesses will normally require a system capable of analysing both labour times and costs. Labour costs include the gross pay of the employee, employer's national insurance, training costs and benefits such as company cars. All employees will give rise to labour costs. Office workers in administration departments, canteen staff, maintenance staff and supervisory staff are examples of **indirect labour. Direct labour** costs arise from the employees that work directly on the goods produced by a manufacturing business, or employees that provide the service in a service business.

8 Remuneration methods

8.1 Time-based system using a time rate

A **time rate** means that a basic amount is paid per hour worked. So wages are determined by the number of hours worked.

Wages = Hours worked × Basic rate of pay per hour

If an employee works more than their basic hours they may be paid an **overtime premium**.

Attendance records usually take the form of **timesheets**. These can be completed by the employee or compiled from **clock cards** that record time in and out.

If employees are working on specific jobs then attendance is sometimes recorded directly on **job cards** rather than timesheets.

If a worker is directly involved in production, their basic hourly rate is always a direct cost when they are working on production.

8.2 Overtime

An overtime premium is the amount paid to an employee over and above the basic hourly wage. For example, if an employee is normally paid £7.50 per hour but is paid £10.00 per hour during **overtime**, the premium is £2.50.

An overtime premium is normally treated as an indirect cost (overhead).

The two exceptions are:

- The overtime is worked at the specific request of a customer for a particular job. In this case the overtime premium is treated as a direct cost of the job.

- The overtime is worked regularly by the production department. In this case the overtime premium may be treated as a usual occurrence and incorporated into an average hourly rate.

Note that in your assessment you may be told exactly how to treat overtime premiums so read the requirements carefully.

Activity 8: Overtime premium

Mark worked from 8am until 5pm with a one-hour lunch break. His normal hours are 9am–5pm with a one-hour lunch break. His basic wage is £15 per hour and overtime is paid at time and a half.

Required

Calculate the basic pay, overtime premium and Mark's total wage for the day.

Basic pay	£	

Overtime premium	£	

Mark's total wage	£		for the day

Activity 9: Job 146

The following data relates to job 146:

Total direct labour hours worked	45,000
Basic hours	12,000
Basic wage rate	£7 per hour
Overtime premium	25%

Required

Calculate the direct labour cost of job 146, assuming that overtime is worked at the specific request of the customer.

Basic pay	£	

Overtime premium	£	

Direct labour cost of Job 146 is	£	

Activity 10: Component C

The following information relates to skilled direct labour costs incurred in producing 500,000 units of Component C during January 20X6:

Normal time hours worked = 5,000 hours

Overtime at time and a half worked = 2,000 hours

Overtime at double time worked = 1,000 hours

Normal time hourly rate = £10 per hour

Overtime premiums paid are included as part of direct labour cost.

Required

(a) **Calculate the correct total cost of direct labour used to produce Component C in January 20X6.**

(b) **Calculate the direct labour cost per unit.**

(a)	Total cost of direct labour	£	

(b)	Direct labour cost per unit	£	

9 The wages control account

Payroll is a record showing each employee's gross pay, net pay and deductions such as PAYE, national insurance and pensions. There is also usually an analysis, which is used for cost accounting purposes. The payroll analysis can analyse gross pay by department, class of labour and product, and be broken down into various constituents such as direct, indirect and idle time.

A wages control account is used to record the payroll costs. Obviously, the amount debited as the wages expense will be the gross pay, as this will be the cost to the business and the cost that needs to be used for costing purposes. However, the constituents of gross pay will be posted separately to the wages control account.

- Net pay is posted from the cash book.
- Deductions are debited with the credit entries being recorded in payables accounts until the amounts are due to be paid to the HMRC/pension scheme.

The credits to the wages control account are:

- Direct labour (debited to production)
- Indirect production labour (debited to a production overheads account)
- Administration labour (debited to a non-production overheads account)

Illustration 4: Wages control account

Gilchrist Chemicals has on its payroll records the following details for the month of June.

	£
Net pay	100,000
PAYE and NIC deductions	25,000
Contributions to company welfare scheme	15,000
Gross pay	140,000

The payroll analysis shows that £110,000 relates to direct labour and £30,000 is for indirect labour.

These details are recorded in the wages control account as follows.

Wages control account

	£		£
Bank	100,000	Production	110,000
HM Revenue & Customs	25,000	Production o/h	30,000
Welfare scheme contributions	15,000		
	140,000		140,000

The other sides of the entries are added to the materials entries in the production control account and the production overheads control account.

Production control account

		£		£
30 June	Inventory control	69,200		
30 June	Wages control	110,000		

Production overhead control

		£		£
30 June	Inventory control	3,600		
30 June	Wages control	30,000		

You will notice that the wages control account has no balance carried down as it simply shares out the total gross wage cost between direct and indirect labour costs. The other two accounts will not yet be balanced as there would be overhead expenses still to enter.

Labour double entry – summary

The process of accounting for labour is similar to the process for accounting for materials.

| (a) | DEBIT | Wages | £X | |
| | CREDIT | Cash | | £X |

Being the payment of staff wages.

| (b) | DEBIT | Direct costs/Production | £X | |
| | CREDIT | Wages | | £X |

Being the transfer of direct labour to production for use in work in progress.

| (c) | DEBIT | Indirect costs/Production overheads | £X | |
| | CREDIT | Wages | | £X |

Being the transfer of indirect labour to production overheads for use in work in progress.

Chapter summary

- Inventory movements are recorded in the inventory control account.

- Direct materials issued to production are debited to the production control account and indirect materials issued are debited to the production overhead control account.

- When a business holds inventories it will incur two main types of costs: the holding costs of that inventory and the ordering costs. The purpose of inventory control is to balance these two costs in order to minimise the overall cost of holding the inventory.

- The reorder level for inventory is calculated to ensure that the inventory levels should never fall to zero during the lead time.

- The economic order quantity is the amount that should be ordered when each order is placed to ensure the minimisation of the overall cost of holding inventory.

- Often a business will set a minimum inventory level below which the inventory level should not be allowed to fall.

- The valuation of inventory normally requires an assumption to be made regarding the valuation method; this will be FIFO or AVCO.

- In order to control the inventory that is held, businesses will regularly count their inventories and compare the physical quantity with the inventory records; any discrepancies should be investigated and corrected.

- At the end of the period there may be some partially completed units, or closing work in progress.

- In order to value the completed units and the closing work in progress the total number of equivalent units must be calculated and the cost per unit determined.

- Employees record their attendance times on attendance records, signing-in books or clock cards.

- Job costing requires more detailed records of time spent on each job, and this is recorded on a timesheet or a job card.

- The wages control account records payroll costs. These may also be charged to the production control account and production overhead control account in a manufacturing business.

Keywords

- **AVCO (average cost):** A weighted average cost is calculated each time a delivery is received, subsequent issues and inventory on hand are valued at this cost

- **Clock card:** A card for each employee that records the start and finish times of periods of work

- **Closing work in progress:** Partially completed units from a process at the end of the period

- **Economic order quantity (EOQ):** The amount to order each time in order to minimise inventory holding costs

- **Equivalent units:** The number of complete units to which the work in progress is equivalent

- **FIFO (first in, first out):** Assumes that the earliest purchases or production are used first. Inventory on hand is valued at the latest prices, issues at earlier prices

- **Holding costs:** Costs of holding inventory, such as storage costs, cost of capital tied up, insurance, obsolescence and security

- **Inventory:** Goods held by the business as a current asset made up of raw materials, work in progress and finished goods

- **Inventory control:** The regulation of inventory levels so that the costs associated with inventory are kept to a minimum

- **Job card:** Details the task to be performed on a particular job, and follows the job round; each employee records the time spent on their operation on the job

- **Lead time:** Time taken from an order being placed to the goods arriving

- **Materials control account:** Cost ledger account where inventory movements are recorded

- **Materials requisition:** A request for materials by the production department sent to the stores

- **Maximum inventory level:** The level above which inventory cannot be allowed to rise

- **Minimum inventory level:** The level below which inventory should not be allowed to fall as a general rule

- **Opening work in progress:** Partially completed units brought forward at the beginning of the period

- **Ordering costs:** Costs of ordering materials, such as administrative costs and transport inwards

- **Overtime:** A higher rate of pay if hours worked in a week exceed a pre-set limit

- **Overtime premium:** The additional cost of overtime hours above the basic rate

- **Payroll:** Record showing each employee's gross pay, net pay and deductions

- **Production control account:** Cost ledger account where all the direct costs of production are gathered

- **Production overhead control account:** Cost ledger account for all production overheads

- **Reorder level:** The inventory level that triggers the placing of an order

- **Salary:** The payment of a set amount at agreed intervals, usually weekly or monthly

- **Timesheet:** A form completed by an employee detailing the time spent on each client's work each day, or week

- **Time rate:** A basic amount paid per hour

Test your learning

1 Using the:

(a) FIFO
(b) AVCO methods

Calculate the cost of materials issues and the value of closing inventory using the information below. Enter your answer into the inventory record cards below. (For AVCO, work to the nearest penny.)

January 3	Balance	100 kg	Valued @ £8.80 per kg
January 16	GRN 423	400 kg	Invoiced @ £9.00 per kg
January 27	Materials requisition 577	250 kg	
February 5	Materials requisition 582	180 kg	
February 9	GRN 439	400 kg	Invoiced @ £9.30 per kg
February 17	Materials requisition 589	420 kg	
February 25	GRN 446	500 kg	Invoiced @ £9.35 per kg

(a) FIFO

	Inventory record card							
	Purchases			Requisitions			Balance	
Date	Quantity kg	Cost £	Total cost £	Quantity kg	Cost £	Total cost £	Quantity kg	Total cost £
3 Jan								
16 Jan								
27 Jan								
5 Feb								
9 Feb								
17 Feb								
25 Feb								

(b) **AVCO**

	Inventory Record Card							
	Purchases			Requisitions			Balance	
Date	Quantity kg	Cost £	Total cost £	Quantity kg	Cost £	Total cost £	Quantity kg	Total cost £
3 Jan								
16 Jan								
27 Jan								
5 Feb								
9 Feb								
17 Feb								
25 Feb								

2   On 1 March a business has £12,400 of materials inventories. During March there were £167,200 of purchases and issues to production totalling £160,400. There were also £8,300 of indirect materials issued to the factory.

Write up the cost ledger accounts to reflect the month's transactions.

Materials control account

	Detail	£			£

Production control account

		£			£

Production overhead control account

		£			£

3   Eagle Printing Company Limited print posters for which they buy paper on rolls. Each roll costs £12.00. Each week, 15 rolls are used; the company operates every week of the year. Each time an order for more rolls of paper is placed, it costs the company £50.00, and the estimated cost of storing one roll is £19.65 per annum.

You are required to calculate the EOQ.

[   ] rolls

4   Kestrel Limited experiences a lead time of 4–8 days for orders of paint. Paint usage is between 150 and 200 litres per day and the buffer inventory is 550 litres.

What is the reorder level?

[   ] litres

5 XYZ Co had an opening inventory value of £880 (275 units valued at £3.20 each) on 1 April.

The following receipts and issues were recorded during April.

8 April	Receipts	600 units @ £3.00 per unit
15 April	Receipts	400 units @ £3.40 per unit
30 April	Issues	900 units

Using the FIFO method, the total value of the issues on 30 April is

£ [   ]

6 2,400 units of component C, valued at a price of £6 each, were in inventory on 1 March. The following receipts and issues were recorded during March.

3 March	Received	4,000 units @ £6.20 per unit
12 March	Received	2,000 units @ £6.86 per unit
23 March	Issued	5,100 units

Using the weighted average price method of inventory valuation, the total value of the components remaining in inventory on 23 March was

£ [   ]

7 2,400 units of component C, valued at a price of £6 each, were in inventory on 1 March. The following receipts and issues were recorded during March.

3 March	Received	4,000 units @ £6.20 per unit
12 March	Received	2,000 units @ £6.86 per unit
23 March	Issued	5,100 units

Using the FIFO method of inventory valuation, the total value of the

components issued on 23 March was   £ [   ]   (to the nearest £)

8 John Gosse is a direct worker who operates a lathe. During one week he works 40 hours, 35 of which are paid at a time rate of £10 per hour, the remainder being overtime which is paid at a premium of £4 per hour.

Calculate the direct and indirect labour cost.

Direct labour cost   £ [   ]

Indirect labour cost   £ [   ]

9   X Co has recorded the following wages costs for direct production workers for November.

Basic pay	£70,800
Overtime premium	£2,000
Gross wages	£72,800

The overtime was not worked for any specific job.

The accounting entries for these wages would be (tick the correct answer):

☐   DEBIT   Production control account   £72,800
      CREDIT   Wages control account   £72,800

☐   DEBIT   Wages control account   £72,800
      CREDIT   Production control account   £72,800

☐   DEBIT   Wages control account   £72,800
      CREDIT   Production overhead control account   £2,000
      CREDIT   Wages control account   £70,800

☐   DEBIT   Production control account   £70,800
      DEBIT   Production overhead control account   £2,000
      CREDIT   Wages control account   £72,800

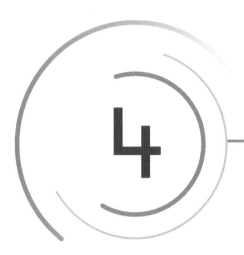

Allocation and apportionment

Learning outcomes

Having studied this chapter you will be able to:

3	Attribute costs according to organisational requirements

3.1	Calculate and attribute overhead costs using traditional methods

- Different methods of indirect cost recovery:
  - Apportionment
  - Allocation
- Attribute overhead costs to production and service cost centres:
  - Apportionment versus allocation
  - Direct method
  - Step-down method

Assessment context

Absorption costing is a core topic and you should expect one or two tasks/questions on this area in the computer-based test.

Qualification context

Overhead treatment is assumed knowledge for Level 4 *Applied Management Accounting*. Specific comparisons of absorption costing with activity-based costing scenarios are a likely assessment question at the higher level.

Business context

Every business needs to understand and control its costs. Overhead costs can sometimes be a very large proportion of a business's total costs.

Chapter overview

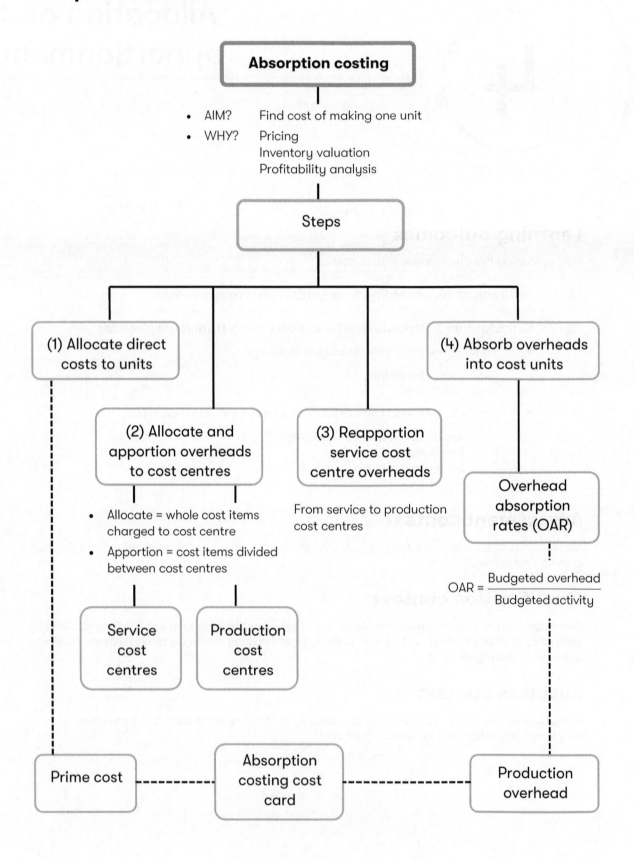

Absorption costing

- AIM?   Find cost of making one unit
- WHY?   Pricing
          Inventory valuation
          Profitability analysis

Steps

(1) Allocate direct costs to units

(4) Absorb overheads into cost units

(2) Allocate and apportion overheads to cost centres

(3) Reapportion service cost centre overheads

From service to production cost centres

Overhead absorption rates (OAR)

- Allocate = whole cost items charged to cost centre
- Apportion = cost items divided between cost centres

$$OAR = \frac{\text{Budgeted overhead}}{\text{Budgeted activity}}$$

Service cost centres

Production cost centres

Prime cost

Absorption costing cost card

Production overhead

BPP LEARNING MEDIA

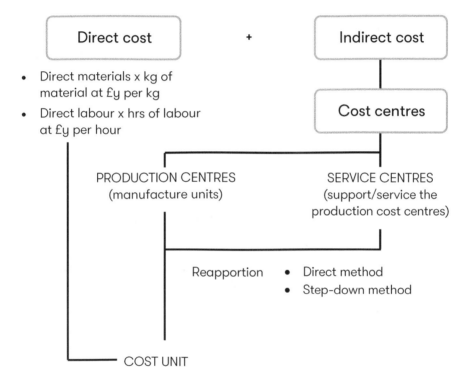

Overheads and absorption costing

- All production costs used to compute value of cost units

Total production costs

Direct cost + Indirect cost

- Direct materials x kg of material at £y per kg
- Direct labour x hrs of labour at £y per hour

Cost centres

PRODUCTION CENTRES
(manufacture units)

SERVICE CENTRES
(support/service the production cost centres)

Reapportion
- Direct method
- Step-down method

COST UNIT

Introduction

One of the key functions of a management accountant is costing. This involves calculating the **cost to produce one unit.** There are different techniques which can be applied to calculate this information. Chapters 4 and 5 will consider one of the key techniques of absorption costing.

AIM? To find the cost of making one unit

WHY? Pricing

Inventory valuation

Profitability analysis

HOW? **Absorption costing** (this chapter and the next chapter)

OR

Activity-based costing (next chapter)

OR

Marginal costing (later chapters)

Under absorption costing, a 'full' production cost per unit is calculated by including both direct production costs and an element of indirect production costs (production overheads).

1 Absorption costing

1.1 Overheads

From previous chapters, we know that the three types of indirect cost are often considered in total and called overheads.

Overheads = Indirect materials + Indirect labour + Indirect expenses

Overheads tend to be grouped as to their function:

- **Production (or factory) overheads** include indirect materials, indirect factory wages, factory rent and rates, and power and light used in the factory

- Non-production overheads:

  - **Administration overheads** include office rent and rates, office salaries, indirect office materials and depreciation of office equipment that is used for administration (rather than the main activity of the business)

  - **Selling and distribution overheads** include delivery costs, salaries of sales staff and depreciation of delivery vehicles

  - **Finance overheads** are bank interest and charges

In most cost accounting systems the aim will be to find the full production cost of the cost units. This means that a method, such as absorption costing, has to be used to include the **production overheads only** in the cost of each cost unit.

Since production overheads are not identified with specific cost units, a process must be followed to charge a share of the total production overhead to each cost unit.

2 Absorption costing overview

Absorption costing uses several stages to attach overhead costs to units of activity. By the final stage, which is absorption, an overhead absorption rate (OAR) is calculated which is used to absorb overheads into cost units. In this way, all cost units have an additional overhead charged to them.

2.1 Method

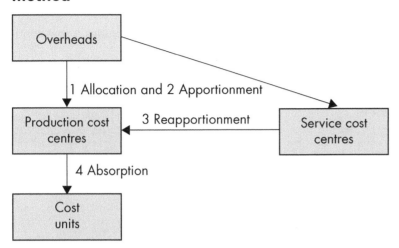

To calculate the overhead cost per unit there are four steps:

(1) **Allocation** – this is where total overheads are charged to the relevant cost centre in full.

(2) **Apportionment** – overheads are shared across each cost centre using a fair basis.

(3) **Reapportionment** – all service cost centre overheads are shared out between the production cost centres.

(4) **Absorption** – Production cost centre overheads are 'absorbed' into cost units using a suitable basis.

3 Allocation and apportionment

3.1 Allocation

Allocation of overheads is the charging of an overhead to a single responsibility centre (department) that has incurred the whole of that overhead. For example, the cost of a supervisor could be allocated to the department supervised and the depreciation of the warehouse could be allocated to the warehouse directly.

Remember that a responsibility centre is a function or department of an organisation that is headed by a manager who has direct responsibility for its performance. Responsibility centres include cost centres, profit centres and investment centres. The process of absorption costing usually focuses on cost centres.

Assessment focus point

Assessment questions may ask you to look at a list of costs for a business and decide whether they can be allocated to particular departments.

Activity 1: Allocation

Below are some overhead costs for a business for last month. This business includes a cost centre for department A and a cost centre for department B.

Required

Using the picklist, decide whether the indirect costs can be allocated or not, and which cost centre they should be allocated to.

Cost	
Wages of the supervisor of department A	▼
Wages of the supervisor of department B	▼
Indirect materials consumed in department A	▼
Rent of the factory shared by departments A and B	▼

Picklist:

Allocate to department A
Allocate to department B
Cannot be allocated

3.2 Apportionment

As you saw in Activity 1, not all overheads can be allocated to a particular cost centre. For costs that cannot be allocated, we use apportionment.

Apportionment of overheads is the charging of a proportion of an overhead to each responsibility centre that incurs part of the overhead. For example, rent of a business premises might need to be shared between the various departments making up the business. When apportioning overheads the basis used should ensure that the share charged to a cost centre reflects its usage of that overhead. This means that each type of overhead needs to be considered separately to find a suitable basis.

Examples of commonly used methods are given in the table below.

Overhead	Suitable basis for apportionment
Buildings costs such as rent, rates, repairs, insurance, heating and lighting	Floor area or volume of space occupied by the cost centre
Canteen costs	Number of employees using the cost centre
Equipment costs such as insurance and depreciation	Cost or carrying amount of equipment (net book value)
Maintenance costs	Amount of usage of maintenance department

Assessment focus point

Assessment questions may ask you to look at a list of costs for a business and decide what the best basis of apportionment is.

Activity 2: Apportionment bases

Below are some overhead costs for a business for last month.

Required

Using the picklist, choose the most appropriate basis of apportionment for each cost.

Cost	Basis of apportionment	
Rent, rates and insurance		▼
Light, heat and power		▼
Depreciation charge of machinery		▼
Canteen costs		▼

Picklist:

Carrying amount
Floor space (square metres)
Number of employees

Illustration 1: Apportionment

McQueen Co has incurred the following overhead costs.

	£000
Depreciation of factory	100
Factory repairs and maintenance	60
Factory office costs (treat as production overhead)	150
Depreciation of equipment	80
Insurance of equipment	20
Heating	39
Lighting	10
Employee welfare	90
	549

Information relating to the production and service departments in the factory is as follows.

	Department				
	Production 1	Production 2	Service 100	Service 101	Totals
Floor space (square metres)	1,200	1,600	800	400	4,000
Volume (cubic metres)	3,000	6,000	2,400	1,600	13,000
Number of employees	30	30	15	15	90
Book value of equipment	£30,000	£20,000	£10,000	£20,000	£80,000

Required

Determine how the overhead costs should be apportioned between the four departments.

Solution

Costs are apportioned using the following general formula.

$$\frac{\text{Value of apportionment base of cost centre}}{\text{Total value of apportionment base}} \times \text{Total overhead cost}$$

For example, heating for department 1 = $\frac{3,000}{13,000} \times £39 = £9$

Item of cost	Basis of apportionment	Total cost	To department			
			1	2	100	101
		£000	£000	£000	£000	£000
Factory depreciation	(floor area)	100.0	30.0*	40.0	20.0	10.0
Factory repairs	(floor area)	60.0	18.0	24.0	12.0	6.0
Factory office costs	(number of employees)	150.0	50.0	50.0	25.0	25.0
Equipment depreciation	(book value)	80.0	30.0	20.0	10.0	20.0
Equipment insurance	(book value)	20.0	7.5	5.0	2.5	5.0
Heating	(volume)	39.0	9.0	18.0	7.2	4.8
Lighting	(floor area)	10.0	3.0	4.0	2.0	1.0
Employee welfare	(number of employees)	90.0	30.0	30.0	15.0	15.0
Total		549.0	177.5	191.0	93.7	86.8

* $\frac{\text{Value of apportionment base of cost centre}}{\text{Total value of apportionment base}} \times \text{Total overhead cost}$

$\frac{1,200}{4,000} \times 100 = £30$ $\frac{1,600}{4,000} \times 100 = £40$ $\frac{800}{4,000} \times 100 = £20$ $\frac{400}{4,000} \times 100 = £10$

Assessment focus point

Assessment questions may ask you to look at a list of costs for a business and decide whether they can be allocated to particular cost centres, or whether they need to be apportioned to cost centres.

Activity 3: Allocation and apportionment basis

Required

Match the overhead with an appropriate basis for allocation and/or apportionment.

Overhead	Basis of apportionment
Rent/rates	Number of employees
Depreciation	Volume of space occupied/floor area
Staff canteen costs	Floor area
Heat, light	Value of equipment insured
Insurance of equipment	Allocate to stores cost centre
Stores costs	Carrying amount or cost of equipment

Activity 4: Overhead apportionment

A company has incurred the following overhead costs for a period:

	£
Factory rent	20,000
Factory heat	5,040
Processing department – supervisor	15,000
Packing department – supervisor	10,000
Depreciation of equipment	7,000
Factory canteen expenses	18,000
Welfare costs of factory employees	5,000
	80,040

Suitable cost centres in the company:

Processing department

Packing department

Canteen

	Processing dept £	Packing dept £	Canteen £
Cubic space	50,000 m³	25,000 m³	5,000 m³
Carrying amount of equipment	£300,000	£300,000	£100,000
Number of employees	50	40	10

Required

Allocate and apportion the overhead costs incurred to the three cost centres using the most suitable basis.

	Basis	Processing dept £	Packing dept £	Canteen £	Total £
Canteen					
Processing dept supervisor					
Packing dept supervisor					
Rent					
Heat					
Depreciation					
Welfare					
Total					

4 Reapportionment

The initial allocation or apportionment will be to production and service cost centres. However, only the production departments manufacture units, which means all the overheads must be charged to these departments only. Reapportionment is the process of removing all overheads from the service cost centres and splitting them on a suitable basis between the production cost centres.

Where there is more than one service cost centre, any work performed for one another (inter service department work) must be split appropriately.

There are two methods to approach this which are assessable in this unit:

(a) Apportion costs of each service department to production departments only. This ignores any work that the service department do for each other (**the direct method**).

(b) Apportion the costs of each service department to production but also allow one service department to allocate costs to the other service department (**the step-down method**).

 Illustration 2: Reapportionment

Let's look at each method individually and see how the reapportionment is achieved.

A company has two production and two service departments (Stores and Maintenance). The following information about activity in the most recent costing period is available.

	Total £	Components shop £	Assembly dept £	Stores £	Maintenance £
Overheads	51,950	24,975	16,925	3,100	6,950

Direct reapportionment

Suppose the Maintenance and Stores departments do no work for each other. This enables us to use the direct method as all the service department costs are incurred in servicing the production departments. All we have to do is find a suitable basis for reapportioning each service cost centre's costs. For Stores, the number or value of materials requisitions could be used. For Maintenance, we could use the number of hours worked or the value of machinery.

Budgeted use of service cost centres:

	By the Components shop	By the Assembly department
Number of materials requisitions from Stores	750	200
Maintenance hours required	300	120

The final apportionment to production cost centres will be as follows.

	Total £	Components shop £	Assembly dept £	Stores £	Maintenance £
Overheads	51,950	24,975	16,925	3,100	6,950
Reapportion maintenance					
300:120 (W1)		4,964	1,986		(6,950)
(hours required as above)					
Reapportion stores					
750:200 (W2)		2,447	653	(3,100)	
(materials requisitions					
as above)	51,950	32,386	19,564	–	–

The total overheads of £51,950 have been apportioned to the two production cost centres, and the figures are now ready for the third stage of the process of finding the overhead cost per unit or absorption.

Workings

		£
1	£6,950 × 300/(300 + 120) =	4,964
	£6,950 × 120/(300 + 120) =	1,986
		6,950

		£
2	£3,100 × 750/(750 + 200) =	2,447
	£3,100 × 200/(750 + 200) =	653
		3,100

The step-down method

This time, let's assume that Maintenance makes use of Stores by requisitioning spare parts for machinery and other materials, but Stores does not use the services of Maintenance at all.

Budgeted use of service cost centres:

	By the Components shop	By the Assembly department	By Maintenance
Number of materials requisitions from Stores	750	200	50
Maintenance hours required	300	120	

The step-down method is appropriate in this case, which means that we must give some thought to which department is reapportioned first. If we empty Maintenance first, when we reapportion Stores costs we will put some costs back into Maintenance, as a charge for the services provided by Stores. Therefore it is more efficient to do Stores first, and then Maintenance, as no further reapportionment will be necessary.

	Total £	Components shop £	Assembly dept £	Stores £	Maintenance £
Overheads	51,950	24,975	16,925	3,100	6,950
Reapportion stores first					
750:200:50 (W1)		2,325	620	(3,100)	155
(materials requisitions)					7,105
Reapportion maintenance next					
300:120 (W2)		5,075	2,030		(7,105)
(maintenance hours)					
	51,950	32,375	19,575	–	–

Notes

1   Stores are reapportioned first as some costs will go to Maintenance too.
2   Maintenance costs are reapportioned **after** Stores costs are added in.

Workings

		£
1	£3,100 × 750/(750 + 200 + 50) =	2,325
	£3,100 × 200/(750 + 200 + 50) =	620
	£3,100 × 50/(750 + 200 + 50) =	155
		3,100
2	£7,105 × 300/(300 + 120) =	5,075
	£7,105 × 120/(300 + 120) =	2,030
		7,105

Activity 5: Overhead reapportionment – direct method

Using the following data, reapportion the overheads of Stores and Maintenance and General administration overheads to production departments X and Y using the direct method.

	Production		Service centres		
	X £	Y £	Stores £	Maintenance £	General administration overheads £
Allocated & Apportioned overheads	70,000	30,000	20,000	15,000	6,000
Value of machinery	8,000	7,000			

- 62.5% of the stores department's time is spent on production department X. The remaining time is spent on production department Y.

- The maintenance costs are to be apportioned between the production departments on the basis of value of machinery.

- General administration overheads are to be apportioned equally between the two production departments.

Direct method

	Production depts		Service centres		
	X £	Y £	Stores £	Maintenance £	General admin overheads £
Overheads					
Reapportion Stores					
Reapportion Maintenance					
Reapportion general admin overheads					
Total					

Activity 6: Overhead reapportionment – step-down method

Using the following data, reapportion the overheads of Stores and Canteen to production departments X and Y using the step-down method starting with Stores

	Production		Service centre	
	X £	Y £	Stores £	Canteen £
Allocated & Apportioned overheads	70,000	30,000	20,000	15,000
Number of employees	45	50	5	–

- 50% of the stores department's time is spent on production department X. 30% of stores department's time is spent on production department Y. 20% is spent on canteen.

- The canteen costs are to be apportioned between the production departments on the basis of number of employees.

Step-down method

	Production depts		Service centre	
	X £	Y £	Stores £	Canteen £
Allocated overhead				
Apportion stores				
Apportion canteen				
Total				

We have now covered allocation, apportionment and reapportionment. We will look at absorption in the next chapter.

Chapter summary

- Absorption costing is a method used to charge an appropriate amount of production overheads to cost units.

- Some overheads can be allocated to a cost centre, others have to be apportioned or split between a number of cost centres.

- The first step in absorption costing is allocation. Allocation is the process by which whole cost items are charged direct to a cost unit or cost centre.

- The second step in absorption costing is overhead apportionment. This involves apportioning general overheads to cost centres.

- The third step then reapportions the costs of service cost centres to production departments. Service cost centre overheads must be reapportioned to the production cost centres; reapportionment of service cost centre costs is achieved using an appropriate method depending upon whether one service cost centre provides services for another cost centre. There are several methods of reapportioning service department overheads to production departments. You need to know:

  - Direct method (ignores inter-service department work)

  - Step-down method (recognises some inter-service department work)

BPP
LEARNING
MEDIA

Keywords

- **Absorption costing:** A way of finding an appropriate amount of overhead per cost unit so that the total cost of producing a product or job can be found

- **Allocation:** Where the whole of an overhead has been incurred by one cost centre, so it is charged in full to that cost centre

- **Apportionment:** Where overheads are shared, on a fair basis, among the cost centres that jointly incurred the cost

- **Overheads:** Indirect labour, indirect materials and indirect expenses

- **Production cost centres:** A cost centre that actually produces cost units

- **Reapportionment:** Apportionment of service cost centres costs to the production cost centres that use their service

- **Service cost centres:** A cost centre that is not directly involved with production, but with supporting production by providing a service, eg maintenance and stores

Test your learning

1   Overhead apportionment is used to (tick the correct answer):

☐ Charge whole items of costs to cost centres

☐ Charge cost units with an appropriate share of overheads

☐ Charge whole items of costs to cost units

☐ Spread common costs over cost centres

☐ Ensure budgeted overheads are not exceeded

2   Bramble Fabrications Limited has three production departments: the machine shop, assembly and painting. There is one service department which usually spends 40% of its time servicing the machine shop and the rest of the time equally in the other two production departments. Budgeted overheads to be apportioned between the departments are:

	£
Factory rent, rates and insurance	9,000
Depreciation of machinery	4,000
Supervisor's salary	8,000
Heat and light	2,000

Information for apportionment purposes:

	Machine shop	Assembly	Painting	Services
Floor area (m²)	500	200	300	200
Value of machinery	£12,000	£4,000	£3,000	£1,000
Number of employees	8	9	5	2

You are required to calculate the final apportionment of budgeted overheads to the three production departments by:

(a)   Apportioning the budgeted overheads to the four departments
(b)   Reapportioning the service department overheads

(a)

	Total £	Machine shop £	Assembly £	Painting £	Services £
Factory rent, rates and insurance	9,000				
Depreciation of machinery	4,000				
Supervisor's salary	8,000				
Heat and light	2,000				
Apportionment to all departments	23,000				

(b)

Reapportionment of services					
Total after reapportionment	23,000				Nil

3   Vine Limited has two production departments, V and W. There are two service departments, S1 and S2. The budgeted costs of each department, along with overheads which have yet to be allocated or apportioned, are listed below, along with details which can be used for allocation and apportionment.

	Total £	V £	W £	S1 £	S2 £
Indirect materials	310,000	160,000	120,000	10,000	20,000
Indirect labour	1,125,000	400,000	650,000	40,000	35,000
Buildings depreciation and insurance	100,000				
Cleaning	25,000				
Machinery depreciation and insurance	1,500,000				
Supervision of production	70,000				
Power	250,000				
Heat and light	20,000				

	Total	V	W	S1	S2
Volume occupied (m³)	10,000	6,000	3,000	800	200
% of power usage		25%	45%	20%	10%
Supervisor hours worked per week		15	20		
Value of machinery	£1,000,000	£380,000	£600,000		£20,000
% use of department S1		40%	60%		
% use of department S2		40%	50%	10%	
Direct labour hours worked		200,000	500,000		

You are required to calculate:

(a)   The total overheads for each department after allocation and apportionment

(b)   The overheads in departments V and W after reapportionment of the service departments using the step-down method

(a) Basis of apportionment

	Total £	V £	W £	S1 £	S2 £
Indirect materials					
Indirect labour					
Buildings depreciation and insurance					
Cleaning					
Machinery depreciation and insurance					
Supervision of production					
Power					
Heat & light					
Total					

(b) Reapportionment

	Total £	V £	W £	S1 £	S2 £
Step down S2 first					
S1 next 40:60					
Total after reapportionment					

BPP
LEARNING
MEDIA

Absorption costing

Learning outcomes

Having studied this chapter you will be able to:

2.2 Prepare cost accounting journals

- Principles of cost accounting journal entries for

    - Direct materials or indirect materials
    - Direct or indirect labour
    - Overhead costs

- Prepare cost accounting journals for

    - Materials
    - Labour
    - Overheads

3.2 Calculate overhead recovery rates using traditional methods

Calculate overhead recovery rates in accordance with suitable bases of absorption:

- For a manufacturer: machine hours or direct labour hours
- For a service business: suitable basis for the specific business

3.3 Calculate overhead recovery rates using activity based costing

- The concept of activity-based costing:

    - Appropriate cost drivers
    - Use of cost pools

- Calculate overhead recovery rates using appropriate cost drivers

3.4 Under- or over-recovery of overheads

- How to account for under- or over-recovered overhead costs in accordance with established procedures:

    - Making under- or over-absorption calculations

    - Interpreting the significance of under or over recoveries of overhead costs on unit costs and total profit

Assessment context

There is likely to be a task asking you to calculate an overhead absorption rate and over- or under-absorption.

Qualification context

Once you have a good foundation of absorption costing you will be using the concept when studying standard costing and variance analysis at Level 4. Absorption costing will be assumed knowledge at Level 4.

Business context

Every business needs to understand and control its costs. Overhead costs can sometimes be a very large proportion of a business's total costs.

Chapter overview

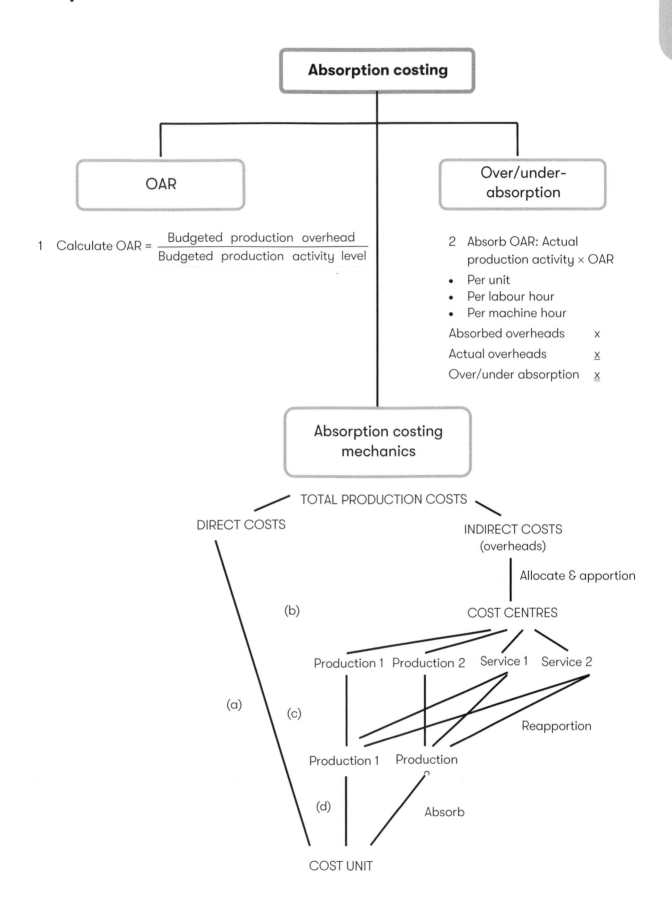

Absorption costing

OAR

1   Calculate OAR = $\dfrac{\text{Budgeted production overhead}}{\text{Budgeted production activity level}}$

Over/under-absorption

2   Absorb OAR: Actual production activity × OAR
  • Per unit
  • Per labour hour
  • Per machine hour

Absorbed overheads   x

Actual overheads   x

Over/under absorption   x

Absorption costing mechanics

TOTAL PRODUCTION COSTS

DIRECT COSTS   INDIRECT COSTS (overheads)

Allocate & apportion

(b)   COST CENTRES

Production 1   Production 2   Service 1   Service 2

(a)   (c)   Reapportion

Production 1   Production

(d)   Absorb

COST UNIT

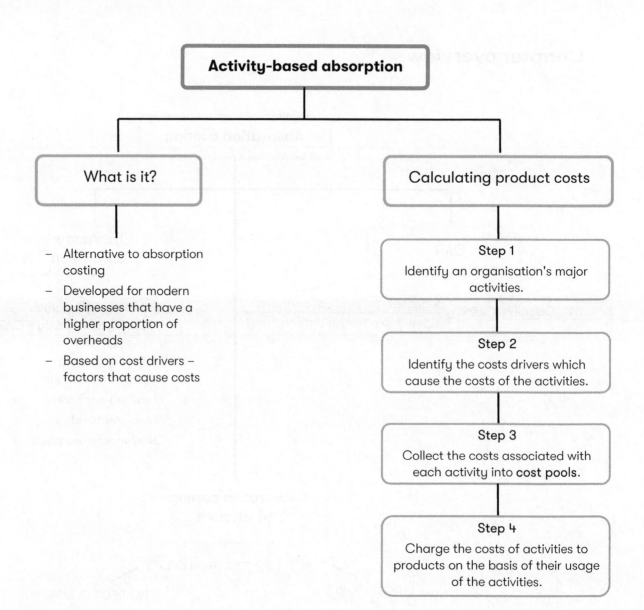

Activity-based absorption

What is it?

- Alternative to absorption costing
- Developed for modern businesses that have a higher proportion of overheads
- Based on cost drivers – factors that cause costs

Calculating product costs

Step 1
Identify an organisation's major activities.

Step 2
Identify the costs drivers which cause the costs of the activities.

Step 3
Collect the costs associated with each activity into **cost pools**.

Step 4
Charge the costs of activities to products on the basis of their usage of the activities.

Introduction

In the previous chapter we covered the first three steps involved in reaching the absorption cost of a unit of production.

To get the full (absorbed) production cost the four steps are:

(1) **Allocation** – charging whole cost items to responsibilty centres
(2) **Apportionment** – sharing production overheads among cost centres
(3) **Reapportionment** – sharing overheads in service cost centres to production cost centres
(4) **Absorption** – absorbing overheads into cost units

In this chapter we will cover step 4 and we will also look at an alternative to absorption costing, called **activity-based costing (ABC)**.

1 Absorption

Overhead absorption is the way that overheads are charged to output (cost units). This is also known as **overhead recovery**. Once all of the production overhead costs have been apportioned to the production cost centres, we need to charge these to the cost units passing through the production cost centres. This is termed **absorption**. We are going to absorb an element of total production overhead into each cost unit.

$$\text{OAR (overhead absorption rate)} = \frac{\text{Production overhead}}{\text{Activity level}}$$

Activity can be expressed in a number of ways – hours worked, machine hours used, costs incurred or units produced – and any of these can be used to calculate the absorption rate.

Ideally, the basis chosen should be the one which most accurately reflects the way in which the overheads are in fact being incurred.

	Basis	Used when
(a)	Per labour hour	The production process is labour intensive
(b)	Per machine hour	The production process is machine intensive
(c)	Per unit	Units are identical (not used in your assessment)

> ### Assessment focus point
>
> Assessment questions may ask you to decide what the most appropriate basis for absorption is for a particular responsibilty centre.

Activity 1: Overhead absorption bases

Mars Ltd has two production departments, mixing and stirring, in which it makes a variety of products.

	Mixing	Stirring
Direct labour hours	20,000	5,000
Direct machine hours	2,000	60,000

Required

Based on the above information, what are the most appropriate overhead absorption bases for the mixing and stirring departments?

Mixing department: OAR should be based on

Stirring department: OAR should be based on

Picklist:

Budgeted direct labour hours
Budgeted direct machine hours

2 Predetermined overhead absorption rates

Businesses need to cost their production throughout the year, not at the end of an accounting period. Therefore they predetermine or estimate their absorption rates for the year in advance, based on the budgeted overheads and the budgeted level of activity.

Formula to learn

$$\text{OAR (overhead absorption rate)} = \frac{\text{Total budgeted production overhead}}{\text{Total budgeted activity level}}$$

Assessment focus point

Assessment questions may ask you to calculate a budgeted overhead absorption rate (OAR) for a manufacturing business, based on budgeted labour hours or budgeted machine hours.

For a service business, the basis for the budgeted overhead absorption rate will depend on the specific business.

Always remember that the OAR is calculated using **budgeted** figures (not actual figures).

Activity 2: Overhead absorption rates (OAR) 1

Budgeted information for department A is as follows:

	Department A
Budgeted overheads	40,000
Direct machine hours	2,000

Required

Calculate the budgeted overhead absorption rate per machine hour for department A?

Budgeted OAR = £ [   ] per machine hour

The amount absorbed into production is:

Formula to learn

Amount absorbed = Actual production activity × OAR

This occurs during the year or month as production takes place.

Illustration 1: Overhead absorption rates

Bluebell Electronics makes two products, the Videobooster and the Blastbox. It is trying to decide on an appropriate basis to absorb overheads. The following budgeted information is provided.

Production units	Videobooster 4,000		Blastbox 6,000	
	Components shop hours	Assembly hours	Components shop hours	Assembly hours
Direct labour				
Hours per unit	1.25	0.50	2.00	1.00
Total hours	5,000	2,000	12,000	6,000
Machine hours				
Hours per unit	2.00	1.00	0.30	0.20
Total hours	8,000	4,000	1,800	1,200

Calculate:

(a)   Separate departmental overhead absorption rates using first labour hours and then machine hours as the absorption basis

(b)   The overhead absorbed by each product under each of the overhead absorption bases

Note. The final apportionment of overheads to the two production cost centres was: Components shop, £32,375; and Assembly, £19,575.

(a)   Departmental absorption rates

		Components	*Assembly*
Rate per direct labour hour			
$\dfrac{\text{Overheads}}{\text{Direct labour hours}}$	=	$\dfrac{£32,375}{5,000+12,000}$	$\dfrac{£19,575}{2,000+6,000}$
	=	£1.90 per direct labour hour	£2.45 per direct labour hour
Rate per machine hour			
$\dfrac{\text{Overheads}}{\text{Machine hours}}$	=	$\dfrac{£32,375}{8,000+1,800}$	$\dfrac{£19,575}{4,000+1,200}$
	=	£3.30 per machine hour	£3.76 per machine hour

(b)   The overhead absorbed by each product

Rate per direct labour hour

	Videobooster	£	*Blastbox*	£
Components shop	£1.90×1.25hrs	2.38	£1.90×2.00hrs	3.80
Assembly	£2.45×0.50hrs	1.23	£2.45×1.00hr	2.45
Total absorbed per unit		3.61		6.25

Rate per machine hour

	Videobooster	£	Blastbox	£
Components shop	£3.30×2.00hrs	6.60	£3.30×0.30hrs	0.99
Assembly	£3.76×1.00hr	3.76	£3.76×0.20hrs	0.75
Total absorbed per unit		10.36		1.74

2.1 Which absorption rate should you use?

As you can see from the example above, the type of absorption rate used can have a huge effect on the cost of a product. The amount of overhead absorbed into the Blastbox varied from £1.74 to £6.25! It is therefore important to consider very carefully which rate is appropriate for each department. The way in which the cost is incurred can guide us towards the best method.

- A rate per direct labour hour would be appropriate if the department is labour intensive and most of the overheads relate to labour (this may apply to Bluebell's Assembly department).

- A rate per machine hour is a fair method if the department is largely mechanised, with relatively little labour input (perhaps Bluebell's Component shop).

Activity 3: Overhead absorption rates (OAR) 2

Mars Ltd has two production departments, mixing and stirring, in which it makes a variety of products. Budgeted overheads are £10,000 and £15,000 respectively, and the following budgeted information has also been collected.

	Mixing	Stirring
Direct labour hours	20,000	5,000
Direct machine hours	2,000	60,000
Number of units	10,000	10,000

Required

Calculate appropriate overhead absorption rates for both the Mixing department and the Stirring department.

Mixing department OAR is £ [ ] per [ ]

Stirring department OAR is £ [ ] per [ ]

2.2 Why do we bother with predetermined OARs?

Many overheads are not known until the end of a period. If we waited until the end of a period, this would cause delays in invoicing, inventory valuation and so on. This is why we calculate an OAR based on budgeted figures. It gives us a way of taking account of overheads before we actually know what they are.

2.3 What basis of absorption would be used in a service sector organisation?

A rate per machine hour or per direct labour hour is suitable for a manufacturing business, but may not be suitable for a service business. For a service business, a suitable basis will depend on the specific business. If you get a service sector organisation in your assessment, you will need to use an appropriate **volume** basis. For example, the number of miles travelled for a bus company.

Activity 4: Overhead absorption rates in the service sector

Bus route X11 has total budgeted overheads for the year of £130,000. The expected miles travelled for the year are 325,000.

Required

Calculate an appropriate overhead absorption rate.

OAR is | £ | | per | |

3 Over- and under-absorption of overheads

3.1 What happens at the end of the year?

At the end of the year, actual overhead costs will be known.

However, using budgeted figures to calculate the overhead absorption rate means that the actual overhead cost is unlikely to be the same as the overheads absorbed into production. This is because we had to rely on two estimates:

* Overhead costs
* Activity levels

These will inevitably differ from the actual values that are experienced during the period. Consequently, at the end of the period when the statement of profit or loss is drawn up, the profit figure will be wrong as the overhead charge will be the absorbed amount (which was based on estimates) rather than the actual amount.

The error in the profit figure results from one of two possibilities.

(1) If more overheads are absorbed than have actually been incurred, this is known as **over-absorption**.

(2) If fewer overheads are absorbed than have actually been incurred, this is known as **under-absorption**.

The amount over- or under-absorbed is adjusted for in the statement of profit or loss after the production cost has been charged. Under-absorption means that too little overhead has been charged in the production cost, so a deduction is made from profit. Over-absorption means that too much overhead has been charged, so there is a compensating addition to profit.

The organisation needs to review the bases of calculation of the OAR as the activity changes over time. For instance, if an organisation becomes more automated and requires fewer workers, it would seem appropriate to change from calculating overheads based on labour hours to those based on machine hours.

Illustration 2: Over- and under-absorption

Cowslip Ltd has annual budgeted overheads of £15,000 and annual budgeted machine hours of 30,000.

The overhead absorption rate will be $= \dfrac{\text{Overheads}}{\text{Machine hours}}$

$$= \dfrac{£15,000}{30,000 \text{ hours}}$$

$$= £0.50 \text{ per machine hour}$$

In year 1, the actual overheads are £15,000 and the actual number of machine hours are 30,000.

What is the over- or under-absorbed overhead?

	£
Actual overheads	15,000
Absorbed overheads (30,000 hrs × £0.50)	15,000
Under/over absorption	Nil

In year 2, the actual overheads are £16,000 and the actual number of machine hours are 29,000.

What is the over- or under-absorbed overhead?

	£
Actual overheads	16,000
Absorbed overheads (29,000 hrs × £0.50)	14,500
Under absorption	1,500

Notice that Cowslip Ltd absorbed fewer overheads than it incurred so it under-absorbed the overhead. At the end of the year, an adjustment will need to be made to the statement of profit or loss account to account for this. As Cowslip Ltd didn't absorb enough, the statement of profit or loss will be debited with £1,500 to increase the expense.

In year 3, the actual overheads are £14,000 and the actual number of machine hours are 32,000.

What is the over- or under-absorbed overhead?

	£
Actual overheads	14,000
Absorbed overheads (32,000 hrs × £0.50)	16,000
Over absorption	2,000

Notice that Cowslip Ltd absorbed more overheads than it incurred so it over-absorbed the overhead. At the end of the year, an adjustment will need to be made to the statement of profit or loss account to account for this. As Cowslip Ltd absorbed too much, the statement of profit or loss will be credited with £2,000 to reduce the expense.

Note. Be very careful to calculate the under- or over-absorption based on actual vs absorbed costs; budgeted costs are not brought into this calculation.

Activity 5: Overhead absorption rates (OAR) 3

Pumpkin Ltd provides you with the following budgeted information for its painting division.

Total overheads: £400,000.

Total budgeted direct labour hours: 3,200

Total budgeted machine hours: 10,000

Required

(a) Calculate the budgeted fixed overhead absorption rate using a direct labour hours basis.

(b) Calculate the budgeted fixed overhead absorption rate using a machine hours basis.

(c) The painting manager informs you that the painting division is highly automated and operates with expensive machinery which is run whenever possible on a 24 hour a day, 7 days a week basis.

Which of the two OARs calculated in (a) and (b) above would be the most appropriate for absorption?

(d) At the end of the accounting period, the painting manager provides you with the following actual data for the painting division:

Total overheads	=	£521,262
Total direct labour hours	=	4,100
Total machine hours	=	12,562

Calculate the amount of overheads over- or under-absorbed for the period using the basis chosen in part (c).

(a) OAR = £ [   ] per direct labour hour

(b) OAR = £ [   ] per machine hour

(c) OAR most appropriate for absorption is £ [   ] per [   ]

(d) Overheads £ [   ] over/under* absorbed

*Delete the incorrect word, ie over or under

Activity 6: Over- or under-absorption

The Assembly department recovers its fixed overheads on the basis of budgeted machine hours.

The Finishing department, however, recovers its fixed overheads on the basis of the budgeted direct labour hours.

The following information relates to these two departments for January 20X6.

	Assembly department	Finishing department
Budgeted fixed overhead absorption rate	£10.00 per hour	£7.50 per hour
Actual machine hours worked	775	810
Actual direct labour hours worked	1,200	1,250
Actual fixed overheads	£8,110	£9,000

Required

(a) Calculate the fixed overheads absorbed in January in the Assembly department.

(b) Calculate the fixed overhead absorbed in January in the Finishing department.

(c) Calculate the over- or under-absorption of fixed overheads during January, stating clearly whether overheads have been over- or under-absorbed, for:

    (i)   The Assembly department
    (ii)   The Finishing department

(a) £ [   ]   Assembly department overhead absorbed

(b) £ [   ]   Finishing department overhead absorbed

(c) (i)   Assembly department £ [   ] over/under* absorbed

    (ii) Finishing department £ [   ] over/under* absorbed

*Delete the incorrect word, ie over or under

4 Advantages and disadvantages of absorption costing

4.1 Advantages

(a) Inventory valuation using absorption costing complies with IAS 2 (which requires that cost includes a fair share of production overheads based on normal activity levels).

(b) Fixed costs must be covered in the long run and absorption costing takes fixed costs into account (unlike marginal costing).

(c) Production cannot be divorced from fixed costs since without them production could not occur.

4.2 Disadvantages

(a) Unit cost includes costs which are not relevant for marginal decision making (see later chapters on marginal costing).

(b) The nature of cost behaviour is obscured.

(c) The method of absorption is to some extent arbitrary.

Activity 7: Mars Ltd

Mars Ltd has the following overhead absorption rates:

Mixing department   50p per labour hour

Stirring department   25p per machine hour

Mars Ltd has a product, the 'Venus', for which you obtain the following information.

Direct materials per unit	£5
Direct labour hours	
– mixing	2.0 hours
– stirring	0.5 hours
Direct machine hours	
– mixing	0.2 hours
– stirring	6.0 hours
Labour is paid £8.60 per hour	

Required

What is the total cost of this product?

	£	£
Direct costs		
Materials		
Labour		
Mixing		
Stirring		
Total direct costs		
Overheads		
Mixing department		
Stirring department		
Total overheads		
Total cost		

5 Accounting for overhead absorption

The process of accounting for production overheads is slightly different.

The initial entry is similar to that for labour and materials:

DEBIT	Production overheads	£X	
CREDIT	Cash (or payables)		£X

The subsequent entry is:

DEBIT	Production	£X	
CREDIT	Production overheads		£X

The amount we debit production and credit production overheads is the amount absorbed into production (overhead absorption rate × actual activity level).

This leaves a balance on the production overheads account which is taken to the statement of profit or loss account. This is known as the under- or over-absorption.

If under-absorption occurs this will be an additional cost in the statement of profit or loss account. Under-absorbed overheads mean that actual overheads incurred are greater than the amount absorbed into the statement of profit or loss account during the period.

Under-absorption accounting double entry is:

DEBIT	Statement of profit or loss	£X
CREDIT	Production overheads	£X

If over-absorption occurs this will reduce the cost in the statement of profit or loss account. Over-absorbed overheads mean that actual overheads incurred are less than the amount absorbed into the statement of profit or loss account during the period.

Over-absorption accounting double entry is:

DEBIT	Production overheads	£X
CREDIT	Statement of profit or loss	£X

 ## Illustration 3: Accounting for overheads

We will return to the cost ledger accounts of Gilchrist Chemicals where neither the production control account nor the production overhead control account were yet completed for the month of June. Gilchrist has incurred other expenses of £16,500 for royalties and £38,900 of indirect expenses. These are debited in the control accounts and credited to the bank account as shown. We are now going to look at how overheads are accounted for.

Production control account

		£			£
30 June	Inventory control	69,200			
30 June	Wages control	110,000			
30 June	Bank	16,500			

Production overhead control

		£			£
30 June	Inventory control	3,600			
30 June	Wages control	30,000			
30 June	Bank	38,900			

The debits in the production overhead control account are the actual overheads incurred during the month. You are now told that the amount of overhead to be absorbed into production based upon the overhead absorption rate is £75,000.

This must be debited to the production control account and credited to the production overhead control account.

Production control account

		£		£
30 June	Inventory control	69,200		
30 June	Wages control	110,000		
30 June	Bank	16,500		
30 June	Prod'n overhead control	75,000		

Production overhead control

	£		£
30 June Inventory control	3,600	30 June Production	75,000
30 June Wages control	30,000		
30 June Bank	38,900		

If we balance the production overhead control account we will find any under- or over-absorbed overhead to transfer to the statement of profit or loss.

Production overhead control

	£		£
30 June Inventory control	3,600	30 June Production	75,000
30 June Wages control	30,000		
30 June Bank	38,900		
30 June Statement of profit or loss	2,500		
	75,000		75,000

The overheads actually incurred total £72,500 (£3,600 + £30,000 + £38,900), whereas the overhead absorbed was £75,000. This is an over-absorption of overhead, which is debited in the production overhead control account and credited to the statement of profit or loss, thereby increasing profit. If the balance had been on the credit side of the production overhead control account this would have been an under-absorption which would then have been debited or charged to the statement of profit or loss.

Assessment focus point

Assessment questions may ask you whether over- or under-absorbed overheads will be debited or credited to the statement of profit or loss. Remember:

An **over**-absorption of overheads is credited to the statement of profit or loss. This will decrease expenses and will increase profit.

An **under**-absorption of overheads is debited to the statement of profit or loss. This will increase expenses and will decrease profit.

We will now finish the cost accounting process by considering the production control account. The total on this account of £270,700 is the total production cost for the period. We are now told that during the period finished products with a production cost of £250,000 have been transferred to the warehouse ready for sale. The accounting entries reflect this with £250,000 being credited to production and debited to a finished goods account.

Production control account

	£		£
30 June Inventory control	69,200	30 June Finished goods	250,000
30 June Wages control	110,000		
30 June Bank	16,500	30 June Closing balance	20,700
30 June Production o/h	75,000		
	270,700		270,700

Finished goods account

	£		£
30 June Production	250,000		

The closing balance on the production control account is the amount of work in progress at the end of the month, that is, cost units that have been started but not yet completed in the month. (This is why the account is sometimes called work in progress instead of production.)

Activity 8: Recording production overheads – Bodger & Co

Bodger & Co incurs production overheads of £6,000.

The production overhead to be absorbed into Production is:

	£
Manufacturing department	4,000
Finishing department	600
Quality control	500

Required

Show how the production overheads will be recorded in the following accounts:

Payables control account, Production overheads control account, Production control account

Payables control account

	£		£
		Inventory materials	5,000

Production overheads control account

	£		£

Production control account

	£		£
Inventory materials	5,000		

6 Activity-based costing (ABC)

Activity-based costing (ABC) is an alternative form of absorption costing. It involves the identification of the factors (called **cost drivers**) which cause the costs of an organisation's major activities.

6.1 Problems of using absorption costing in today's environment

Absorption costing assumes all products consume all resources in proportion to their production volumes.

- It tends to allocate too great a proportion of overheads to high-volume products (which cause relatively little diversity and hence use fewer support services).

- It tends to allocate too small a proportion of overheads to low-volume products (which cause greater diversity and therefore use more support services).

ABC attempts to overcome these problems.

6.2 ABC and using it to calculate product costs

Activities cause costs	Activities include ordering and despatching.
The costs of an activity are caused or driven by factors known as cost drivers	The cost of the ordering activity might be driven by the number of orders placed, the cost of the despatching activity by the number of despatches made.
The costs of an activity are assigned to products on the basis of the number of the activity's cost driver products generate	If product A requires 5 orders to be placed, and product B 15 orders, ¼ (ie 5/(5 + 15)) of the ordering cost will be assigned to product A and ¾ (ie 15/(5 + 15)) to product B.

6.2.1 Cost drivers

KEY
TERM

A **cost driver** is a factor influencing the level of cost.

Costs associated with a particular activity are collected in a **cost pool**.

For those costs that vary with production levels in the short term, ABC uses volume-related cost drivers such as labour hours or machine hours.

For costs that vary with some other activity and not volume of production, ABC uses transaction-related cost drivers such as the number of production runs for the production scheduling activity.

6.2.2 Calculating product costs using ABC

Step 1

Identify an organisation's major activities

Step 2

Identify the factors (cost drivers) which cause the costs of the activities

Step 3

Collect the costs associated with each activity into cost pools

Cost pools are equivalent to cost centres used with traditional absorption costing.

Step 4

Charge the costs of activities to products on the basis of their usage of the activities. A product's usage of an activity is measured by the number of the activity's cost driver it generates

Suppose the cost pool for the ordering activity totalled £100,000 and that there were 10,000 orders (orders being the cost driver). Each product would therefore be charged with £10 for each order it required. A batch requiring five orders would therefore be charged with £50.

Here are some examples of costs and possible cost drivers. An absorption rate is calculated for each cost pool.

Cost pool	Possible cost driver
Ordering costs	Number of orders
Materials handling costs	Number of production runs
Machine set-up costs	Number of machine set-ups
Production scheduling costs	Number of production runs
Despatching costs	Number of orders despatched

 ## Illustration 4: ABC

Lasanya Ltd makes two products, X and Y and uses activity based costing. The following bases are used to calculate overhead recovery:

Cost pool	Cost driver
Ordering costs	Number of orders
Materials handling costs	Number of production runs
Machine set-up costs	Number of machine set-ups

Budgeted overhead costs and drivers are:

Cost pool	Budget £	Cost driver	X	y	Total
Ordering costs	9,100	Number of orders	12	16	28
Materials handling costs	10,920	Number of production runs	6	8	14
Machine set-up costs	7,700	Number of machine set-ups	1	6	7

What are the overhead absorption rates for each overhead?

As with traditional absorption costing, the rates are calculated by dividing the budgeted overheads by the budgeted activity (cost driver) level.

Ordering costs

The overhead absorption rate will be

$$= \frac{\text{Ordering cost overheads}}{\text{Number of orders}}$$

$$= \frac{£9,100}{28\,\text{orders}}$$

$$= £325\,\text{per order}$$

Materials handling costs

The overhead absorption rate will be

$$= \frac{\text{Materials handling cost overheads}}{\text{Number of production runs}}$$

$$= \frac{£10,920}{14\,\text{production runs}}$$

$$= £780\,\text{per production run}$$

Machine set-up costs

The overhead absorption rate will be

$$= \frac{\text{Machine set-up cost overheads}}{\text{Number of set-ups}}$$

$$= \frac{£7,700}{7\,\text{machine set-ups}}$$

$$= £1,100\,\text{per set-up}$$

The actual numbers were as follows:

Cost driver	X	y	Total
Number of orders	10	19	29
Number of production runs	6	8	14
Number of machine set-ups	1	4	5

What is the overhead absorbed for product X, product Y and in total?

As with traditional absorption costing, the absorbed amount is calculated by multiplying the actual activity level (cost driver) by the overhead absorption rate.

BPP
LEARNING
MEDIA

	Product X	Product Y	Total
Ordering costs absorbed	£325 × 10 = £3,250	£325 × 19 = £6,175	£325 × 29 = £9,425
Materials handling costs absorbed	£780 × 6 = £4,680	£780 × 8 = £6,240	£780 × 14 = £10,920
Machine set-up costs absorbed	£1,100 × 1 = £1,100	£1,100 × 4 = £4,400	£1,100 × 5 = £5,500

The actual overheads were as follows:

Cost pool	Actual cost £
Ordering costs	10,540
Materials handling costs	9,500
Machine set-up costs	5,500

What is the over- or under-absorbed overhead for each overhead cost?

As with traditional absorption costing, the under- or over-absorbed amount is calculated by deducting the absorbed amount from the actual overhead amount.

	Ordering costs £	Materials handling costs £	Machine set-up costs £
Actual overheads	10,540	9,500	5,500
Absorbed overheads	9,425	10,920	5,500
Under/(over) absorption	1,115	(1,420)	0

Activity 9: Activity-based costing

Having attended an AAT course on activity-based costing (ABC) you decide to experiment by applying the principles of ABC to the four products currently made and sold by your company. Details of the four products and relevant information are given below for one period.

	P1	P2	P3	P4
Output in units	120	100	80	120
Costs per unit:	£	£	£	£
Direct material	40	50	30	60
Direct labour	28	21	14	21

The total of the production overhead for the period has been analysed as follows.

	£
Set-up costs	5,250
Stores receiving	3,600
Inspection/quality control	2,100
Materials handling and despatch	4,620

You have ascertained that the following 'cost drivers' are to be used for the costs shown.

Cost	Cost driver
Set-up costs	Number of production runs
Stores receiving	Requisitions raised
Inspection/quality control	Number of production runs
Materials handling and despatch	Orders executed

	P1	P2	P3	P4	Total
Number of production runs	6	5	4	6	21
Number of requisitions raised	20	20	20	20	80
Number of orders executed	12	10	8	12	42

Required

(a) Fill in the table below to calculate the cost per driver for each overhead cost.

$\dfrac{\text{Set-up costs}}{\text{Number of production runs}}$		=	£	per production run
$\dfrac{\text{Stores receiving}}{\text{Number of requisitions raised}}$		=	£	per requisition raised
$\dfrac{\text{Inspection / quality control}}{\text{Number of production runs}}$		=	£	per production run
$\dfrac{\text{Materials handling and despatch}}{\text{Number of orders executed}}$		=	£	per order executed

(b) Using your answers from (a), calculate the overhead costs for each product.

	P1	P2	P3	P4
Number of production runs	6	5	4	6
Cost per production run				
Set up costs per product				

	P1	P2	P3	P4
Number of requisitions raised	20	20	20	20
Cost per requisition raised				
Stores receiving costs per product				

	P1	P2	P3	P4
Number of production runs	6	5	4	6
Cost per production run				
Inspection/quality control costs per product				

	P1	P2	P3	P4
Number of orders executed	12	10	8	12
Cost per order executed				
Materials handling and despatch per product				

(c) Fill in the table below to calculate the total costs for each product.

	P1 £	P2 £	P3 £	P4 £
Direct material				
Direct labour				
Production overhead				
Set-up costs				
Stores receiving				
Inspection/quality control				
Material handling and despatch				
Total cost				
Unit costs				

Chapter summary

- In absorption costing, it is usual to add overheads into product costs by applying a predetermined overhead absorption rate. The predetermined rate is set annually, in the budget.

- The absorption rate is calculated by dividing the budgeted overhead by the budgeted level of activity. For production overheads, the level of activity is often budgeted direct labour hours or budgeted machine hours.

- Management should try to establish an absorption rate that provides a reasonably 'accurate' estimate of overhead costs for jobs, products or services.

- The use of separate departmental absorption rates instead of blanket (or single factory) absorption rates will produce more realistic product costs.

- The rate of overhead absorption is based on estimates and it is quite likely that either one or both of the estimates will not agree with what actually occurs. Actual overheads incurred will probably be either greater than or less than overheads absorbed into the cost of production.

  - Over-absorption means that the overheads charged to the cost of production are greater than the overheads actually incurred.

  - Under-absorption means that insufficient overheads have been included in the cost of production.

- Activity-based costing (ABC) is an alternative form of absorption costing. It involves the identification of the factors (cost drivers) which cause the costs of an organisation's major activities.

Keywords

- **Activity-based costing:** An alternative approach to absorption costing using cost drivers to assign activity costs to units

- **Cost driver:** Factor influencing the level of cost

- **Cost pool:** This is a collecting place for activity based costs (equivalent to a cost centre used with traditional absorption costing)

- **Overhead absorption rate:** The rate at which overheads are charged to cost units calculated by dividing budgeted overheads by the budgeted level of activity

- **Over-absorption:** More overheads are absorbed into production than have actually been incurred

- **Under-absorption:** Fewer overheads are absorbed into production than have actually been incurred

Test your learning

1   Which of the following statements about overhead absorption rates are true?

    (i)   They are predetermined in advance for each period
    (ii)   They are used to charge overheads to products
    (iii) They are based on actual data for each period
    (iv) They are used to control overhead costs

    A   (i) and (ii) only
    B   (i), (ii) and (iv) only
    C   (ii), (iii) and (iv) only
    D   (iii) and (iv) only

2   Over-absorbed overheads occur when

    A   Absorbed overheads exceed actual overheads
    B   Absorbed overheads exceed budgeted overheads
    C   Actual overheads exceed budgeted overheads
    D   Budgeted overheads exceed absorbed overheads

3   A company absorbs overheads on machine hours which were budgeted at 11,250 with overheads of £258,750. Actual results were 10,980 hours with overheads of £254,692.

    Overheads were

    A   Under-absorbed by £2,152
    B   Over-absorbed by £4,058
    C   Under-absorbed by £4,058
    D   Over-absorbed by £2,152

The following information relates to questions 4 and 5

Budgeted labour hours	8,500
Budgeted overheads	£148,750
Actual labour hours	7,928
Actual overheads	£146,200

4   Based on the data given above, what is the labour hour overhead absorption rate?

    A   £17.20 per hour
    B   £17.50 per hour
    C   £18.44 per hour
    D   £18.76 per hour

5   Based on the data given above, what is the amount of under-/over-absorbed overhead?

    A   £2,550 under-absorbed overhead
    B   £2,550 over-absorbed overhead
    C   £7,460 over-absorbed overhead
    D   £7,460 under-absorbed overhead

Job, batch and service costing

Learning outcomes

Having studied this chapter you will be able to:

2.5 Differences between costing systems

- The appropriate choice of costing system for different business sectors and individual organisations.
- The effect of waste on costing inputs and outputs
- Record cost information, using different costing systems:
  - Job costing
  - Batch costing
  - Unit costing
  - Service costing

Assessment context

There is likely to be a task on this topic. For example, you may be asked to calculate a cost per batch.

Qualification context

This chapter introduces some tools that will be used throughout your studies and included within the later *Applied Management Accounting* unit, such as costing particular jobs.

Business context

Many businesses will use these techniques when calculating charges to clients for work performed.

Chapter overview

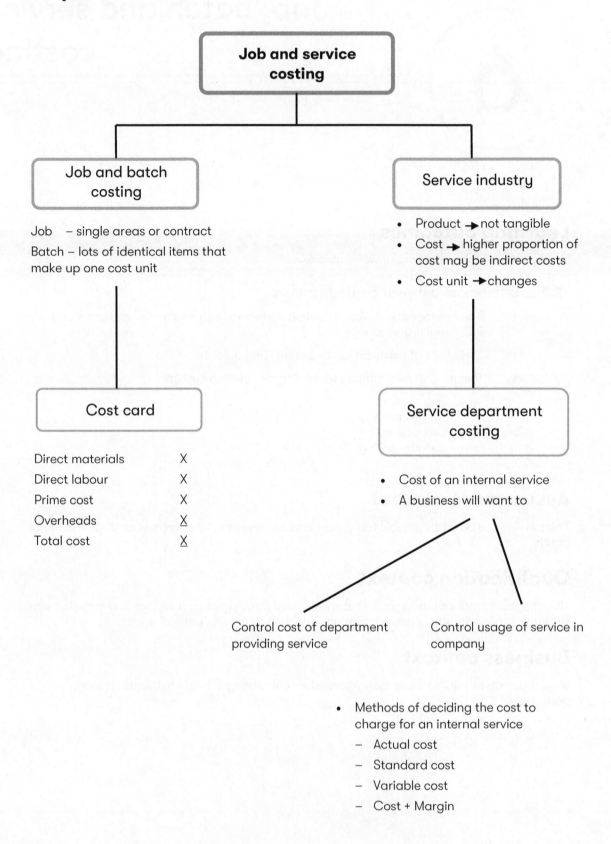

Job and service costing

Job and batch costing

Job – single areas or contract

Batch – lots of identical items that make up one cost unit

Cost card

Direct materials	X
Direct labour	X
Prime cost	X
Overheads	X
Total cost	X

Service industry

- Product → not tangible
- Cost → higher proportion of cost may be indirect costs
- Cost unit → changes

Service department costing

- Cost of an internal service
- A business will want to

Control cost of department providing service

Control usage of service in company

- Methods of deciding the cost to charge for an internal service
  - Actual cost
  - Standard cost
  - Variable cost
  - Cost + Margin

Introduction

So far we have concentrated on gathering together the costs for individual cost units – the products that a business makes – and this is known as unit costing. However, there are other costing systems depending upon the type of product or service that a business provides. We will now consider some alternative costing systems and finish with a section on waste.

1 Job costing

1.1 What is a job?

It is a cost unit that consists of a single order or contract carried out to the special requirements of the customer.

> **Jobs** are customer orders which last a relatively short time.

Jobs differ and it is necessary to keep a separate record of each job and the costs incurred on that job.

Job costing is used by builders, electricians, plumbers and so on.

The problem with jobbing businesses is that there is no price list as such, as there is no standard product. Each individual job will be different with different costs.

When a customer approaches the business requesting a quote for a price for the job, they will provide details of the precise requirements they have for this particular job. The business must then decide how much the job is going to cost and how much profit it is to earn on the job and then come up with a price that satisfies this.

It is important to realise that not only must the price of the job cover the direct costs of materials, labour and any direct expenses, but it must also cover a portion of the overheads, so that all of the overheads for a period are covered by the prices of the jobs done in that period.

1.2 Collection of job costs

Materials requisitions are sent to stores requesting the necessary materials.

The materials requisition is used to cost materials allocated to a job. This is recorded on a job cost sheet or job cost card.

1.3 Labour costs

A **job card** or job ticket is completed by an employee recording start and finish times and then passed on to the employee who undertakes the next function and so on.

Direct labour is recorded on the job cost card.

Remember that where overtime is done at the specific request of the customer, it is treated as a direct cost. For job costing, it will be included on the job card.

1.4 Expenses

Direct expenses are recorded on the job cost card.

1.5 Overheads

Once direct costs have been recorded on the job cost card, the job needs to be charged with overheads.

Overheads are absorbed using predetermined overhead absorption rates. A job may pick up overheads from several departments.

If the overheads of the business are not included in the job quote then the overheads will never be covered by the income from jobs. Only by including the overheads before any profit element is added can the business be sure of earning enough to cover its overheads as well as the direct costs.

1.6 Reworking

Where reworking occurs as a one-off (ie specifically because of the job) rather than as an expected part of production, its cost should be included on the job card as a direct cost.

Activity 1: Job 4321

The following information is available for job 4321, which is being produced at the request of a customer.

	Department A	Department B	Department C
Materials consumed	£4,000	£1,000	£1,500
Direct labour: wage rate per hour	£6	£8	£5
Direct labour hours	300	200	400

In accordance with company policy, the following are chargeable to jobs:

Fixed production overheads	£5 per labour hour
Fixed administration overhead	80% of total production cost
Profit	20% mark-up on cost

Required

Calculate the total cost and selling price of job 4321.

		Job 4321	
		£	£
Direct materials: department	A		
	B		
	C		
Direct labour: department	A		
	B		
	C		
Fixed production overhead:			
Total production cost			
Fixed administration overhead:			
Total cost			
Profit			
Selling price			

Activity 2: Splodge Ltd

Splodge Ltd has been asked to undertake a particular job for a customer. The relevant information is as follows:

- 40 kg of bricks will be used @ £5 per kg.
- Louis will need to work 2 hours and is paid £8.00 per hour.
- Ben will need to work 3 hours and is paid £8.50 per hour.
- Overtime is to be done if necessary as the customer wants the job completed ASAP.
- Overtime is paid at triple time.
- Due to unforeseen complexities, Louis had to stay late on Tuesday and work 2 hours' overtime to finish the job.
- Due to Ben's cold, he had to redo his work on Wednesday morning as he hadn't done it properly the first time.
- Ben had to use 10 kg extra of bricks to rework the job.
- Ben doesn't normally have to rework his tasks.

Required

Complete the job card below.

Job 08/10/04 No 111	Workings	£
Materials – bricks		
Issued		
Issued for rework		
Labour		
Louis		
Basic hours		
Overtime premium		
Ben		
Basic hours		
Reworked hours		
Total direct cost		
Overheads (£200 per job)		
Total job cost		

2 Batch costing

2.1 What is a batch?

A batch is a cost unit that consists of a separately, readily identifiable group of units. It is used in manufacturing businesses that make batches of different products rather than single products. For example, a shoe manufacturer may make a batch of 400 shoes of one style in size 4 and then a batch of 300 shoes of a different style in size 7.

Batch costing is a costing system that gathers together the costs of production of an entire batch of a similar product in order to find the cost of each individual item in that batch.

The costing is the same as for a job. The necessary information and procedures are set out below.

A batch card must be set up for each batch, carrying a unique identifying number. This card will be used to collect information on the costs of the batch.

2.2 Materials requisition document

Quantities of materials issued to each batch should be documented by some form of materials requisition document. This will be a record of materials issued from stores. A similar document should be used to record materials returned to stores, or transferred for use on other batches.

2.3 Perpetual inventory system

The materials issued from stores need to be priced in some way. One method is to maintain a perpetual inventory system on ledger cards. The cards would be updated for materials receipts from goods inward notes, which would have to be priced at actual cost. The materials requisition document would be the source for updating the cards for materials issues. A decision would have to be taken on the basis for pricing such issues; possible bases include FIFO and AVCO.

2.4 Cost per unit

Once all of the costs of the batch have been determined the cost of each individual unit of product in that batch can be found as follows:

$$\text{Cost per unit} = \frac{\text{Cost of the batch}}{\text{Number of units in the batch}}$$

Assessment focus point

In your assessment, a task could ask you to calculate a cost per batch and then a cost per unit.

3 Service costing

3.1 Service organisations

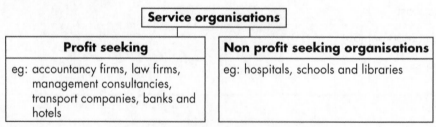

Service organisations	
Profit seeking	**Non profit seeking organisations**
eg: accountancy firms, law firms, management consultancies, transport companies, banks and hotels	eg: hospitals, schools and libraries

Service organisations do not make or sell tangible goods.

Service costing is a costing system adapted for services or functions.

Service costing differs from product costing methods for a number of reasons.

(a)   With many services, the cost of direct materials consumed will be relatively small compared to the labour, direct expenses and overheads cost. In product costing the direct materials are often a greater proportion of the total cost.

(b)   The output of most service organisations is difficult to define and hence a unit cost is difficult to calculate.

(c)   The service industry includes such a wide range of organisations which provide such different services and have such different cost structures that costing will vary considerably from one to another.

3.2   Charging customers for services

The procedure for charging customers for services is similar to that which applies in job costing. A mark-up will be added to the cost per unit to give a selling price that will provide the required level of profit.

The choice of the cost unit by the organisation is important to ensure that a fair charge is made to the users of the service.

3.3   Cost per unit

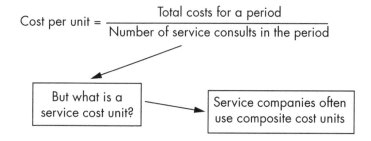

$$\text{Cost per unit} = \frac{\text{Total costs for a period}}{\text{Number of service consults in the period}}$$

But what is a service cost unit?

Service companies often use composite cost units

3.4   Composite cost units

Organisations in the service industry often use **composite cost units** to analyse and monitor their costs, particularly when a 'single' cost unit would not be appropriate. As an example, an airline may base a charge for paying for excess baggage on:

(a)   How far in km the baggage will be transported
(b)   The weight of the baggage

Both of these will have an impact on the airline's fuel cost, so it would be inappropriate to base the charge on distance or weight alone.

An appropriate composite cost unit would therefore be £X per kg per km.

Typical cost units used by companies operating in a service industry are shown below.

Service	Cost unit
Road, rail and air transport services	Passenger–kilometre, tonne–kilometre
Hotels	Occupied bed–night
Education	Full-time student
Hospitals	Patient–day
Catering establishments	Meal served

3.5   Service department costing

Service department costing is used to establish a specific cost for an 'internal service', which is a service provided by one department for another, rather than sold externally to customers. Service departments therefore include canteens and data-processing departments.

The purposes of service department costing:

(a)   To control the costs and efficiency in the service department

(b)   To control the costs of the user departments and prevent the unnecessary use of services

The 'cost' of support services charged to user departments could be based on any of the following:

(a)   No charge at all
(b)   Total actual cost
(c)   Standard absorption cost
(d)   Variable cost
(e)   Cost plus a mark-up for profit

4 Waste

Sometimes losses or waste occur either before, during or after production. For example, there may be losses in cooked products due to evaporation in the cooking process, or ingredients and materials may become out of date or obsolete before use, or a manufacturing process may produce defective units. If some part of the waste is still usable, then it can sometimes be sold for a reduced price called a scrap value.

We mentioned in Chapter 4 that one of the key functions of a management accountant is costing, ie calculating the cost to produce one unit. It's therefore important to record the cost of any losses or waste because otherwise, a business cannot establish an accurate cost of its product or service. Recording losses or waste will also help to highlight to management areas of inefficiency.

Losses can be classified as 'normal' losses or 'abnormal' losses and they are accounted for differently.

4.1 Normal loss

> **Normal loss** is the expected loss from production.

The normal loss is the amount of loss that is expected from a production process. This is usually expressed as a percentage of the materials input to the process.

As the normal loss is part of the normal manufacturing process, no value is given to the normal loss units; instead the process costs are averaged out over the good units of production. In other words, the cost of the normal loss is included in the standard cost of the products.

In some instances the loss units are defective units or waste materials that can be sold for a scrap value. Any scrap value arising from selling the normal loss can be used to reduce the cost of the good units. The net costs are spread over the 'good' units of output.

Formula to learn

Cost per 'good' unit = $\dfrac{\text{Total costs - scrap proceeds from normal loss}}{\text{Unit input - normal loss units}}$

4.2 Abnormal loss

> **Abnormal loss** is any actual loss in excess of the normal loss.

Sometimes the actual loss will differ from the expected or normal loss. If the actual loss is greater than the expected loss, the difference is known as an abnormal loss.

Whereas the normal loss is expected and unavoidable, any abnormal losses or gains are not expected and are considered avoidable, so the accounting treatment of abnormal losses is different from that of the normal loss. An abnormal loss is written off as a loss and valued at the full cost per unit.

Illustration 1: Waste

Oscy Ltd produces fruit flavoured drinks using several liquid ingredients including fizzy water. It expects to have a loss of 10% of the fizzy water that it puts into the drink making process. Last month 1,300 litres of fizzy water were entered into the process and 1,105 litres of fruit flavoured drink were produced at a cost of £585.00. There was no scrap value.

(a)   What is the expected loss in litres?

(b)   What is the actual loss in litres?

(c)   What is the abnormal loss in litres?

(d)   How much of the actual loss should be written off?

(e)   What is the cost per litre of fruit flavoured drink?

(f)   What is the cost of the abnormal loss written off?

(g)   If the loss could be sold as animal feed for £0.18 per litre, what would the cost per litre of fruit flavoured drink be?

Answers

(a)   The expected loss is 10% of the fizzy water litres. 1,300 litres × 10% = 130 litres

(b)   The actual loss = the amount input less the output amount.

Actual loss = 1,300 litres − 1,105 litres = 195 litres

(c)   The abnormal loss = Actual loss − normal loss

Abnormal loss = 195 litres − 130 litres = 65 litres

(d)   65 litres. The abnormal loss should be written off as a loss.

(e)   Using the formula for cost per good unit (per good litre in this case):

$$\text{Cost per 'good' litre} = \frac{\text{Total costs - scrap proceeds from normal loss}}{\text{Unit input - normal loss units}}$$

= (£585.00 − £0) / (1,300 − 130) = £0.50 per litre

(f)   The abnormal loss is valued at the same cost as 'good' litre.

Therefore the amount written off = £0.50 × 65 litres = £32.50

(g)   The scrap proceeds from the normal loss would be 130 litres × £0.18 = £23.40.

Using the formula for cost per good unit (per good litre in this case):

$$\text{Cost per 'good' litre} = \frac{\text{Total costs - scrap proceeds from normal loss}}{\text{Unit input - normal loss units}}$$

= (£585 − £23.40) / (1,300 − 130) = £0.48 per litre

Activity 3: Waste

Jaspy Ltd expects a 20% normal loss from the input of 2,000 kg of materials into a machine. The output from the machine was 1,500 kg. The cost of materials input was £400.

What is the normal loss and abnormal loss in kg and the cost per kg of good output?

	kg
Normal loss	
Abnormal loss	
Cost per kg	£

Chapter summary

- Job costing is a costing system that is used in a business that provides individual, 'one-off' products for customers.

- In a job costing system the accounting function must first produce a schedule of the expected costs of the product that the customer wants; this schedule must include not only the direct costs of producing the product but also any overheads that need to be absorbed into the job to ensure that all of the overheads of the business for the period are eventually covered by the prices set for the jobs done.

- Once the price has been agreed and the job is started, all of the costs of the job must be gathered together by the accounting function. Any materials requisitions must quote the job number and all job cards for employees' hours must also show which job was worked on.

- The accounting function will then absorb overheads into the job according to the organisation's policies.

- Batch costing is used in businesses where instead of there being production runs of identical products there are a number of production runs of batches of different products.

- The purpose of batch costing is to find the cost of an entire batch of a product and then to divide that cost by the number of units produced in the batch; this will then give the unit cost of each unit of that product.

- Service costing is used in service businesses where services are provided rather than goods made. The measurement of activity often involves more than one activity as a composite cost unit.

- The cost of a normal loss (normal waste) is included in the standard cost of the products.

Keywords

- **Abnormal loss:** Any actual loss in excess of the normal loss
- **Batch costing:** A costing system that gathers together the costs of production of an entire batch of a similar product in order to find the cost of each individual item in that batch
- **Composite cost unit:** A cost unit where the service combines more than one activity
- **Job card:** An individual employee's record of the time spent on each job
- **Job costing:** A costing system that allocates costs to individual, 'one-off' jobs for customers
- **Normal loss:** The expected loss from production
- **Service costing:** A costing system adapted for services or functions

Test your learning

1   A kitchen manufacturer has been asked to supply a kitchen to a customer. The estimates of costs are given below:

Materials for manufacturing the units – £12,500

Direct labour for fitting the units – 23 hours @ £8.60 per hour

Direct labour for redecorating – 5 hours @ £6.50 per hour

Overheads are absorbed on the basis of £12.40 per direct labour hour.

Profit on each job is taken at 25% of total costs.

How much will the kitchen cost the customer?

£ [   ]

2   A pie factory operates on a batch production system. The latest batch to have been produced is 1,200 cheese and mushroom pies. The costs of this batch are:

Ingredients	£840.00
Labour	7 hours @ £6.50

Overheads are absorbed on the basis of £1.20 per labour hour.

What is the cost of each pie (to one decimal place)?

[   ] pence

3   Which of the following would be appropriate cost units for a transport business?

(i)   Cost per tonne–kilometre
(ii)   Fixed cost per kilometre
(iii)   Maintenance cost of each vehicle per kilometre

[ ] (i) only

[ ] (i) and (ii) only

[ ] (i) and (iii) only

[ ] All of them

4   Which of the following organisations should NOT be advised to use service costing?

[ ] Distribution service

[ ] Hospital

[ ] Maintenance division of a manufacturing company

[ ] An engineering company

Standard costing and budgeting

Learning outcomes

4.1	Principles of standard prices/costs and budgeting
	• A product's standard price and standard cost
	• How standard prices and costs can be used to develop budgets
	• Different types of budget:
	– Fixed
	– Flexed
	– Rolling
	• How operating statements are used to compare budgeted volume and standard revenue/cost versus actual performance.
	• Prepare budgets for multi-product organisations:
	– Revenue
	– Materials
	– Labour
	– Variable overheads
	– Fixed overheads
	– Non-manufacturing overheads
	• Flex fixed budgets for actual volume.

Assessment context

You should make sure that you are happy with using the information from a cost card to prepare simple cost and revenues budgets at different activity levels. Assessment tasks may ask you prepare a flexed budget and to calculate variances and indicate whether they are adverse or favourable.

Qualification context

The fundamental aspects of budgeting learnt in this paper give the ground work for Level 4 *Applied Management Accounting*. At Level 4, budgetary control and types of budgets are looked at and flexed budgets are prepared and used for variance analysis calculations.

Business context

A core part of any business is to determine its objectives and come up with a plan of how they will achieve these objectives (strategy). Budgeting provides details of how the business should operate in order to achieve its objectives.

Chapter overview

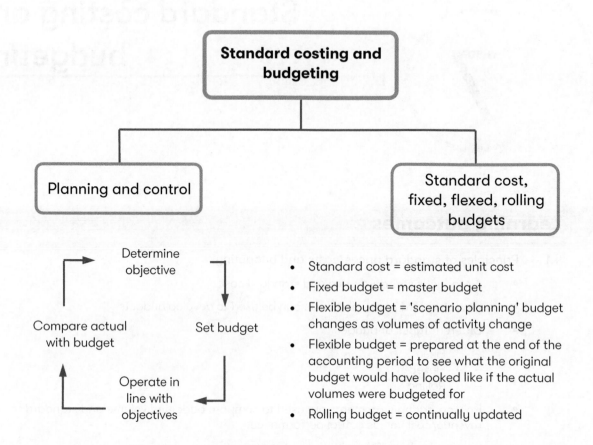

Standard costing and budgeting

Planning and control

Standard cost, fixed, flexed, rolling budgets

Determine objective

Set budget

Operate in line with objectives

Compare actual with budget

- Standard cost = estimated unit cost
- Fixed budget = master budget
- Flexible budget = 'scenario planning' budget changes as volumes of activity change
- Flexible budget = prepared at the end of the accounting period to see what the original budget would have looked like if the actual volumes were budgeted for
- Rolling budget = continually updated

Introduction

A **standard costing system** is used where a business produces a number of standard products. Every unit of a standard product is expected to use the same quantity of direct materials and requires the same amount of time to make.

The standard cost is the planned unit cost of a standard product or service, and is therefore the expected cost of producing one unit of that product or service.

A budget is a financial and/or quantitative plan of operations for a forthcoming period.

Budgeting is part of the overall process of planning and control. A budget is a plan which will assist in achieving objectives.

The cycle of planning and control:

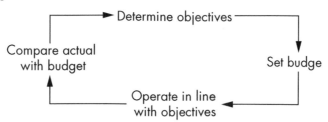

1 Standard costing

> **Standard cost** is an estimated unit cost.

A **standard cost** is calculated from management expectations of:

- Usage and efficiency levels of materials and labour
- Prices of materials, labour and overheads
- Budgeted overhead costs and budgeted levels of activity

A standard cost is a predetermined calculation of how much costs should be under specified working conditions. To aid control, it is important that the standard cost is accurate and reviewed regularly.

The standard cost of each unit is set out in a **standard cost card**, which is then used for control within an organisation.

Illustration 1: Example of a standard cost card for a cost unit

		£/unit
Direct costs:		
Direct materials	(5 kg @ £3/kg)	15.00
Direct labour	(3 hrs @ £6/hr)	18.00
		33.00
Indirect costs:		
Variable overheads		2.00
Fixed overheads		3.00
Full product cost		38.00

1.1 Use of standard costing in budgetary control

Standard costing is used to:

- Value inventories
- Prepare cost budgets for production
- Provide control information (variances)

This chapter will focus on preparing budgets.

A budget can be compared with actual performance to monitor and control a business. This comparison effectively compares standard costs with actual costs, leading to the calculation of differences (variances). Variances are discussed in the next chapter.

The variances are investigated by management, and actions are taken to rectify any performance issues. The action may lead to the setting of new standards, and so there is a cycle of continuous improvement.

The purposes of a budget in planning and control are therefore facilitated by standard costing but here we look at constructing budgets using standard costs.

Activity 1: Latt

Latt expects to make 5,000 units of production in the coming year.

The following has been estimated:

Each unit will require 3 kg of material with a total cost of £15.

Each unit will require 2 hours of labour paid at £7 per hour.

Fixed overheads are expected to be £50,000.

Required

Complete the standard cost card below:

Unit	Quantity	Cost per unit	Total unit cost
Material			
Labour			
Fixed overheads			
Total			

2 Preparing budgets

2.1 Revenue budget

The **sales budget** will normally be in two parts. There will be a forecast for the number of units that it is anticipated will be sold, and a **sales revenue budget** calculated by multiplying the estimated unit sales by the expected selling price per unit.

Once the expected quantity of sales has been determined, then the anticipated price to be charged for the products or services can be applied. This gives us the budgeted income, usually referred to as the sales revenue budget (in £). From the sales budget, the resource budgets for production can then be prepared.

Illustration 2: Sales budget

Oliver Engineering produces a single product, the Stephenson. For budgeting purposes, the year is divided into 13 four-week periods, with five working days each week and therefore 20 working days per period. The forecast sales quantities for the first five periods of 20X0 are as follows:

Period 1 Units	Period 2 Units	Period 3 Units	Period 4 Units	Period 5 Units
10,000	12,000	15,000	13,000	11,000

The current selling price of the Stephenson is £40, although it is anticipated that there will be a 10% price increase in Period 4.

The sales revenue budget can now be prepared.

	Forecast revenue £
Period 1 (10,000 × £40)	400,000
Period 2 (12,000 × £40)	480,000
Period 3 (15,000 × £40)	600,000
Period 4 (13,000 × £44)	572,000
Period 5 (11,000 × £44)	484,000
	2,536,000

2.2 Production budget

Once the sales budget has been prepared, the next stage is to prepare the **production budget** in finished goods units. There are two factors that will affect the amount of production required:

- Any changes in inventory levels of finished goods that are anticipated
- The level of defective finished goods that are forecast

2.3 Changes in finished goods inventory levels

If all goods produced can be sold, and there is to be no change in the levels of finished goods held in inventory, then the amount that must be produced is the same as the quantity of forecast sales.

However, if the level of finished goods held in inventory is to change, then this will affect the quantity that is to be produced.

Once the sales quantity has been determined, then the production quantity will be calculated as:

Sales quantity	X
Less opening inventories of finished goods	(X)
Add closing inventories of finished goods required	X
Production quantity	X

The opening inventories of finished goods are deducted from the sales quantity as we already have these in inventory and therefore do not need to make them.

Waste

If, during production, the quantity of material input is likely to reduce (due to wastage, evaporation etc) the quantity input must be greater than the quantity of the finished product and a material standard must take account of this.

 ## Illustration 3: Waste

Suppose that the fresh raspberry juice content of a litre of Purple Pop is 100 ml and that there is a 10% loss of raspberry juice during the process because of evaporation. The standard material usage of raspberry juice per litre of Purple Pop will be:

100 ml × (100% / 90%) = 111.11 ml

Defective output

In many production processes, a certain percentage of finished goods will be defective and not saleable.

If there is an anticipated level of defective production, then the production quantity must be increased to ensure that there are enough units of the product available for sale after the defective products have been deducted. Therefore, the production quantity must be adjusted as follows:

Sales quantity	X
Less opening inventories of finished goods	(X)
Add closing inventories of finished goods required	X
Quantity required to meet sales demand	X
Add anticipated defective units	X
Production quantity	X

 ## Activity 2: Production budget

A business has budgeted sales for the following period of 3,500 units of its product. The inventories at the start of the period are 800 units and these are to be reduced to 600 units at the end of the period.

In previous periods 5% of production units fail quality control checks and need to be reworked.

Required

What is the production quantity for the period?

☐ units

2.4 Materials budget

The next stage is to determine the amount of material required for each unit of the product for the purposes of calculating the **materials usage budget**. This will normally come from the standard cost card.

This quantity per unit will then be applied to the number of units to be produced, in order to determine the amount of material required to be used in production in each period.

Wastage of material must also be taken into account when determining the amount of materials that are required in order to produce the quantity of products set out in the production budget.

The material usage budget is therefore constructed as follows:

Quantity required to meet production	X
Add wasted material	X
Materials usage	X

Assessment focus point

As per the defective units when preparing the production budget, always round wasted materials up (not down) to the nearest whole kg.

Illustration 4: Materials usage budget

Continuing the Oliver Engineering example, we know that the production quantities required for each of the first four periods of the year are as follows:

Production budget

Period 1 Units	Period 2 Units	Period 3 Units	Period 4 Units
10,205	13,011	14,796	12,756

From the standard cost card, each unit of production requires 2 kg of material X. However, we also know that the production process has a normal loss of 20% of the materials input into the process.

This means that although each unit of product requires 2 kg of material X, this represents only 80% of the actual amount required. 20% more than 2 kg per unit must be inputted into the process.

The amount of material X required for each unit is therefore:

2 kg × 100/80 = 2.5 kg

The amount of normal loss can be calculated separately as:

$$2 \text{ kg} \times \frac{20}{80} = 0.5 \text{ kg}$$

The materials usage budget can now be prepared:

Materials usage budget

	Period 1	Period 2	Period 3	Period 4
Quantity of production	10,205	13,011	14,796	12,756
Materials usage (Quantity × 2.5 kg)	25,513 kg	32,528 kg	36,990 kg	31,890 kg

Activity 3: Material usage budget

A business requires 15,400 units of production in a period and each unit uses 5 kg of materials. 10% of materials are wasted during the production process.

Required

What is the total amount of the material required for the period (to the nearest kg)?

☐ kg

Once the materials usage budget has been set, then this can be translated into the **materials purchases budget** in units of materials and £.

Just as with the production budget, the opening and closing levels of materials inventories must be taken into account, in order to determine how many materials must be purchased during each period. The quantity of purchases will be determined as follows:

Materials usage	X
Less opening inventory of materials	(X)
Add closing inventory of materials	X
Quantity to be purchased	X

Finally, once the quantity to be purchased is known, then the anticipated purchase price can be applied to this to determine the materials purchases budget in terms of value.

Illustration 5: Materials purchases budget

We know the materials usage budget for Oliver Engineering is as follows:

Materials usage budget

	Period 1 kg	Period 2 kg	Period 3 kg	Period 4 kg
Materials usage	25,513	32,528	36,990	31,890

It is the policy of the company to hold enough materials to cover 10 days of the following period of production. The inventory level at the start of Period 1 is 12,000 kg of material and the materials usage in Period 5 is calculated as 28,000 kg.

First, we must determine the inventory levels of materials required at the end of each period. This has to be enough to cover 10 days out of the 20 days of production for the next period.

The closing inventories of materials are as follows:

Period 1	32,528 kg × 10 days/20 days	=	16,264 kg
Period 2	36,990 kg × 10 days/20 days	=	18,495 kg
Period 3	31,890 kg × 10 days/20 days	=	15,945 kg
Period 4	28,000 kg × 10 days/20 days	=	14,000 kg

Now the materials purchases budget can be prepared, first in units.

Materials purchases budget

	Period 1 kg	Period 2 kg	Period 3 kg	Period 4 kg
Materials usage	25,513	32,528	36,990	31,890
Less opening inventories of materials	(12,000)	(16,264)	(18,495)	(15,945)
Add closing inventories of materials	16,264	18,495	15,945	14,000
Materials to be purchased	29,777	34,759	34,440	29,945

The cost of each kg of material X has been, and will continue to be, £5. Therefore, the value of the materials purchases budget can also be set by taking the quantity to be purchased for each period and applying the unit price. For example, for Period 1, 29,777 kg must be purchased at a cost of £5 per kg = £148,885.

Materials purchases budget

Period 1 £	Period 2 £	Period 3 £	Period 4 £
148,885	173,795	172,200	149,725

Activity 4: Materials purchases budget

A business requires 124,000 litres of a material for its next month's production run. The material costs £2.60 per litre and current inventories are 14,000 litres. The business aims to increase its inventory levels by 15% by the end of the month.

Required

What is the budgeted cost of materials for the month?

£

2.5 Labour budget

Once the production budget has been set, then it is necessary to determine the number of hours of labour that are required for the production level in the **labour usage budget**. This can be determined by referring to the standard cost card, which will state the number of hours of labour required for each unit of product.

Once we know the number of hours to be worked in each period, then the **labour cost budget** (in £) can be set by applying the wage rate to the number of hours. However, care must be taken with any overtime hours that are to be worked.

Illustration 6: Labour cost budget

The labour usage budget for Oliver Engineering is as follows:

Labour usage budget

	Period 1 Hours	Period 2 Hours	Period 3 Hours	Period 4 Hours
Labour hours	12,756 hrs	16,264 hrs	18,495 hrs	15,945 hrs

The Grade A labour are paid at a rate of £9 per hour but only 16,000 hours can be worked within the normal working hours. Any hours above 16,000 are overtime hours that are paid at time and a third.

We will now produce the figures for the **labour cost budget**:

Period 1	12,756 hours × £9	£114,804
Period 2	(16,000 hours × £9) + (264 hours × £12)	£147,168
Period 3	(16,000 hours × £9) + (2,495 hours × £12)	£173,940
Period 4	15,945 hours × £9	£143,505

The labour cost budget will look like this:

Labour cost budget

Period 1 £	Period 2 £	Period 3 £	Period 4 £
£114,804	£147,168	£173,940	£143,505

2.6 Overheads budget

Budgets must also be set for the **overheads** and production facilities related costs, which can include, for example, factory rent and costs of running machinery. Overheads will also include depreciation charges.

Overheads may be variable, semi-variable, fixed or stepped costs.

Illustration 7: Overheads budget

Oliver Engineering is now trying to produce estimates for its overheads for the first four periods of the year.

The cost of machine power is considered to be a true variable cost and it has been estimated that each Stephenson uses £2.40 of machine power.

The cost of the maintenance department has been estimated at £12,000 if 8,000 units are produced; and £16,000, if 12,000 units are produced.

The factory rent is £104,000 for each year.

The cost of production supervisors depends upon the level of activity within the factory. For an activity level of up to 12,000 units, the production supervisors' costs are £2,000 per period; for up to 14,000 units, this increases to £3,000; and for activity up to 16,000 units, the cost rises to £4,000 per period.

Before we can prepare the overhead budget, we must use the high low method to determine the variable and fixed elements of the maintenance department costs.

Maintenance department costs

	Production level Units	Total cost £
Level 1	8,000	12,000
Level 2	12,000	16,000
Increase	4,000	4,000

Variable cost = £4,000/4,000 units = £1 per unit

At 8,000 units:

	£
Variable cost 8,000 × £1	8,000
Fixed element (bal fig)	4,000
Total cost	12,000

We can produce the budgeted figures for each of these overheads based as usual on the production budget:

Machine power is a variable cost = units × £2.40

Maintenance department is a semi-variable cost = (units × £1) + £4,000

Rent is a fixed cost = £104,000 × 4/52 = £8,000 per period

Supervisors' costs are a stepped cost:

≤ 12,000 units	= £2,000
≤ 14,000 units	= £3,000
≤ 16,000 units	= £4,000

Production budget

	Period 1 Units	Period 2 Units	Period 3 Units	Period 4 Units
	10,205	13,011	14,796	12,756

Overhead budget

	Period 1 £	Period 2 £	Period 3 £	Period 4 £
Machine power @ £2.40/unit	24,492	31,226	35,510	30,614
Maintenance department @ £1/unit + £4,000	14,205	17,011	18,796	16,756
Rent – £8,000 per period	8,000	8,000	8,000	8,000
Supervisors' costs	2,000	3,000	4,000	3,000
	48,697	59,237	66,306	58,370

3 Fixed and flexed budgets

The **fixed budget** is the master budget prepared before the beginning of the budget period.

It is based on budgeted volumes, costs and revenues.

Fixed budgets are usually 'fixed' but occasionally it may be appropriate to change a budget. This usually happens when changes occur that were out of the control of the managers or the organisation as a whole. Reasons for revising a fixed budget include:

- Unexpected changes in regulations which impact on costs or revenue
- Unexpected changes in economic conditions, such as inflation, which impact on costs or revenue
- Unexpected technological changes which impact the business
- Unexpected radical change in customer attitudes

Illustration 8: Fixed budgets

Martin Engineering prepares detailed budgets for each quarter of the year. The budget for Quarter 4 of 20X8 was set as follows:

	Quarter 4 budget £
Sales 1,000 units	40,000
Material	(10,000)
Labour	(12,000)
Production overhead	(3,000)

	Quarter 4 budget £
Gross profit	15,000
Overheads	(8,000)
Operating profit	7,000

This budget was set on the basis of both production and sales of 1,000 units and no opening or closing inventory.

It is now the first week in January 20X9 and the actual results for Quarter 4 are being compared to the budget:

	Quarter 4 budget £	Actual units	Quarter 4 actual £
Sales 1,000 units	40,000	1,200	45,600
Material	(10,000)		(12,480)
Labour	(12,000)		(13,800)
Production overhead	(3,000)		(3,200)
Gross profit	15,000		16,120
Overheads	(8,000)		(9,080)
Operating profit	7,000		7,040

As part of the process of control, the management accountant of Martin Engineering now prepares a report showing the variances between the budget and the actual results (remember from your earlier studies that variances will be described either as adverse or favourable).

Variance report

	Quarter 4 budget £	Actual units	Quarter 4 actual £	Variance £
Sales 1,000 units	40,000	1,200	45,600	5,600 Fav
Material	(10,000)		(12,480)	2,480 Adv
Labour	(12,000)		(13,800)	1,800 Adv
Production overhead	(3,000)		(3,200)	200 Adv
Gross profit	15,000		16,120	1,120 Fav
Overheads	(8,000)		(9,080)	1,080 Adv
Operating profit	7,000		7,040	40 Fav

It would appear that there are a mixture of variances with favourable variances for sales and profit but adverse variances for all of the costs.

The problem however is that the budget and the actual figures are not strictly comparable: the budget was based upon sales and production of 1,000 units whereas the actual activity level was production and sales of 1,200 units. This is where flexed budgets can be used.

KEY TERM

Flexible budgets are budgets designed to change as volume of activity changes. This can be done by recognising the behaviour of different costs (fixed or variable).

Flexed budgets are budgets that have been prepared based on actual volumes for budgetary control purposes.

3.1 Purpose of flexible budgets

(a)   Designed to cope with **different activity levels** to keep the budget meaningful and hence preserve the relevance of variances for effective control.

(b)   Useful at the **planning** stage to show different results from possible activity levels. This is an example of 'what if?' analysis.

(c)   Necessary as a **control** device because we can meaningfully compare actual results with relevant flexed/flexible budget, ie budgetary control. They are used at the end of a control period to aid with budgetary control – to compare actual results with what should have been achieved based on budgeted costs/revenues at the actual volumes.

When used within this context of budgetary control the **flexible** budget is referred to as the **flexed budget**. A flexed budget is a budget that has been prepared based on actual volumes for budgetary control purposes.

Differences between the flexible/flexed budget figures and actual results are called **variances**.

Illustration 9: Flexed budgets

Given below again is the Quarter 4 budget for Martin Engineering:

	£
Sales 1,000 units	40,000
Material	(10,000)
Labour	(12,000)
Production overhead	(3,000)
Gross profit	15,000
Overheads	(8,000)
Operating profit	7,000

The details of the cost behaviour of each of the costs is given below:

Materials	The materials cost is totally variable.
Labour	Each operative can only produce 250 units each quarter – the cost of each operative is £3,000 each quarter.
Production overhead	The production overhead is a totally fixed cost.
Overheads	The general expenses are made up of a budgeted fixed cost of £8,000.

We will now flex the budget to the actual activity level of 1,200 units.

Sales

| Budgeted selling price | = | £40,000/1,000 units |
| | = | £40 per unit |

BPP
LEARNING
MEDIA

Therefore the budgeted sales revenue for 1,200 units is:

| Sales | = | 1,200 × £40 |
| | = | £48,000 |

Materials are totally variable

Budgeted materials per unit	=	£10,000/1,000 units
	=	£10 per unit
Budgeted materials cost for 1,200 units	=	1,200 × £10
	=	£12,000

Labour is a stepped cost

One operative is required for each 250 units; therefore for 1,200 units five operatives will be required. For 1,000 units, four operatives would be used. So the cost per operative = £12,000/4 = £3,000.

| Budgeted labour cost | = | 5 × £3,000 |
| | = | £15,000 |

Production overheads is a fixed cost

| Budgeted cost for 1,200 units | = | £3,000 |

General overheads is a fixed cost | = | £8,000 |

The flexed budget will appear as follows:

	Quarter 4 flexed budget £
Sales 1,200 units	48,000
Materials	(12,000)
Labour	(15,000)
Production overhead	(3,000)
Gross profit	18,000
Overheads	(8,000)
Operating profit	10,000

The flexed budget can then be compared to the actual figures in the form of an operating statement and the true variances calculated.

Martin Engineering: Quarter 4 operating statement

	Budget £	Units	Actual £	Variance £
Sales 1,200 units	48,000	1,200	45,600	2,400 Adv
Material	(12,000)		(12,480)	480 Adv
Labour	(15,000)		(13,800)	1,200 Fav
Production overhead	(3,000)		(3,200)	200 Adv
Gross profit	18,000		16,120	1,880 Adv
General expenses	(8,000)		(9,080)	1,080 Adv
Operating profit	10,000		7,040	2,960 Adv

We can now see that instead of an overall favourable profit variance being reported there is in fact a significant adverse profit variance with all the variances other than the labour variance being adverse. This is quite a different picture to the variances calculated using the fixed budget. Note that a report like this, that allows actual figures to be compared with budget figures and variances to be calculated, is called an **operating statement**.

Activity 5: Country soups

The marketing manager of Country Soups believes that the sales of mushroom soup next quarter will be between 350,000 and 450,000 cans. The budgeted cost schedule below contains cost information relevant over this range.

Required

Complete the budgeted cost schedule for the three possible levels of production shown below, calculating the cost per can in £ to three decimal places.

Cans made:		350,000 £	400,000 £	450,000 £
Cost element	Cost			
Direct materials	10p per can			
Direct labour	8p per can			
Canning costs	2p per can			
Depreciation	£16,000			
Rent and rates	£28,000			
Other overheads	£36,000			
Total cost (£)				
Cost per can (£)				

Note. Depreciation, rent and rates, and other overheads are all fixed costs.

Activity 6: Charter flights

The Charter Flights profit centre has just revised its forecasts for the number of miles it expects to fly during the next month on a particular charter contract. Originally it expected the contract would be for flights totalling 5,000 miles. It now expects that the total miles to be flown will increase to either 6,000 or 7,000 miles.

Notes

- The company chartering the flights has negotiated with Charter Flights a reduction on the sales price of 10% per mile, paid on all miles flown in excess of the 5,000 miles agreed in the original contract.

- Landing and servicing fee are a semi-variable cost. There is a fixed charge of £600,000 plus £50 per mile.

Required

Use the table below to estimate the profit per mile (in pounds, to 2 decimal places) of this contract at both 6,000 and 7,000 miles flown.

Likely miles	5,000 £000	6,000 £000	7,000 £000
Sales revenue	2,500		
Variable/semi-variable costs:			
Aviation fuel	400		
Landing and servicing fees	850		
Other variable overheads	135		
Fixed costs:			
Wages and salaries	420		
Other fixed overheads	625		
Total cost	2,430		
Total profit	70		
	£	£	£
Profit per mile flown	14.00		

Activity 7: TV dinners

A company has produced three forecasts of activity levels for the next three months for its TV dinners range. The original budget involved producing 5,000 batches but, due to an increase in demand, production levels of between 6,000 and 7,000 batches now seem likely.

Overheads are semi-variable and they should be calculated using the high–low method. If 8,000 batches are sold the total overheads will be £20,800 and the unit variable cost is constant up to this volume. At 5,000 units total overheads are £16,300.

Required

Complete the table below to estimate the profit per batch (to 3 decimal places) of the TV dinners range at the different activity levels.

Batches made and sold	5,000 £	6,000 £	7,000 £
Sales revenue	30,000		
Costs:			
Direct materials	1,250		
Direct labour	3,000		
Overheads			
Variable element			
Fixed element			

Batches made and sold	5,000 £	6,000 £	7,000 £
Total cost			
Total profit			
Profit per batch			

Assessment focus point

An assessment task may ask you to flex a budget, calculate variances and indicate whether they are adverse or favourable.

4 Rolling budgets

KEY TERM

Rolling budgets are budgets that are continually updated in order to project a continual amount of time into the future.

A rolling budget is compiled by adding the next accounting period when the current accounting period is over. By doing this, a set amount of time is always included within the budget.

For example, a budget is set on a quarterly basis for the next year. The January to March budget is set out in detail while the budget for the period from April to December is usually less detailed. At the end of March, the detailed budget is created for April to June, along with an additional outline budget for the quarter from January to March of the following year, which is added in later.

This has the advantage of giving budget holders an opportunity to react to changes in circumstances. It will also enable a more accurate budget to be produced if any items could not be accurately forecast when the original budget was set. However, it also means that budgeting will tend to be done more frequently, and take up more management time.

- In a standard costing system, all output is valued at a standard cost per unit.

- The direct materials standard cost is set by determining the estimated quantity of material to be used per unit and the estimated price of that material.

- The direct labour standard cost is set by determining the estimated labour time per unit and the estimated rate per hour.

- The fixed overhead standard cost is determined by finding a realistic estimate of each of the elements of the fixed overhead.

- A budgeted costing system which allows the budgeted cost of production to be compared to the actual costs and variances calculated can help management perform their three main roles of decision making, planning and control.

- A fixed budget is set in advance of a budgeting period as a predetermined plan of activity for all areas of a business.

- A flexed budget is used in the control aspect of the budgetary system as the actual results are compared to the flexed budget in order to determine any variances.

- In order to flex a budget a distinction must be drawn between variable costs and fixed costs. The variable elements of cost will increase or decrease with changes in activity level whereas the fixed elements of cost do not vary with changes in activity levels.

- Rolling budgets are compiled by adding the next accounting period when the current accounting period is over.

Keywords

- **Budgeted costing system:** A system that assigns budgeted costs to each cost unit and allows a comparison of budgeted costs to actual costs and the calculation of variances
- **Variance:** The difference between the budgeted costs and the actual costs for a period
- **Fixed budget:** A budget set in advance of a period in order to act as a plan of action for the whole organisation
- **Flexed budget:** A budget prepared based on actual volumes for budgetary control purposes
- **Flexible budget:** A budget designed to change as volume of activity changes. This can be done by recognising the behaviour of different costs (fixed or variable)
- **Operating statement:** A report allowing actual figures to be compared with budget figures and variances calculated
- **Rolling budget:** A budget that is continually updated in order to project a continual amount of time into the future
- **Standard cost:** An estimated unit cost

Test your learning

1   The budget for a production company for the month of December and the actual results for the month are given below:

	Budget 4,000 units £	Actual 3,600 units £
Sales	96,000	90,000
Materials	18,000	15,120
Labour	27,200	25,200
Production overhead	5,700	5,900
Gross profit	45,100	43,780
General expenses	35,200	32,880
Operating profit	9,900	10,900

The materials and labour costs are variable costs, the production overhead is a fixed cost and the general expenses are fixed.

(a)   Calculate variances between the fixed budget and the actual results and state whether they are adverse or favourable.

	Budget 4,000 units £	Actual 3,600 units £	Variance £	Adv/Fav
Sales	96,000	90,000		
Materials	18,000	15,120		
Labour	27,200	25,200		
Production overhead	5,700	5,900		
Gross profit	45,100	43,780		
General expenses	35,200	32,880		
Operating profit	9,900	10,900		

(b)   Prepare a flexed budget for the actual activity level and show the variances for each of the figures.

	Flexed budget 3,600 units £	Actual 3,600 units £	Variance £	Adv/Fav
Sales		90,000		
Materials		15,120		
Labour		25,200		
Production overhead		5,900		
Gross profit		43,780		
General expenses		32,880		
Operating profit		10,900		

2 Vanquish Ltd has the following original budget and actual performance for its product zephyr for the year ending 31 December.

	Budget	Actual
Volume sold	50,000	72,000
	£000	£000
Sales revenue	1,000	1,800
Less costs:		
Direct materials	175	265
Direct labour	200	240
Overheads	350	630
Operating profit	275	665

Both direct materials and direct labour are variable costs, but the overheads are fixed.

Complete the table below to show a flexed budget and the resulting variances against this budget for the year. Show the actual variance amount, for sales and each cost, in the column headed 'Variance' and indicate whether this is Favourable or Adverse by entering F or A in the final column. If neither F nor A enter 0.

	Flexed budget	Actual	Variance	Favourable F or Adverse A
Volume sold		72,000		
	£000	£000	£000	
Sales revenue		1,800		
Less costs:				
Direct materials		265		
Direct labour		240		
Overheads		630		
Operating profit		665		

Variance analysis

Learning outcomes

4.2 Calculate variances

- Recognise variances as being either favourable or adverse
- Calculate variances using flexed budgets
- Compare flexed budget versus actual costs and revenues to calculate:
    - Sales price variance (total)
    - Raw material variance (total)
    - Labour variance (total)
    - Variable overhead variance (total)
    - Fixed production variance (total)

4.3 Analyse and investigate variances

- Determine the cause and effects of revenue and cost variances
- Recognise significant variances for investigation
- Report on remedial action to address adverse variances

Assessment context

Variance calculation is a very important part of your *Management Accounting Techniques* studies and it is vital that you are able to calculate all of the different types of variance included in the syllabus for this unit.

Qualification context

Variances examined in this unit are also examinable in the Level 4 *Applied Management Accounting (AMAC)*. This is taken a step further by including a few further calculations and the interpretation and behavioural aspects of variances.

Business context

Actual costs and revenues are compared against forecasts within a business on a frequent basis. This is part of the budgetary control process and helps to identify problems within the production process.

Chapter overview

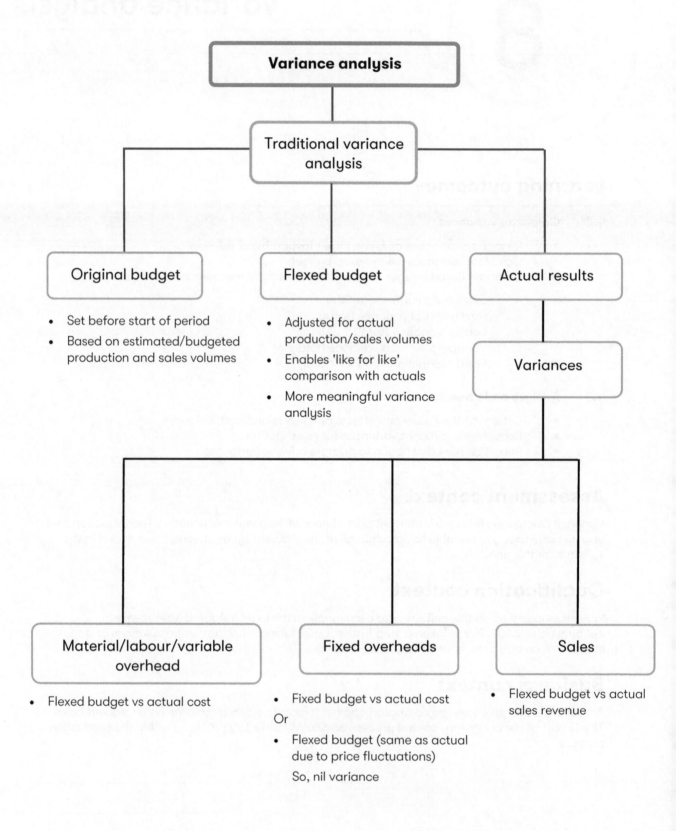

Variance analysis

Traditional variance analysis

Original budget
- Set before start of period
- Based on estimated/budgeted production and sales volumes

Flexed budget
- Adjusted for actual production/sales volumes
- Enables 'like for like' comparison with actuals
- More meaningful variance analysis

Actual results

Variances

Material/labour/variable overhead
- Flexed budget vs actual cost

Fixed overheads
- Fixed budget vs actual cost
Or
- Flexed budget (same as actual due to price fluctuations)
  So, nil variance

Sales
- Flexed budget vs actual sales revenue

Introduction

As you know, **variances** can be either favourable (F), ie better than expected, or adverse (A), ie worse.

Overview

	Fixed (original) budget	Flexed budget		Actual results
Sales volume	X	X		X
	£	£		£
Sales revenue	X	X	Sales variance	X
Cost of sales:				
Materials	X	X	Material variance	X
Labour	X	X	Labour variance	X
Variable overhead	X	X	Variable overhead variance	X
Fixed overheads	<u>X</u>	<u>not flexed</u>	Fixed overhead variance	<u>see note below</u>
Profit	<u>X</u>	<u>X</u>		<u>X</u>

Budget	Actual units × standard cost or selling price per unit	Actual units × actual cost or selling price per unit

Fixed overhead variances will just be the difference between actual and budgeted (original) fixed overheads. Fixed overheads should not be flexed. Hence the variance will not be due to under/over absorption.

1 Calculating variances

You need to know how to flex a budget and show the resulting variances.

Illustration 1: Flexed budgets and variances

Vanquish Ltd has the following original budget and actual performance for product ZT4 for the year ending 31 December.

	Budget	Actual
Volume sold	100,000	144,000
	£000	**£000**
Sales revenue	2,000	3,600
Less costs:		
Direct materials	350	530
Direct labour	400	480
Variable overheads	100	120
Fixed overheads	980	980
Operating profit	170	1,490

The direct materials, direct labour and variable overheads are variable costs, but the fixed overheads are fixed.

Complete the table below to show a flexed budget and the resulting variances against this budget for the year. Show the actual variance amount, for sales and each cost, in the column headed 'Variance' and indicate whether this is Favourable or Adverse by entering F or A in the final column. If neither F nor A enter 0.

	Flexed budget	Actual	Variance	Favourable F or Adverse A
Volume sold		144,000	–	
	£000	£000	£000	
Sales revenue		3,600		
Less costs:				
Direct materials		530		
Direct labour		480		
Variable overheads		120		
Fixed overheads		980		
Operating profit		1,490		
Volume sold	144,000	144,000	–	
	£000	£000	£000	
Sales revenue	2,880	3,600	720	F
Less costs:				
Direct materials	504	530	26	A
Direct labour	576	480	96	F
Variable overheads	144	120	24	F
Fixed overheads	980	980	0	0
Operating profit	676	1,490	814	F

Workings

Sales revenue

Budgeted sales price per unit = £2,000,000/100,000 units = £20 per unit

So, 144,000 units of revenue should have been 144,000 × £20 = £2,880,000

Direct materials

Budgeted material cost per unit = £350,000/100,000 = £3.5 per unit

So, 144,000 units of material should have cost 144,000 × £3.5 = £504,000

Direct labour

Budgeted labour cost per unit = £400,000/100,000 = £4 per unit

So, 144,000 units of material should have cost 144,000 × £4 = £576,000

Variable overheads

Budgeted variable overhead cost per unit = £100,000/100,000 = £1 per unit

So, 144,000 units of material should have cost 144,000 × £1 = £144,000

Notice that for the **variable** costs and for revenue, we have taken each original budget figure and divided it by 100,000 units and multiplied it by 144,000 units. 144,000/100,000 = 1.44 or 144%. So a slightly quicker of calculating the flexed revenue and flexed variable costs would be to multiply the original budget by 144%:

	Original budget × 144%	Flexed budget £
Sales revenue	2,000 × 144%	2,880
Direct materials	350 × 144%	504
Direct labour	400 × 144%	576
Variable overheads	100 × 144%	144

You can calculate the decimal to multiply the original budget using:

Actual number of units ÷ Original budgeted number of units

You can multiple this by 100 to obtain a percentage, or you can use a percentage button if you are using a spreadsheet (see Chapter 9).

Remember however, that you can only use this to flex costs that vary with the number of units produced (variable costs). You can also use it for revenue, provided that the number of units made and sold are the same.

Fixed overheads

Fixed overheads do not change as volume/activity changes. Actual fixed overheads were £980,000.

Operating profit

Operating profit = £2,880,000 – £504,000 – £576,000 – £144,000 – £980,000 = £676,000

In the illustration above, we calculated the sales price variance, the total direct material variance, the total direct labour variance, the total variable overhead variance and the fixed overhead variance. So you now know that:

(a)   The sales price variance is the difference between the actual revenue received and the budgeted sales revenue for the actual level of sales.

(b)   The total direct **materials variance** is the difference between the actual cost of materials used in production and the budgeted cost for the actual level of production.

(c)   The total direct labour variance is the difference between the actual cost of labour for the period and the budgeted cost of labour for the actual production in the period.

(d)   The total variable overhead variance is the difference between the actual cost of variable overhead for the period and the budgeted cost of variable overhead for the actual production in the period.

(e)   The total fixed overhead cost variance is the difference between the actual fixed overhead and the budgeted fixed overhead.

Activity 1: Protec Ltd

Protec Ltd has the following original budget and actual performance for product PT5 for the year ending 31 December.

	Budget	Actual
Volume sold	100,000	100,000
	£000	£000
Sales revenue	3,000	5,400
Less costs:		
Direct materials	525	795
Direct labour	600	720
Overheads	1,470	1,842
Operating profit	405	2,043

Both direct materials and direct labour are variable costs, but the overheads are fixed.

Required

Complete the table below to show a flexed budget and the resulting variances against this budget for the year. Show the actual variance amount, for sales and each cost, in the column headed 'Variance' and indicate whether this is Favourable or Adverse by entering F or A in the final column. If neither F nor A enter 0.

	Flexed budget	Actual	Variance	Favourable F or Adverse A
Volume sold				
	£000	£000	£000	
Sales revenue				
Less costs:				
Direct materials				
Direct labour				
Overheads				
Operating profit				

Fixed overheads do not change as volume/activity changes. But actual fixed overheads may change due to price effects.

Activity 2: Zetec Ltd

Zetec Ltd has the following original budget and actual performance for product ZT4 for the year ending 31 December.

	Budget	Actual
Volume sold	10,000	12,350

	£	£
Sales revenue	300,000	407,550
Less costs:		
Direct materials	50,000	53,000
Direct labour	40,000	49,000
Fixed overheads	110,000	178,000
Operating profit	100,000	127,550

Both direct materials and direct labour are variable costs, but the overheads are fixed.

Required

Complete the table below to show a flexed budget and the resulting variances against this budget for the year. Show the actual variance amount for sales and each cost in the column headed 'Variance' and indicate whether this is Favourable or Adverse by entering F or A in the final column. If neither F nor A enter 0.

	Flexed budget	Actual	Variance	Favourable F or Adverse A
Volume sold				
	£	£	£	
Sales revenue				
Less costs:				
Direct materials				
Direct labour				
Fixed overheads				
Operating profit				

2 Investigating variances

2.1 Causes of variances

When reporting variances to management a simple table is a useful starting point. However, management will also wish to know the reasons for the variances. In this unit we only look at total material, labour, fixed overhead and sales variances.

Variance	Favourable	Adverse
Material	Unforeseen discounts received	Price increase
	Greater care in purchasing	Careless purchasing
	More efficient use of material	Defective material
	Errors in allocating material to jobs	Excessive waste or theft
		Stricter quality control
		Errors in allocating material to jobs

Variance	Favourable	Adverse
Labour	Use of workers at a lower rate of pay Output produced more quickly than expected because of worker motivation, better quality materials etc	Wage rate increase Output lower than standard set because of lack of training, sub-standard materials etc Idle time – waiting for materials, machine breakdown etc
Fixed overhead/ Variable overhead	Savings in costs incurred More economical use of services	Increase in cost of services used Excessive use of services Change in type of service used
Sales revenue	Units sold at a higher selling price More units sold than budgeted due to increase in demand	Lower price charged due to competition Demand has fallen as better product available in the market

2.2 Interdependence of variances

You may have noticed from some of the possible causes of variances given above that many of these are likely to be inter-related. This is known as the **interdependence of variances**.

For example, if lower-grade material is purchased at a cheaper price than standard, this would lead to a favourable material variance. However, this **favourable variance** may be cancelled out by an **adverse variance**, if the lower grade of material means that there is greater wastage than standard.

2.3 Responsibility for variances

Investigating the causes of variances and determining any interdependence between them is an important aspect of management control, as in a system of responsibility accounting the managers responsible for various elements of the business will be held accountable for the relevant variances.

Take the example of a favourable material price variance caused by purchasing a lower grade of material, which leads directly to an adverse materials usage variance. The initial reaction might be to praise the purchasing manager for the favourable variance and to lay blame for the adverse usage variance on the production manager. However, the true picture is that, in the absence of any further reasons for the variance, the responsibility for both variances lies with the purchasing manager.

2.4 Other reasons for variances

Further causes of variances may be one-off events such as a power cut, breakdown of machinery or annual staff holidays.

Assessment focus point

An assessment task may ask you to flex a budget, calculate variances and indicate whether they are adverse or favourable. You could also be given variances and asked which one has the greatest impact on profit. You could also be asked about the likely cause of a particular variance.

Chapter summary

- The sales variance is the difference between the actual revenue received and the budgeted sales revenue for the actual level of sales.

- The materials variance is the difference between the actual cost of materials used in production and the budgeted cost for the actual level of production.

- The labour variance is the difference between the actual cost of labour for the period and the budgeted cost of labour for the actual production in the period.

- The variable overhead variance is the difference between the actual cost of labour for the period and the budgeted cost of variable overhead for the actual production in the period.

- The fixed overhead cost variance is the difference between the actual fixed overhead and the budgeted fixed overhead.

- Management like to know the causes of variances as well as see the numbers. This helps them understand why variances have arisen and how they might avoid them in the future.

Keywords

- **Adverse variance:** Where the actual cost is greater than the budgeted cost, or the actual sales were less than budgeted sales

- **Favourable variance:** Where the actual cost is less than the budgeted cost, or the actual sales were more than budgeted sales

- **Fixed overhead variance:** The difference between the budgeted and actual fixed overhead for the period

- **Interdependence of variances:** Causes of variances are often inter-related. This is called the interdependence of variances

- **Labour variance:** The difference between the budgeted labour cost for the actual production and the actual cost

- **Materials variance:** The difference between the budgeted materials cost for the actual production and the actual cost

- **Variable overhead variance:** The difference between the budgeted variable overhead cost for the actual production and the actual cost

- **Variance:** The difference between the budgeted costs or sales and the actual costs or sales for a period

Test your learning

1   Flower budgeted to sell 200 units and produced the following budget.

	£	£
Sales		71,400
Variable costs		
Labour	31,600	
Material	12,600	
		44,200
Contribution		27,200
Fixed costs		18,900
Profit		8,300

Actual sales turned out to be 230 units, which were sold for £69,000. Actual expenditure on labour was £27,000 and on material £24,000. Fixed costs totalled £10,000.

Prepare a flexible budget that will be useful for management control purposes

	Budget 200 units £	Budget per unit £	Flexed budget 230 units £	Actual 230 units £	Variance £ (A)/(F)
Sales					
Variable costs					
Labour					
Material					
Fixed costs					
Profit					

9

Marginal costing

Learning outcomes

Having studied this chapter you will be able to:

1.2 Differences between marginal and absorption costing

- The difference between product and period costs:
  - some period costs are carried forward in the value of closing inventory under absorption costing
  - in marginal costing only variable costs are included in inventory and period costs are written off in full
- The impact on reported performance of marginal versus full absorption costing in both the short run and the long run
- When each method is appropriate
- Calculate prime cost, marginal cost and full absorption cost

6.1 Learning outcome 2

- The concept of contribution, ie revenue minus variable costs

Assessment context

Look out for questions in your examination which require you to calculate profit or losses using absorption and marginal costing. The concept of contribution is frequently tested in the assessment and is used when making short-term decisions involving profit volume analysis (covered in the next chapter).

Qualification context

At Level 4, costing techniques in the modern business environment will be studied. These are often compared with the more traditional techniques of absorption costing and marginal costing.

Business context

Marginal costing is an alternative to absorption costing. The marginal cost is the part of the cost of one unit of product that would be avoided if the unit were not produced. This information is extremely useful for making decisions such as pricing decisions or whether to continue producing a particular type of unit.

Chapter overview

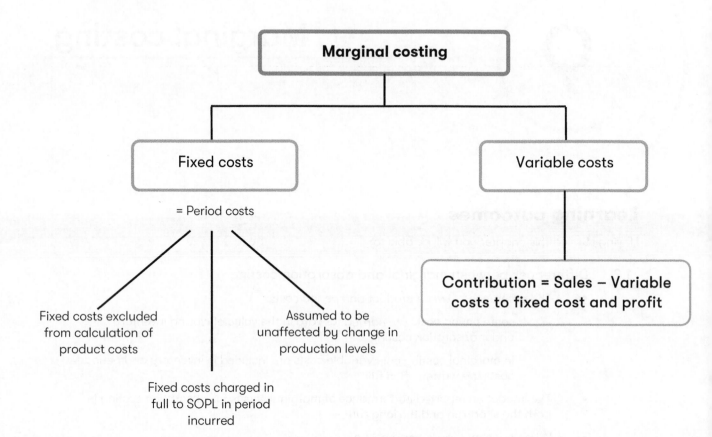

Marginal costing

Fixed costs

= Period costs

Fixed costs excluded from calculation of product costs

Fixed costs charged in full to SOPL in period incurred

Assumed to be unaffected by change in production levels

Variable costs

Contribution = Sales – Variable costs to fixed cost and profit

Introduction

In an earlier chapter we mentioned that there were a number of approaches we could apply to calculate the cost of producing an item or providing a service. So far we have seen how all of the production overheads can be allocated, apportioned and then absorbed into the cost of the product giving a total production cost for each cost unit. This is known as **absorption costing** (or **full costing**).

However, there is a different method of costing known as **marginal costing** (or **variable costing**), which may be preferred by some organisations and can be more useful for some reporting purposes.

Under a marginal costing system the cost unit is valued at just the variable (or marginal) cost of production. The fixed production costs for the period are charged to the statement of profit or loss as an expense for the period rather than being included as part of the cost of the cost unit.

1 Marginal costing

1.1 Contribution

Marginal costing treats all fixed costs as **period costs**. The fixed costs are not included when calculating **product costs**.

Only variable costs are charged as a cost of sale. Instead of profit, a figure known as **contribution** is calculated:

	£
Sales revenue	X
Less: all variable costs	(X)
Contribution to fixed cost and profit	X

> **Contribution** – Contribution = Sales value – Variable cost of sales.
>
> **Period costs** are costs relating to a time period rather than to the output of products.
>
> **Product costs** are costs of a product made up from its cost elements.

Activity 1: Contribution

Required

Calculate the contribution for the following products:

	J	K	L
Sales price	£10.00	£5.00	£3.00
Costs:			
Materials	£3.00	£2.50	£0.50
Labour	£1.00	£1.50	£1.25
Variable sales costs	£0.25	£0.15	£0.30
Variable overheads	£0.75	£0.10	£0.25
Fixed overheads	£1.00	£1.00	£1.00

	J	K	L
Contribution per unit	£	£	£

If we sell one extra unit:

- We will generate additional revenue for one extra unit
- We will incur variable costs of one extra unit
- Profit will increase by the contribution (sales price – variable costs) of that one extra unit
- There will be no impact on fixed overheads

Illustration 1: Absorption costing and marginal costing

Graham Associates produce just one product in their factory. The factory has two production departments, assembly and packaging. The anticipated production for the next month, March, is 50,000 units and the expected costs are as follows:

Direct materials	£20 per unit
Direct labour	3 hours assembly at £8.00 per hour
	1 hour packaging at £6.00 per hour
Assembly variable overheads	£240,000
Assembly fixed overheads	£120,000
Packaging variable overheads	£100,000
Packaging fixed overheads	£40,000

Overheads are absorbed on the basis of labour hours.

We will start by calculating the cost of each cost unit using absorption costing.

Absorption costing

		Assembly	Packaging
Total overhead (variable + fixed)		£360,000	£140,000
Total labour hours	50,000 × 3	150,000	
	50,000 × 1		50,000
Overhead absorption rate		£360,000	£140,000
		150,000	50,000
Total overhead/Total labour hours	=	£2.40 per	£2.80 per
		labour hour	labour hour

Unit cost

		£
Direct materials		20.00
Direct labour	assembly 3 hours × £8.00	24.00
	packaging 1 hour × £6.00	6.00
Overheads	assembly 3 hours × £2.40	7.20
	packaging 1 hour × £2.80	2.80
Total unit cost		60.00

Marginal costing

Now we will calculate the same unit cost using marginal costing and therefore only including the variable costs, which are direct materials, direct labour and variable overheads.

		Assembly	Packaging
Variable overhead		£240,000	£100,000
Total labour hours		150,000	50,000
Variable overhead cost per hour		£240,000	£100,000
		150,000	50,000
	=	£1.60 per	£2.00 per
		labour hour	labour hour

Unit cost

		£
Direct materials		20.00
Direct labour	assembly	24.00
	packaging	6.00
Variable overhead	assembly 3 hours × £1.60	4.80
	packaging 1 hour × £2.00	2.00
Prime cost		56.80

Activity 2: Unit cost

A factory produces a single product with the following budgeted costs:

Direct materials	£3.40
Direct labour	£6.80
Variable overheads	£1.20
Fixed overheads	£340,000

Overheads are absorbed on the machine hour basis and it is estimated that in the next accounting period machine hours will total 100,000. Each unit requires two hours of machine time.

What is the cost per unit using:

(a)   Absorption costing?
(b)   Marginal costing?

(a)

Absorption costing – unit cost	£
Direct material	
Direct labour	
Variable overhead	
Total variable cost	
Fixed overhead	
Absorption cost	

(b)

Marginal costing – unit cost	£
Direct material	
Direct labour	
Variable overhead	
Marginal cost	

Activity 3: MC vs AC cost per unit

The following information relates to the manufacture of product E during the month of December 20X6:

Direct materials per unit	£12.00
Direct labour per unit	£13.50
Total variable overheads	£88,000
Total fixed overheads	£110,000
Number of units produced	11,000

Required

Calculate the cost per unit of product E under:

(a)   Marginal costing
(b)   Full absorption costing

(a)

Marginal costing	£
Direct materials	
Direct labour	
Variable overheads per unit	
Total variable (marginal) cost	

(b)

Full absorption costing	£
Total variable cost	
Add: overhead absorption rate	
Full product cost	

1.2 Absorption versus marginal costing – effect on profit

We can now have a look at what effect the two different accounting methods have on the profits that are reported. Under absorption costing the full production cost of the units actually sold in the period is charged as part of cost of sales. The only other entry may be some adjustment for under- or over-absorption of overheads.

However, under marginal costing the lower, variable, cost per unit is charged as part of cost of sales and deducted from sales. This resulting figure is called contribution – it is sales minus variable costs of production and is the contribution towards the fixed costs and any profit. The fixed overheads are then charged to the statement of profit or loss as a period cost.

In the long run, the total profit for a company will be the same whether marginal costing or absorption costing is used. Different accounting conventions merely affect the profit of individual accounting periods.

 Illustration 2: Effect on profit

Returning to Graham Associates the budgeted sales and production for each of the next three months, March, April and May, are 50,000 units. The budgeted cost figures for each month remain the same at:

Direct materials	£20.00 per unit
Direct labour	3 hours assembly at £8.00 per hour
	1 hour packaging at £6.00 per hour
Assembly variable overheads	£240,000
Assembly fixed overheads	£120,000
Packaging variable overheads	£100,000
Packaging fixed overheads	£40,000

The actual production and sales for each of the three months turned out to be:

	March	April	May
Sales	50,000	45,000	52,000
Production	50,000	50,000	50,000

There were no inventories of the product at the beginning of March. In each month both variable and fixed overheads were exactly as budgeted. Sales were at a selling price of £70.00 per unit.

Remember that the cost per unit for absorption costing is £60.00 and for marginal costing is £56.80.

Statement of profit or loss for March

Absorption costing

	£000	£000
Sales (50,000 × £70.00)		3,500
Less: cost of goods sold		
Opening inventory	–	
Cost of production (50,000 × £60.00)	3,000	
	3,000	
Less: closing inventory	–	
		3,000
Profit		500

Marginal costing

	£000	£000
Sales		3,500
Less: cost of goods sold		
Opening inventory	–	
Cost of production (50,000 × 56.80)	2,840	
	2,840	
Less: closing inventory	–	
		2,840
Contribution		660
Less: fixed costs (120,000 + 40,000)		160
Profit		500

In this month the profits under absorption costing and under marginal costing are exactly the same. The reason for this is that there has been no change in inventory levels. There was no opening inventory and as production and sales were for equal amounts there is also no closing inventory. **When opening and closing inventory amounts are equal then absorption costing profit and marginal costing profit will be equal.**

Statement of profit or loss for April

In April sales were 45,000 units and production was 50,000 units leaving closing inventory of 5,000 units.

Absorption costing

	£000	£000
Sales (45,000 × £70.00)		3,150
Less: cost of goods sold		
Opening inventory	–	
Cost of production (50,000 × £60.00)	3,000	
	3,000	
Less: closing inventory (5,000 × £60.00)	300	
		2,700
Profit		450

Marginal costing

	£000	£000
Sales		3,150
Less: cost of goods sold		
Opening inventory	–	
Cost of production (50,000 × 56.80)	2,840	
	2,840	
Less: closing inventory (5,000 × 56.80)	284	
		2,556
Contribution		594
Less: fixed costs (120,000 + 40,000)		160
Profit		434

In this month there is a difference in profit:

	£000
Absorption costing profit	450
Marginal costing profit	434
Difference	16

The difference in reported profit under the two costing methods is due to the fixed overheads absorbed into inventory. Under marginal costing the entire fixed overhead for the month is charged to the statement of profit or loss. However, under absorption costing the fixed overhead is included in the cost per unit and therefore any fixed overhead in the closing inventory is carried forward to the next period rather than being charged in this period.

As inventory levels have risen from zero opening inventory to 5,000 units of closing inventory this means that the fixed overhead amount included in the inventory valuation for those 5,000 units has been deducted from this month's cost of sales and carried forward to the next month. This has not happened under marginal costing, therefore the absorption costing profit is higher.

The two profit figures can be reconciled as **the difference is due solely to the increase in inventories and the fixed overhead included in that inventory valuation.**

Fixed overheads per unit $= \dfrac{£120,000 + £40,000}{50,000} = £3.20$

Remember that the difference in profit was £16,000. This has been caused by:

Fixed overhead included in increase in inventory

(5,000 units × £3.20)   £16,000

Statement of profit or loss for May

Absorption costing

	£000	£000
Sales (52,000 × £70.00)		3,640
Less: cost of goods sold		
Opening inventory (5,000 × £60.00)	300	
Cost of production (50,000 × £60.00)	3,000	
	3,300	
Less: closing inventory (3,000 × £60.00)	180	
		3,120
Profit		520

Marginal costing

	£000	£000
Sales		3,640
Less: cost of goods sold		
Opening inventory (5,000 × 56.80)	284	
Cost of production (50,000 × 56.80)	2,840	
	3,124	
Less: closing inventory (3,000 × 56.80)	170.4	
		2,953.6
Contribution		686.4
Less: fixed costs (120,000 + 40,000)		160.0
Profit		526.4

	£000
Absorption costing profit	520.00
Marginal costing profit	526.40
Difference	6.40

In May the marginal cost profit is £6,400 higher than the absorption cost profit as in this month inventory levels have decreased from 5,000 units to 3,000 units. Therefore under absorption costing more of the brought forward fixed costs have been charged to the statement of profit or loss in the month than have been carried forward to the following month in closing inventory.

The difference is made up of:

Fixed overhead in inventory decrease 2,000 × £3.20 = £6,400

Activity 4: Marginal costing profit statement

Sanctuary Catering has established the following budgeted annual sales and cost information meal types.

'STANDARD' and 'VEGETARIAN'

Meal type	Standard	Vegetarian
Meals prepared and sold	130,000 meals	200,000 meals
Staff hours required	3,250	6,000
Sales revenue	£1,040,000	£1,500,000
Direct materials (ingredients etc)	£468,000	£600,000
Direct labour	£260,000	£400,000
Variable overheads	£260,000	£300,000

The fixed costs attributable to Standard and Vegetarian meals are budgeted to be £212,000.

Required

Complete the table below to show the budgeted contribution per type of meal and Sanctuary Catering's budgeted profit or loss for the year from these two meals.

	Standard £	Vegetarian £	Total £
Selling price per meal			
Less: variable costs per meal			
Direct materials			
Direct labour			
Variable overheads			
Contribution per unit			
Sales volume (units)			
Total contribution			
Less: fixed costs			
Budgeted profit or loss			

1.3 Absorption vs marginal costing – advantages and disadvantages

- Absorption costing has the advantage of allowing managers to see whether the sales of their products are covering all of the production costs of those products.

- However, it is argued that contribution is a much more useful figure for management decision-making purposes.

- Under absorption costing, we have seen that it is possible to report a higher profit figure by increasing the closing inventory levels. Although this will increase absorption costing profit, it is not in the best interests of the organisation. It is unethical behaviour.

  - It is argued, however, that **absorption costing is preferable to marginal costing in management accounting, in order to be consistent with the requirement of current accounting standards and financial reporting.**

  - It is also argued that absorption costing is more appropriate for a business which uses cost plus pricing.

It is, however, important to appreciate that the differences in reported profits occur only in the short run, ie in reporting the profit of individual accounting periods. This is because, in the long run, total costs will be the same using either method of accounting. Short-term differences are the results of changes in the level of inventory.

Activity 5: MC vs AC

CPL is considering what the effect would be of costing its products under marginal costing (MC) principles, instead of under the full absorption costing (FAC) principles that it currently follows.

The following information relates to one of the company's products:

Selling price per unit	£12
Prime cost per unit	£4
Variable production overhead per unit	£3
Budgeted fixed production overhead	£30,000 per month
Budgeted production	15,000 units per month
Budgeted sales	12,000 units per month
Opening inventory	2,000 units

Required

(a) Calculate the contribution per unit (on a MC basis).

	£
Selling price/unit	
Prime cost/unit	
Variable production cost/unit	
Marginal cost (MC)/unit	
= Contribution/unit	

(b) Calculate the profit per unit (on a FAC basis).

	£
Selling price/unit	
Marginal cost/unit	
Fixed production cost/unit	
FAC cost/unit	
= Profit/unit	

(c) Complete the table below to produce a statement of profit or loss for the product for the month under marginal costing (MC) principles.

	£	£
Sales		
Less: cost of sales		
Opening inventory		
Variable production costs		
Closing inventory		
Cost of sales (MC basis)		
Contribution		
Fixed costs		
Profit		

(d) Complete the table below to produce a statement of profit or loss for the product for the month under full absorption costing (FAC) principles.

	£	£
Sales		
Less: cost of sales		
Opening inventory		
Production costs		
Closing inventory		
Cost of sales (FAC basis)		
Profit		

(e) Explain why the two profit figures differ by selecting the correct words from the brackets in the statement below.

The two profit figures differ by £ [   ] because under FAC the

_____(decrease/increase) in the valuation of inventory during the month is
_____(higher/lower) than the _____(decrease/increase) under MC.

This is because fixed overhead cost has been carried forward in the statement of financial position in the inventory valuation as an asset under FAC principles, but written off against profit under MC principles.

Assessment focus point

In your assessment, a task could ask you to calculate the marginal cost of a batch or the marginal cost of a unit.

Chapter summary

- Under absorption costing all production overheads are allocated and apportioned to production cost centres and then absorbed into the cost of the products on some suitable basis.

- Under marginal costing the cost of the products is the variable cost of production with all fixed production costs being charged to the statement of profit or loss as a period charge.

- If inventory levels are constant then both absorption costing and marginal costing will report the same profit figure.

- If inventory levels are increasing, absorption costing profit will be higher as more fixed overheads are carried forward to the following period in closing inventory than those brought forward in opening inventory.

- If inventory levels are falling, marginal costing profit will be higher as less fixed overheads are carried forward under absorption costing in the closing inventory figure than those brought forward in opening inventory.

- The difference in profit will be the fixed production overhead included in the increase/decrease in inventory levels under absorption costing.

- The contribution figure shown in marginal costing can be argued to be more use to management than the full absorption costing profit figure.

- It is possible to manipulate profit reporting under absorption costing by increasing inventory levels and thereby increasing reported profit. However, differences in reported profits occur only in the short run, and in the long run total costs will be the same by either method of accounting.

Keywords

- **Absorption (full) costing:** Both variable and fixed production overheads are included in unit cost

- **Contribution:** Sales value less variable cost of the goods sold

- **Marginal (variable) costing:** Unit cost includes only variable production costs

- **Period cost or a cost relating to a time period:** Usually, fixed overheads which aren't affected by changes in production level

- **Production or product cost:** The cost of a finished product built up from its cost elements

Test your learning

1   Given below is the budgeted information about the production of 60,000 units of a single product in a factory for the following quarter:

Direct materials		£12.50 per unit
Direct labour	– assembly	4 hours @ £8.40 per hour
	– finishing	1 hour @ £6.60 per hour
Assembly production overheads		£336,000
Finishing production overheads		£84,000

It is estimated that 60% of the assembly overhead is variable and that 75% of the finishing overhead is variable.

What is the budgeted cost of the product using:

(a)   **Absorption costing?**

£ | |

(b)   **Marginal costing?**

£ | |

Short-term decision making

10

Learning outcomes

6	Use management accounting techniques to support short-term decision making

6.1	Estimate and use short-term future revenue and costs

- Use estimates of relevant future revenue and costs
- Use cost-volume-profit (CVP) analysis (both by calculation and by linear breakeven chart) to calculate
    - Breakeven analysis
    - Margin of safety and margin of safety percentage
    - Target profit
    - Profit-volume ratio
- Interpret and report on CVP analysis

Assessment context

Cost-volume-profit (CVP) analysis is an important tool that management accountants can use in decision making. Assessment questions may require you to recall the formulae included in this chapter – make sure you learn them so that you can apply them when you need to.

Qualification context

CVP analysis is a basic tool that a company can use for decision making, particularly for short-term decision making. It is therefore a tool that can be useful at all levels of your studies.

Business context

When using a marginal costing system, there is more risk that fixed costs will not be covered. Using CVP, the business can plan to ensure fixed costs are covered and target profit figures can also be calculated.

Chapter overview

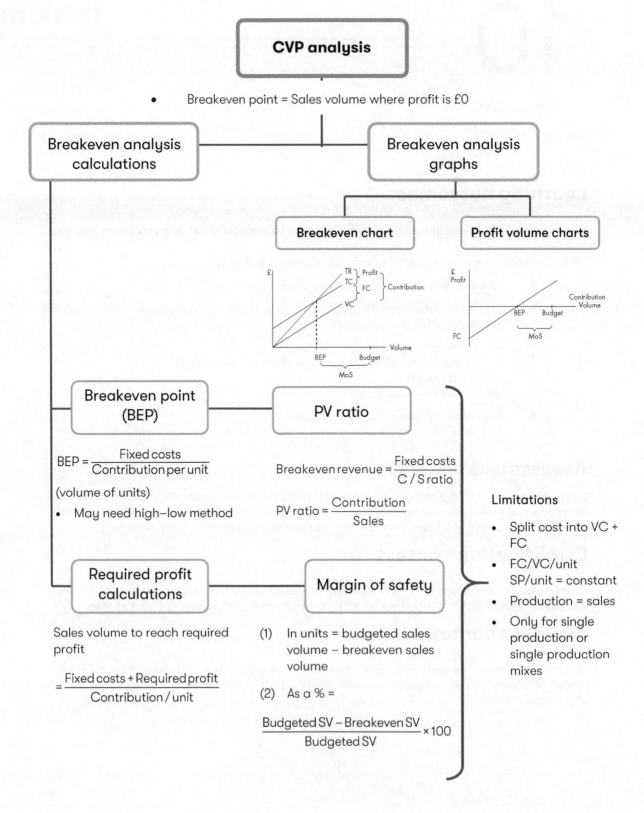

CVP analysis

- Breakeven point = Sales volume where profit is £0

Breakeven analysis calculations

Breakeven analysis graphs

Breakeven chart

Profit volume charts

Breakeven point (BEP)

PV ratio

$$BEP = \frac{Fixed\ costs}{Contribution\ per\ unit}$$

(volume of units)

- May need high–low method

$$Breakeven\ revenue = \frac{Fixed\ costs}{C\ /\ S\ ratio}$$

$$PV\ ratio = \frac{Contribution}{Sales}$$

Required profit calculations

Margin of safety

Sales volume to reach required profit

$$= \frac{Fixed\ costs + Required\ profit}{Contribution\ /\ unit}$$

(1) In units = budgeted sales volume – breakeven sales volume

(2) As a % =

$$\frac{Budgeted\ SV - Breakeven\ SV}{Budgeted\ SV} \times 100$$

Limitations

- Split cost into VC + FC
- FC/VC/unit SP/unit = constant
- Production = sales
- Only for single production or single production mixes

Introduction

This chapter considers a useful technique for making decisions that will affect the business in the next few months (in the short term). It is commonly examined.

Cost–volume–profit (CVP) analysis is concerned with the relationship between sales volume and profit level. CVP analysis identifies the **breakeven point** for a company and the **margin of safety**.

1 Relevant future income and costs for short-term decision making

When providing management information for decision making, you must work out which costs and revenues are **relevant** to the decision.

In the context of short-term decision making, the **relevant cost** is **contribution**. The fixed costs do not affect the decision made and are **irrelevant costs**.

A relevant cost (sometimes known as an **avoidable cost**) is a future, incremental cash flow arising as a direct consequence of a decision. In other words, relevant costs are those costs that are changed by a decision.

2 Breakeven analysis and contribution

2.1 Assumption

We will assume that selling price per unit, variable cost per unit and fixed costs are all constant, that is, they do not change with varying output. This is a reasonable assumption for short-term decisions although, of course, in the long term or for very high levels of output this might not apply.

2.2 Contribution

As discussed in the previous chapter, **contribution** shows us how much profit increases as sales increase.

Contribution per unit = Selling price per unit less all variable costs per unit

We will need this definition to set up the breakeven formula.

3 Breakeven point

> The **breakeven point** is the volume of sales which will give a company a profit of £nil.

If sales exceed the breakeven point the company will make a profit.

Breakeven analysis is often referred to as **cost–volume–profit analysis**.

Formula to learn

Breakeven point = Number of units of sale required to breakeven

$$= \frac{\text{Fixed costs}}{\text{Unit contribution}}$$

When calculating the breakeven point, always round the number of units **up** to the next whole unit.

Illustration 1: Breakeven point

Reardon Enterprises sells a single product with a selling price of £10 per unit. The variable costs of producing the product are £6 per unit and the fixed costs of the business are £200,000.

What is the breakeven point in units?

$$\text{Breakeven point} = \frac{£200,000}{£10-£6}$$

$$= 50,000 \text{ units}$$

We can prove that this is the point where no profit or loss is made.

	£
Sales (50,000 × £10)	500,000
Variable costs (50,000 × £6)	300,000
Contribution	200,000
Fixed costs	(200,000)
Profit	–

Therefore the management of Reardon Enterprises will know that they must ensure that sales volumes exceed 50,000 units per annum in order for the business to cover its total costs and make any profit.

Activity 1: Breakeven units

A business has a single product that it sells for £28. The variable costs of producing the product are £19 per unit and the fixed costs of the business are £360,000.

Required

What is the breakeven point in units?

Breakeven point = [   ] units

Activity 2: Breakeven revenue

A company has different output levels, and incurs different total production costs at each level, as follows:

Output Units	Total costs £
6,000	44,700
8,000	57,700

Required

If the selling price is £8 per unit at all levels, what is the breakeven point? What is the breakeven revenue? (Use a rough sheet for workings.)

Breakeven point = [   ] units

Breakeven revenue = £ [   ]

4 The profit volume (PV) ratio

KEY TERM

The **PV ratio** (or **contribution/sales C/S ratio**) is a measure of how much contribution is earned from each £1 of sales. PV ratio = contribution ÷ sales

The higher the PV ratio, the better. A higher PV ratio means that more contribution is earned per £1 of sales. This is useful for making decisions, particularly if a business wants to compare two different scenarios.

The ratio of contribution to sales is an alternative method of finding the breakeven point.

Formula to learn

$$\text{Breakeven revenue} = \frac{\text{Fixed costs}}{\text{PV ratio}}$$

$$\text{PV ratio} = \frac{\text{Contribution}}{\text{Sales}}$$

Activity 3: Profit volume ratio

Required

Using details from the breakeven revenue activity (Activity 2) above, find the PV ratio and breakeven revenue.

PV ratio = [   ] %

Breakeven revenue = £ [   ]

The company realises that it can increase the selling price to £10 per unit if fixed costs were increased to £6,000. Variable costs would remain at £6.50 per unit. What is the revised PV ratio?

PV ratio = [   ] %

Which option is the most financially beneficial for the company?

☐ Original selling price and fixed cost

☐ Revised selling price and fixed cost

5 The margin of safety

As well as being interested in the breakeven point, management may also be interested in the amount by which actual sales can fall below anticipated sales without a loss being made. This measure, of the amount by which sales must fall before we start making a loss, is the **margin of safety**.

A loss is made if sales volume is less than the breakeven point.

Formula to learn

Margin of safety = Budgeted sales volume less breakeven sales volume Or, as a percentage:

$$\text{Margin of safety} = \frac{\text{Budgeted sales volume} - \text{Breakeven sales volume}}{\text{Budgeted sales volume}} \times 100$$

Activity 4: Margin of safety

Required

Using details as per the breakeven revenue example in Activity 2, and with budgeted sales being 5,000 units, calculate the margin of safety.

Margin of safety = [   ] units

Margin of safety = [   ] %

6 Target profit

The approach used to find an expression for the breakeven sales volumes can be extended to find the volume needed to attain a required or **target profit** level.

Formula to learn

$$\text{Sales volume to reach required profit level} = \frac{\text{Fixed costs} + \text{Required profit}}{\text{Unit contribution}}$$

The required profit is like an additional fixed cost which must be covered before the company 'breaks even'.

Activity 5: Target profit level

Required

Using the data from the breakeven revenue example in Activity 2, if we need to make a profit of £10,000, calculate the required sales volume.

Sales volume to achieve target profit = [   ] units

7 Breakeven charts and profit–volume graphs

7.1 Breakeven chart

A breakeven chart shows the profit or loss at different levels of sales.

It shows, in diagrammatic form, the relationship between sales volume or value, total revenue, and total costs. Breakeven occurs when total costs are equal to total revenue.

The horizontal axis is used for sales volume or value and the vertical axis for money (costs and revenue).

Three lines are plotted on the graph:

- First the sales revenue line (which will pass through the origin, since when sales volume is nil, revenue is nil);

- Then the fixed costs line (which will be parallel to the horizontal axis);

- And finally the total costs line.

Illustration 2: Breakeven chart

The following information relates to Reardon Enterprises.

Selling price per unit	£10
Variable cost per unit	£6
Contribution per unit	£4
Fixed costs	£200,000
Breakeven point	50,000 units or £500,000
Budgeted sales	70,000 units

Breakeven chart

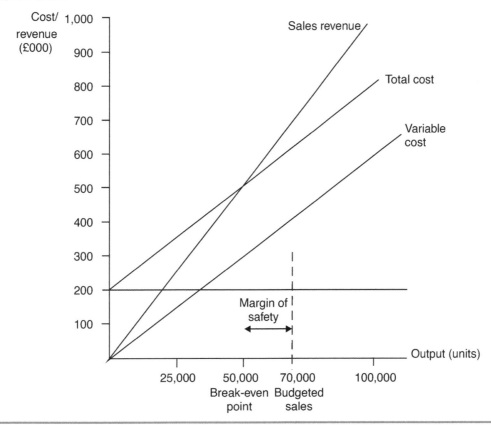

This chart shows variable costs, fixed costs, total costs and sales revenue at various different activity levels.

Assessment focus point

You will not be asked to sketch a graph in the computer based assessment but you could be asked to label one.

7.2 How to interpret the breakeven chart

- The fixed cost line is a horizontal line at £200,000.

- Variable costs start at the origin – if there are no sales then there are no variable costs. You can see, for example, variable costs at 100,000 units are £600,000.

- The total cost line is parallel to the variable cost line but starts at £200,000, the level of the fixed costs.

- Sales revenue again starts at the origin. You can see that the revenue is £1,000,000 if sales are 100,000 units.

7.3 What the breakeven chart shows

- The breakeven point is the point where the sales revenue line crosses the total costs line.

- The margin of safety is the horizontal distance between budgeted sales of 70,000 units and breakeven sales of 50,000 units.

- The amount of profit or loss at each activity level is the vertical distance between the sales revenue line and the total cost line.

7.4 Profit–volume chart

 Illustration 3: Profit–volume chart

Profit–volume chart

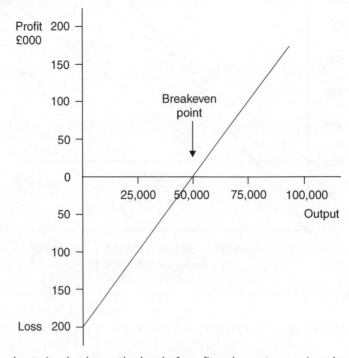

The profit–volume chart simply shows the level of profit or loss at any given level of activity.

7.5 How to interpret a P/V chart

- The loss when there are zero sales is equal to the fixed costs, £200,000.
- The profit at the 100,000 units activity level is £200,000.

7.6 What the P/V chart shows

- The profit or loss at any level of activity can be read off the chart.

- The breakeven point is where the profit line crosses the horizontal axis – where profit is zero.

- The horizontal axis could alternatively have shown sales revenue rather than activity level.

8 Limitations of breakeven analysis

CVP analysis is a useful technique for managers. It can provide simple and quick estimates, and breakeven charts provide graphical representations of breakeven arithmetic. It does, however, have a number of limitations.

The limitations are the assumptions that it makes.

8.1 Assumptions

(a) All costs can be split into fixed and variable elements
(b) Fixed costs are constant
(c) Variable cost per unit is constant
(d) Selling price is constant
(e) Constant inventory levels (sales = production)
(f) Analysis only possible for single products or for single product mixes

Chapter summary

- In the context of short-term decision making, the relevant cost is contribution. Fixed costs are generally irrelevant.

- The breakeven point in units is found by dividing the fixed costs by the contribution per unit.

$$\text{Breakeven point} = \frac{\text{Fixed costs}}{\text{Unit contribution}}$$

- If a target profit is required the unit sales to achieve this can be found by dividing the fixed costs plus target profit by the contribution per unit.

- The difference between budgeted or actual sales and the breakeven point is the margin of safety, which can be expressed as a percentage of budgeted or actual sales.

- The profit volume ratio can be used to find the breakeven point in terms of sales revenue.

- Sales revenue, costs, contribution, profit and breakeven point can be illustrated by a breakeven chart or a profit–volume chart.

Keywords

- **Avoidable costs:** Costs that would not be incurred if the activity to which they relate did not exist

- **Breakeven analysis:** Calculations to determine the breakeven point

- **Breakeven point:** Level of sales whereby sales revenue is equal to total costs

- **Contribution:** Sales revenue or selling price per unit less variable costs

- **Cost-volume-profit analysis:** Analysis of the relationships between activity levels, costs and profits

- **Incremental cost:** The increase in costs that occur as a result of a decision

- **Irrelevant cost:** A cost incurred in the past (a past cost or **sunk cost**) that is irrelevant to any decision being made now; it includes committed costs which are future cash flows that will be incurred anyway, regardless of the decision taken now

- **Margin of safety:** Excess of budgeted or actual sales over the breakeven point sales

- **Profit–volume (P/V) ratio:** Ratio of contribution to sales, also known as the contribution to sales (C/S) ratio

- **Relevant cost:** A future incremental cash flow arising as a direct consequence of a decision

- **Target profit:** A planned level of profit, and from this the target profit units can be worked out

Test your learning

1   A business has budgeted sales of its single product of 38,000 units. The selling price per unit is £57 and the variable costs of production are £45. The fixed costs of the business are £360,000.

Calculate the breakeven point in units

☐ units

and the margin of safety (to the nearest whole per cent)

☐ %

2   A business has fixed costs of £910,000. It sells a single product at a selling price of £24 and the variable costs of production and sales are £17 per unit.

How many units of the product must the business sell in order to make a profit of £500,000?

☐ units

3   A business sells its single product for £40. The variable costs of this product total £32. The fixed costs of the business are £100,000.

What is the sales revenue required in order to make a profit of £200,000?

£ ☐

11 Cash management

Learning outcomes

7.1 Principles of cash budgeting

- The key differences between cash and profit
- Principles of forecasting cash receipts and payments for:
    - Sales, purchases and production
    - The acquisition and disposal of non-current assets
    - Accounts receivable and payable
    - Capital/new loans, repayment of loans and drawings

- The funding methods available for the acquisition of non-current assets:
    - Cash
    - Part-exchange
    - Borrowing – loans, hire purchase

- The suitability of each funding method for the acquisition of non-current assets
- The importance of liquidity and use of resources ratios
- The working capital cycle
- Produce cash budgets
- Calculate working capital using resources ratios:

    - Inventory holding period (days) = Inventories / Cost of sales × 365

    - Trade receivables collection period (days) = Trade receivables / Revenue × 365

    - Trade payables payment period (days) = Trade payables / Cost of sales × 365

    - Working capital cycle (days) = Inventory days + Receivable days – Payable days

7.2 Improving cash flow

- The importance of liquidity for businesses' survival
- The actions that can be taken if insufficient liquidity:
    - Raise additional finance from owners in the form of capital
    - Raise additional finance externally in the form of debt

- Other methods of improving cash flow:
    - Chase receivables
    - Delay supplier payments
    - Offer prompt payment discounts (PPD)
    - Dispose of non-current assets
    - Reduce inventory
- How accounting software and the use of automation and visualisation can aid cash flow planning

Assessment context

You need to understand the meaning of liquidity, how to reconcile profit with cash, how to calculate working capital ratios and how to improve cash flow in the short term.

Qualification context

The distinction between cash and profit is a fundamental concept that you need to fully understand throughout your accounting career.

Business context

Cash flow is the life blood of any business; without proper financial management, even solid, profitable business ideas run the risk of failure.

Chapter overview

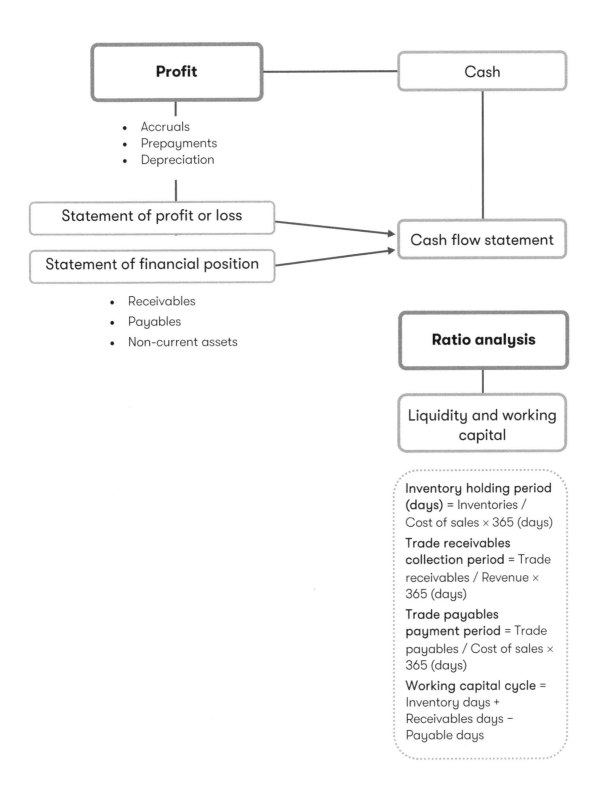

Profit

- Accruals
- Prepayments
- Depreciation

Cash

Statement of profit or loss

Statement of financial position

- Receivables
- Payables
- Non-current assets

Cash flow statement

Ratio analysis

Liquidity and working capital

Inventory holding period (days) = Inventories / Cost of sales × 365 (days)

Trade receivables collection period = Trade receivables / Revenue × 365 (days)

Trade payables payment period = Trade payables / Cost of sales × 365 (days)

Working capital cycle = Inventory days + Receivables days − Payable days

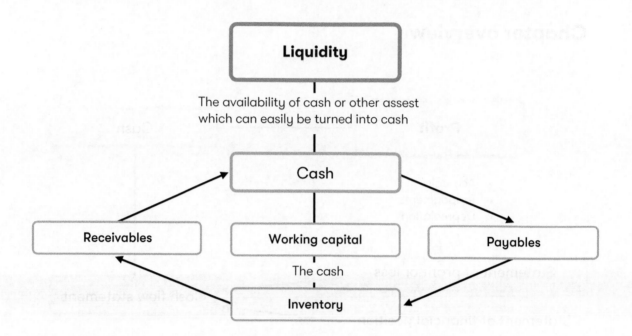

Introduction

This chapter is designed to enable you to distinguish between cash and profit and to understand the importance of liquidity.

The aim of most businesses is to make a **profit** for its owners. If a business is profitable, this means that it is making more by selling its goods or services than it is spending on the purchase of goods and the payment of expenses.

Profit is **not** the same as cash. A profitable business may still fail if it cannot pay its bills.

Liquidity is vital to the success of a business and this chapter looks at how the working capital cycle plays a part in the liquidity of the business.

The chapter finishes by covering ways to improve cash flow and how accounting software can aid cash flow planning.

1 The difference between cash and profit

Cash is ready money, most easily thought of as banknotes and coins, and money in a current bank account. It has been described many times as the lifeblood of business in a modern economy.

1.1 The accruals concept

The profit for a period is calculated using the accruals concept. Under the accruals concept revenue from sales and the cost of goods and expenses are accounted for in the period in which they are earned or incurred rather than in the period in which the cash is received or paid. Therefore, even though a business may appear to have made a profit in a period, it may not yet have the cash to show for it.

1.2 Non-cash expenses

Generally, expenses of a business will reduce the amount of cash that the business has, as these expenses will have to be paid for. However, there are some expenses which have no effect on cash at all; these are known as non-cash expenses. The most obvious of these is the annual depreciation charge on non-current assets. Although this is an expense of the business, it is not an amount of cash leaving the business. The cash impact only arises on the initial purchase of the non-current asset (see below).

KEY TERM

> **Depreciation** An accounting charge made to the statement of profit or loss to write off capital expenditure of a tangible asset over its useful life.

Depreciation charge or a **loss on the sale of a non-current asset** appear in the statement of profit or loss but are **non-cash expenses**.

A **provision** for an expense in the future is also a non-cash expense.

1.3 Receipts/payments not affecting profit

Many businesses will find that on occasions they have receipts of cash into the business which do not affect profit. For example, if a sole trader pays more capital into the business or a company issues additional equity shares for cash, there are receipts of cash into the business but the profit of the business is not affected.

Conversely, if a sole trader takes drawings out of the business or a company pays its shareholders a cash dividend, then these are reductions in the cash balance of the business but do not reduce the profit level.

1.4 Purchase of non-current assets

When non-current assets are purchased by a business, this will often mean a large payment of cash in order to acquire the asset. However, as you will have seen in your earlier accounting studies this does not directly affect the statement of profit or loss. The statement of profit or loss is affected by the annual depreciation charge on the new asset, which is charged as an expense, rather than the full cash cost.

1.5 Sale of non-current assets

When a non-current asset is sold, this will mean cash coming into the business (ie the cash received from the sale). However, the profit of the business is only increased or decreased by any amount of **profit or loss** on the sale of this asset (the difference between the sale proceeds received for the asset and its carrying amount (cost less accumulated depreciation)), rather than the cash received.

Activity 1: Differences between cash flow and profit

Required

Give four examples highlighting why profits and cash differ.

Solution

(a)

(b)

(c)

(d)

1.6 Reconciling profit with cash

Assessment focus point

A question in your assessment may ask you to demonstrate how to reconcile the profit figure to the cash figure. You need to know whether to add or deduct the transaction amounts from the profit figure to reach the cash figure. This means understanding whether the transactions have an effect on cash, profit or both.

Activity 2: Reconciling profit to cash

Identify, by selecting Add or Deduct, how a business reconciles profit with cash.

Profit	Add ✓	Deduct ✓
Drawings by owner		
Receipt for the sale of a non-current asset		
Depreciation		
Loan repayment		
Receipt of a loan		
= Cash		

2 Forecasting cash

Cash forecasting ensures that there will be enough funds to sustain the activities of the organisation. It also helps the organisation plan its financial transactions to be more efficient, so that it can minimise the costs of borrowings and maximise the return from investing surplus funds.

KEY TERM

A **cash budget** is a detailed budget of estimated cash inflows and outflows.

For a cash budget to be useful, it should incorporate the following:

- Analysis of the sources of receipts leading to total receipts for the period
- Analysis of the sources of payments leading to total payments for the period
- Net cash flow for the period
- Bank balance brought forward
- Bank balance carried forward

Cash budget for the three months ending 31 March 20X5

	Jan £	Feb £	Mar £
Cash receipts:			
Receivables	X	X	X
Loan		X	
Total receipts	X	X	X
Cash payments:			
Payables	X	X	X
Wages	X	X	X
Overheads	X	X	X
Purchase of non-current assets	X		
Total payments	X	X	X

	Jan £	Feb £	Mar £
Net cash flow (receipts – payments)	X	(X)	X
Opening balance (b/f)	X	X	(X)
Closing balance (c/f)	X	(X)	X

2.1 Sales receipts

When preparing a cash budget, one of the most complicated areas is normally cash receipts from sales.

> If cash is received at a later time to when the sale was recorded, there is a **lagged receipt**.

For example, a sale could be made on credit terms if payment is required 30 days after the invoice date. A business should know from experience the probable payment times for its customers.

Activity 3: Lagged receipts

Fred has just started in business and has forecast sales as follows:

January   £125,000
February   £150,000
March   £175,000

All sales are on credit and 75% of each month's sales revenues will be received one month later.

The remaining revenue will be received two months after the sale.

Required

Forecast the cash receipts from January to March.

Solution

	January £	February £	March £
Cash received from invoices issued in:			
January			
February			
March			
Total receipts from sales			

2.2 Purchases payments

If cash is paid at a later time to the recording of the purchase or expense, it is a **lagged payment**.

Activity 4: Lagged payments

Arthur has produced the following purchasing estimates for the budgeted statement of profit of loss:

January	£45,000
February	£65,000
March	£80,000

Purchases made in January must be paid for immediately. From then on, Arthur will get one month's credit from suppliers.

Required

How will the cash payments be forecast?

Solution

	January £	February £	March £
Payments for purchases			

2.3 Calculating cash received on disposal of non-current assets

If a non-current asset is disposed of, and information is given about its carrying amount and the profit or loss on disposal, it is possible to find the amount of cash received for the asset.

Illustration 1: Non-current assets

A business has an opening balance for non-current assets in the statement of financial position of £100,000 and a closing balance of £120,000. The statement of profit or loss shows a £10,000 charge for depreciation during the period.

The amount of cash spent on additional non-current assets is:

	£
Opening balance	100,000
Less depreciation charge	(10,000)
	90,000
Closing balance	120,000
Cash expenditure	30,000

The logic for this is that the balance for non-current assets has increased by £20,000 in the statement of financial position but this is after charging £10,000 of depreciation. Therefore, in order to have increased this much, there must have been £30,000 of new expenditure on non-current assets.

Note. This assumed that no non-current assets were sold in the period.

Illustration 2: Calculating cash received on disposal of non-current assets

If a non-current asset is disposed of and information is given about its carrying amount and the profit or loss on disposal it is possible to find the amount of cash received for the asset.

During the year a business disposed of equipment which originally cost £20,000 and on which the accumulated depreciation was £12,000. This transaction gave rise to a profit on disposal of £2,500.

The amount of cash received on disposal of the non-current asset is:

	£
Cost	20,000
Less: accumulated depreciation	(12,000)
Carrying amount	8,000
Profit on disposal	2,500
Cash proceeds	10,500

The logic for this is that if a profit has been made on disposal, the cash proceeds must be £2,500 greater than the carrying amount of the equipment at the time of disposal.

Activity 5: Cash on disposal of non-current assets

A business decides to sell one of its buildings which originally cost £105,000. At the date of disposal, accumulated depreciation on the building amounted to £48,500. The sale generated a profit on disposal of £35,000.

Required

What were the cash proceeds on disposal of the building?

	✓
£21,500	
£56,500	
£70,000	
£91,500	

2.4 Funding non-current assets

Funding method	Details/suitability
Cash	If a business has a surplus of cash, it may want to use cash to purchase the non-current asset. Paying cash is not a suitable method if the business is short of cash.
Part-exchange	This involves supplying part cash and part goods. For example, a business may want to upgrade a piece of machinery to a newer model by trading in the old machine and paying additional cash.
Loans	A loan is suitable for a long-term finance such as the purchase of non-current assets. The business will usually repay the loan in monthly instalments.
Hire purchase	The business pays for the non-current asset in instalments to lease the asset from the seller, with an option to buy the asset once the full amount of the contract has been paid.

Activity 6: A simple cash budget

Rakesh intends to start up in business on 1 October 20X6, using £15,000 which he currently has invested, and a bank loan of £10,000.

The following additional information is available:

(a) The bank loan receipt of £10,000 is expected in November and the monthly repayment amount of £250 will start in December.

(b) Arrangements have been made to purchase non-current assets costing £8,000. These will be paid for in October.

(c) Inventories costing £5,000 will be acquired in September and subsequent monthly purchases will be: October £2,000, November £4,000. Cash is paid to the suppliers a month after purchase.

(d) Forecast monthly sales are £3,000 for October, £6,000 for November and December. Customers pay a month after sale.

(e) Running expenses, including rent, are estimated at £1,600 per month, all paid in cash.

(f) Rakesh intends to make monthly cash drawings of £1,000.

Required

Prepare a forecast cash budget for the 3 months to December 20X6.

	October £	November £	December £
Cash receipts			
Loan			
Receivables			
Total receipts			
Cash payments			
Non-current asset			
Payables			
Running expenses			

	October £	November £	December £
Loan repayment			
Drawings			
Total payments			
Net payments			
Opening balance			
Closing balance			

3 Liquidity

> **Cash** Ready money, most easily thought of as banknotes and coins, and money in a current bank account. A business may be profitable but if it is unable to pay its bills, it will fail.
>
> **Liquidity** The ease and speed with which an investment can be converted into cash.

Liquidity is the amount of cash a company can obtain quickly to settle its debts (and possibly to meet other unforeseen demands for cash payments too). It is the ability of a company to pay its suppliers on time, meet its operational costs such as wages and salaries, and to pay any longer-term outstanding amounts such as loan repayments. Adequate liquidity is often a key factor in contributing to the success or failure of a business. The liquidity of a business depends on the availability of cash or assets which can easily be converted into cash; therefore liquidity is not just about holding cash in hand or in a bank current account, as there are also other liquid assets.

Liquid assets include:

- Cash (the most liquid)
- Short-term investments which can easily be sold and converted into cash (ie those for which there is a ready market, such as listed shares)
- Fixed-term deposits with a bank or building society – for example, six-month deposits with a bank
- Trade receivables

Liquidity is a measure of how safe the business is in terms of its cash availability. Even if a business is profitable, it must also have enough cash to pay amounts due when they become payable.

Some assets are more liquid than others. Inventories of goods are fairly liquid in some businesses. Inventories of finished production goods might be sold quickly, and a supermarket will hold consumer goods for resale that could well be sold for cash very soon. Raw materials and components in a manufacturing company have to be used to make a finished product before they can be sold to realise cash, and so they are less liquid than finished goods. Just how liquid they are depends on the speed of inventory turnover and the length of the production cycle.

Cash is the most liquid of assets and is part of the **working capital** of the business. It is also important to realise that the time taken to convert trade receivables into cash and the time taken to pay trade payables affects the liquidity position of the business.

Non-current assets are not liquid assets. A company can sell off non-current assets, but unless they are no longer needed, or are worn out and about to be replaced, they are necessary to continue the company's operations. Selling non-current assets is certainly not a long-term solution to a company's cash needs, and so although there may be an occasional non-current asset item which is about to be sold off, probably because it is going to be replaced, it is safe to disregard non-current assets when measuring a company's liquidity.

In summary, **liquid assets** are current asset items that will, or could soon, be converted into cash, and cash itself. Two common definitions of liquid assets are **all current assets** or **all current assets with the exception of inventories**.

The main source of liquid assets for a trading company is **sales**. A company can obtain cash from sources other than sales, such as the issue of shares for cash, a new loan or the sale of non-current assets. But a company cannot rely on these at all times and in general, obtaining liquid funds depends on making sales and profits.

Activity 7: Liquid and non-liquid assets

Required

Identify examples of liquid and non-liquid assets from the following by placing a tick under the correct heading.

Solution

	Liquid assets	Non-liquid assets
Notes and coins		
Receivables		
Property		
Inventory		
Bank balance		

4 Working capital

Working capital is the value of current assets less the value of current liabilities.

> **Current assets** Cash, inventory, receivables
>
> **Current liabilities** Payables, loans falling due within one year, overdraft

The two main objectives of working capital management are:

- To increase the **profits** of a business
- To provide sufficient **liquidity** to meet short-term obligations as they fall due

4.1 The working capital cycle

There is often a **conflict** between the two main objectives of working capital management. Management therefore, need to carefully consider the level of investment in working capital and to consider the **impact** that this is having on a company's liquidity position. An overview of this is given by the **working capital cycle** (also known as the **cash operating cycle**).

Working capital cycle

The working capital cycle is the period of time between the **outflow** of cash to pay for raw materials and the **inflow** of cash from customers.

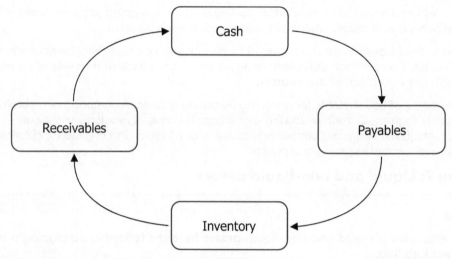

The optimal length of the cycle depends on the industry.

4.2 Calculating the working capital cycle

Formula to learn

Trade receivables collection period	$\dfrac{\text{Trade receivables}}{\text{Revenue}}$	× 365	=	days
Inventory holding period	$\dfrac{\text{Inventory}}{\text{Cost of sales}}$	× 365	=	days
Trade payables payment period	$\dfrac{\text{Trade payables}}{\text{Cost of sales}}$	× 365	=	days
	Working capital cycle =			

Illustration 3: Working capital cycle

Set out below are the statement of profit or loss and statement of financial position for Hampton Manufacturing Ltd:

Hampton Manufacturing Ltd

Statement of profit or loss for the year ended 30 September 20X8

	£
Revenue	1,350,400
Cost of sales	837,200
Gross profit	513,200
Less expenses	274,000
Profit from operations	239,200

Statement of financial position as at 30 September 20X8

	£	£
Non-current assets		2,428,300
Current assets:		
Inventory	156,300	
Trade receivables	225,000	
Cash and cash equivalents	10,200	
	391,500	
Trade payables	(169,800)	
Net current assets		221,700
		2,650,000
Equity		2,000,000
Retained earnings		650,000
		2,650,000

We will now calculate the individual working capital ratios.

Inventory holding period
$$= \frac{\text{Inventory}}{\text{Cost of sales}} \times 365$$

$$= \frac{£156,300}{£837,200} \times 365$$

$$= 68 \text{ days}$$

Trade receivables' collection period
$$= \frac{\text{Trade receivables}}{\text{Credit sales}} \times 365$$

$$= \frac{£225,000}{£1,350,400} \times 365$$

$$= 61 \text{ days}$$

Trade payables' payment period
$$= \frac{\text{Trade payables}}{\text{Cost of sales}} \times 365$$

$$= \frac{£169,800}{£837,200} \times 365$$

$$= 74 \text{ days}$$

Using ratios in this way to assess the working capital cycle has certain limitations:

- Figures extracted from the statement of financial position are a snapshot of a single point in time and may not be representative of the normal level of investment in working capital, eg due to seasonal fluctuations. Also, the working capital needs of a business will fluctuate with changes in the level or nature of its business activities.

- The appropriate level of working capital will vary from business to business, eg a retailer making mainly cash sales would be expected to have a low trade receivables balance, whereas a manufacturer of aeroplanes would have a high working capital requirement because of the length of the production period.

Nevertheless, considering the working capital cycle is a useful starting point in the management of cash.

For Hampton, the length of the working capital cycle is as follows:

	Days
Inventory holding period	68
Trade receivables' collection period	61
Less trade payables' payment period	(74)
Working capital cycle	55

Therefore, 55 days elapses between Hampton paying for its raw materials and then getting cash in from the customer who has purchased the goods that these materials have been made into.

Activity 8: Working capital cycle

The table below gives information extracted from the annual accounts of Management Co for the past year.

Management Co – Extracts from annual accounts

	Year 1 £
Inventory	270,000
Purchases of raw materials	518,400
Cost of production	675,000
Cost of goods sold	756,000
Sales	864,000
Receivables	172,800
Payables	86,400

Required

Calculate the length of the working capital cycle (assuming 365 days in the year).

Solution

Trade receivables collection period	$\dfrac{\text{Receivables}}{\text{(credit) sales}}$	× 365	=	days
Inventory holding period	$\dfrac{\text{Inventory}}{\text{Cost of sales}}$	× 365	=	days
Trade payables payment period	$\dfrac{\text{Payables}}{\text{(credit) purchases}}$	× 365	=	(days)

Working capital cycle =

By comparing the working capital cycle from one period to the next, or one company to another, it should be possible to identify potential problems.

A **lengthening** of the working capital cycle, with more inventory and receivables or fewer payables, will **slow down** cash receipts.

A **shorter** working capital cycle, with less inventory and receivables or more payables, will **speed up** a company's cash receipts and should improve its cash balances.

Is there an **optimum cash cycle length**? The answer will depend upon the following:

- Whether the cash cycle is too long, and investment in working capital should be reduced by shortening the cycle; or

- Whether the cash cycle is too short and becoming unsustainable, indicating a need at some time in the future for an increase in working capital investment.

4.3 Calculating the ratios for a shorter time period

Assessment focus point

An assessment question could ask you to calculate a ratio for a period of less than a year, for example, a trade payables payment period for 90 days instead of 365 days. You need to adapt the ratio by multiplying by the appropriate number of days instead of 365 days.

Illustration 4: Short time period

Six months to	30 June 20X4 £
Trade payables	80,000
Cost of sales	380,000

Calculate the trade payables payment period for the six months ended 30 June 20X4 to the nearest whole day, assuming each month has 30 days.

Solution

Trade payables payment period = Trade payables / Costs of sales × 180 days

= £80,000 / £380,000 × 180 days = 38 days (to the nearest whole day)

4.4 Calculating a ratio by rearrangement

Assessment focus point

An assessment question could give you some of the figures in the working capital cycle and ask you to rearrange the working capital formula to calculate a missing ratio.

Illustration 5: Rearranging the working capital cycle formula

The following information is available for WCC Ltd:

	Days
Working capital cycle	27
Inventory holding period	25
Trade payables payment period	30

Calculate the trade receivables collection period.

Solution

Working capital cycle = Trade receivables collection period + Inventory holding period – Trade payables payment period

Therefore

Trade receivables collection period = Working capital cycle – Inventory holding period + Trade payables payment period

$$= 27 - 25 + 30 = 32 \text{ days}$$

5 Improving cash flow

A cash budget is a useful method of determining whether it is likely that the business will have enough cash to keep going. If a **cash deficit** is forecast in the cash budget, then management will want to find suitable financing options to cover this deficit.

5.1 Raising finance

Finance can be raised:

- From owners in the form of capital

  This should be used for long term investment, not short-term cash management.

- Externally in the form of debt

  For example, borrowing from the bank in the form of a loan.

There are a number of reasons why a business may need additional finance. A company must **match** the situation with an appropriate financing option.

Why we need additional finance	Appropriate ways of meeting these needs
• Short-term deficit, eg as support for working capital	• Overdraft • Short-term loan • Lease finance • Trade credit
• Long-term deficit, eg for the purchase of non-current assets	• Debt via long-term loan, loan stock or bonds • Equity share capital • Lease finance • Issue of preference shares

5.2 Other methods of improving cash flow

Instead of seeking credit from a bank, management may consider whether operational cash flows could be improved in the short term.

Liquidity management is about control of not just cash but also inventory, receivables and payables. The shorter the working capital cycle, the sooner cash is received which can be used elsewhere in the business. Thus a business can improve its cash position by making changes to its working capital management policies, eg by improving its debt collection, by taking full advantage of credit terms offered by suppliers and by not holding unnecessary inventory.

Improving cash flow	Notes
Chase receivables or reduce credit terms offered to customers	Eg credit terms could be reduced from 60 days to 30 days.
	However, this may lead customers to go elsewhere to receive extended credit terms.
Delay supplier payments or negotiate extended credit terms with suppliers	If supplier payments are simply delayed:
	• Prompt payment discounts may be lost.
	• May lead to a loss of supplier goodwill.
	• If the supplier resorts to legal action, this may affect the organisation's future credit rating.
	The organisation must weigh up the cost of lost discounts against the value of the number of days borrowing obtained.
Offer prompt payment discounts (PPD)	The benefit must outweigh the cost.
Dispose of non-current assets	A business must be sure to retain the non-current assets that it needs to produce goods or services.
Reduce inventory	A balance must be struck between the cost of holding inventory and the risk of running out of inventory.

Activity 9: Reducing the working capital cycle

A business wishes to reduce its working capital cycle which is currently 71 days.

In each case indicate whether it needs to increase or decrease each of the following to help it achieve its objective:

	Increase ✓	Decrease ✓
Inventory turnover		
Receivables' days		
Payables' days		

Activity 10: Working capital cycle changes

The following information relates to a business:

Receivables' collection period – 46 days

Payables' payment period – 35 days

Inventory turnover period – 27 days

The business is budgeting to improve the efficiency of its production process which will reduce inventory turnover by 3 days. At the same time it is intending to reduce its costs by taking advantage of prompt payment discounts offered by its suppliers. As a result all suppliers will now need to be paid after 30 days.

BPP
LEARNING
MEDIA

(i)

	Increase ✓	Decrease ✓
Will this increase or decrease the working capital cycle of the business?		

(ii)   Calculate the working capital cycle before the budgeted changes.

(iii)   Calculate the working capital cycle after the budgeted changes.

6 Accounting software

Instead of spreadsheets, businesses may use specialist cash flow forecasting software to identify cash shortages or surpluses in advance. Cash flow forecasting software is often quicker and more accurate than using a spreadsheet. The software can provide real-time cash forecasting and a visual dashboard to aid understanding. Visual tools are a key way of sharing and presenting data because seeing images can sometimes aid understanding and therefore improve decision making. Graphs are often used for visualising data.

For example, software can be used to produce a forecast graph that clearly shows when a business will reach its overdraft limit of, say £1,500.

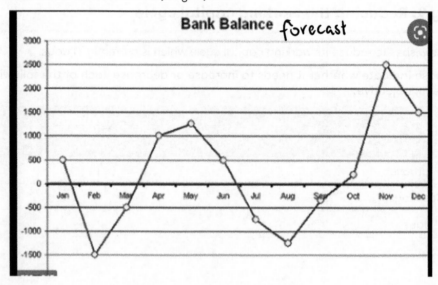

6.1   Automation

Cash flow forecasting uses forecast data and actual data and inputting this data into the cash flow forecast can sometimes be automated. For example, the trade payables and trade receivables amounts which are recorded in the accounting system can be automated to appear in the cash flow forecast.

Automation can reduce the risk of human error, increase efficiency by saving time and improve the quality of the forecast.

Chapter summary

- It is important to realise how vital cash is to a business, even if the business is profitable, as it must be able to meet its payments as and when they fall due.

- There are a number of differences between profit and cash such as; the accruals concept, non-cash expenses, receipts or payments which do not affect profit, and purchases and sales of non-current assets.

- When preparing a cash budget, one of the most complicated areas is normally cash receipts from sales.

- Receipts from cash sales will take place at the same time as the sale, but receipts from credit sales may be spread over a number of subsequent months. Any cash from credit sales still outstanding at the end of a particular period becomes the closing trade receivables balance.

- Payments for purchases on credit will also typically be spread over a number of future months. Any cash not yet paid to suppliers at the end of a particular period becomes the closing trade payables.

- Liquidity is the ability of a business to meet its payments, as and when they are due.

- The most liquid asset of all is cash but other major assets which can be converted into cash may include bank deposits, investments, inventory and trade receivables.

- Working capital is made up of inventory, trade receivables and trade payables and the working capital cycle is an important indicator of the liquidity of a business.

- A business can try to reduce its working capital cycle by making changes to its working capital policies.

Keywords

- **Accruals concept:** Revenue and expenses are accounted for in the period in which they are incurred, rather than the period in which the cash is received or paid

- **Cash budget:** A detailed budget of estimated cash inflows and outflows

- **Cash transaction:** A transaction by cash, cheque, credit card or debit card

- **Credit transaction:** A transaction where receipt or payment of cash is delayed for a period of time

- **Current assets:** Cash, inventory, receivables

- **Current liabilities:** Payables, loans falling due within one year, overdraft

- **Depreciation:** An accounting expense spreading the depreciable amount (initial cost – scrap value) of a non-current asset over the period of ownership

- **Inventory holding period:** The amount of time that inventory is being held by a business

- **Lagged payment:** Payment of cash which takes place some time after the related transaction

- **Lagged receipt:** Receipt of cash which takes place some time after the related transaction

- **Liquidity:** The ease and speed with which an investment can be converted into cash

- **Non-cash expenses:** Expenses of the business which are charged to profit but do not affect the amount of cash in the business, for example, depreciation of a non-current asset

- **Trade payables' payment period:** The amount of time it takes for a business to pay its trade payables

- **Trade receivables' collection period:** The amount of time that it takes for trade receivables to pay the amounts that they owe

- **Working capital:** The total of the current assets of a business less its current liabilities

- **Working capital cycle:** The period of time between cash being paid for raw materials and cash being received from customers for goods sold

Test your learning

1   Selecting from the picklists, complete the following sentence:

Although it is important for a business to [   ], it can be argued that it is even more important for a business to [   ] in order to be able to pay amounts when they are due.

Picklist 1:

make a profit
have a healthy cash balance

Picklist 2:

have a healthy cash balance
make a profit

2   Which of the following are factors that account for the difference between the amount of profit a business makes and its cash balance? Tick the relevant reasons:

	✓
Prepayment of rent	
Purchase of a non-current asset	
Purchases of inventory for cash	
Depreciation	
Cash sales	

3   A business had sales of £790,000 during the year and cost of sales of £593,000. Inventory at the year end was valued at £68,000, trade receivables were £102,000 and trade payables were £57,000.

What is the working capital cycle of the business?

	✓
30 days	
40 days	
54 days	
124 days	

4   A business has a working capital cycle of 35 days. Its inventory holding period is 21 days and its trade receivables' collection period is 60 days.

What is the trade payables' payment period?

	✓
25 days	
39 days	
46 days	
56 days	

5   Select the three most liquid assets that the majority of businesses are likely to have from
      the list below.

      -
      -
      -

      Inventory of raw materials
      Trade receivables
      Fleet of cars used in the business
      Cash in hand
      Business computers
      Bank deposit account
      Business head office
      Investment in shares
      Bank current account
      Inventory of finished goods

6   Which of the following might be associated with a lengthening cash operating cycle?

      ☐   Longer inventory holding period

      ☐   Taking longer to pay suppliers

      ☐   Lower investment in working capital

      ☐   Improved debt collection

12 Spreadsheets

Learning outcomes

5.1 Organise, record and format data

- Organise data

  Design spreadsheets to support:
  - Flexing budgets
  - The calculation and analysis of variances
  - Production of operating statements
  - Overhead absorption and allocation
  - Short-term decision making
  - Cash budgeting

- Ensure data is valid and reliable:

  - Select data from different sources

  - Enter data manually into appropriate cells and worksheets

  - Link data from different sources within the same worksheet/across different worksheets:

    (1) Copying and pasting special values
    (2) Linking

  - Remove duplications in data

- Format data:

  - Formatting cells:

    (1) advanced formatting i.e. data manipulation, data security, data statistics

    (2) decimals, whole numbers, thousand separator, %

    (3) currency, accountancy, general, number

    (4) show adverse/negative figures with () or −

  - Produced/format/adjust charts and graphs:

    (1) chart production: 3D, exploded, bar, column, pie
    (2) changing chart type

  - Chart labelling:

    (1) axis scale
    (2) titles
    (3) legend
    (4) data tables

5.2 Use tools to manipulate, analyse and verify data

- use a range of formulas and functions to perform calculations
    - mathematical and logical functions using absolute and relative cell referencing:
        - (1) sum
        - (2) average
        - (3) minimum
        - (4) maximum
        - (5) round
        - (6) roundup
        - (7) rounddown
        - (8) sumif
        - (9) count
        - (10) counta
        - (11) countif
        - (12) IF (simple and nested)
        - (13) VLOOKUP
        - (14) HLOOKUP
        - (15) days
    - statistical techniques:
        - (1) goal seek
        - (2) forecast
- use tools to support analysis of data:
    - data sort/data filter using single and/or multiple criteria
    - conditional formatting (using function)
    - lookup tables:
        - (1) pivot tables
        - (2) pivot charts
    - subtotals
        - (1) average
        - (2) sum
        - (3) maximum
        - (4) minimum
    - comments box:
        - (1) show
        - (2) hide
    - edit and update data:
        - (1) include new data (worksheet/chart)
        - (2) consider if any new data is included in any existing analysis/existing charts
    - verify accuracy of data by using formula auditing tools:
        - (1) trace precedents
        - (2) trace dependents
        - (3) show formulas

5.3 Use tools to prepare, protect and present accounting information

- use a range of formulas and functions to perform calculations
    - protect integrity of data:
        - (1) use data validation to restrict data entry and editing
        - (2) protect individual and ranges of cells

- enhance the visual presentation of data:

    (1) insert/edit headers and footers
    (2) hide/unhide rows/columns

- format columns and rows to enhance understanding of data: font type, font colour, size, bold, italics, alignment

- freezing rows and columns

- adjust margins, orientation and print area

- use a range of charts to summarise and present information

- chart alteration: moving and resizing, changing chart type, in stacked, 3D, exploded formats

- changing data series: chart colour/format, add/change cell fill colour

- format charts: altering and formatting scales, axes, labels, data series, data tables

Assessment context

You should expect to see questions using spreadsheets in every computer-based test.

Qualification context

Some of the concepts in this chapter may be familiar to you from your earlier studies, from use of spreadsheets or from experience using other software packages.

Business context

The use of spreadsheet packages is a vital part of business life. Spreadsheets are known for their speed and accuracy in calculations and also their data manipulation capabilities. This means that spreadsheets are indispensable in the work of accountants and other finance professionals.

Chapter overview

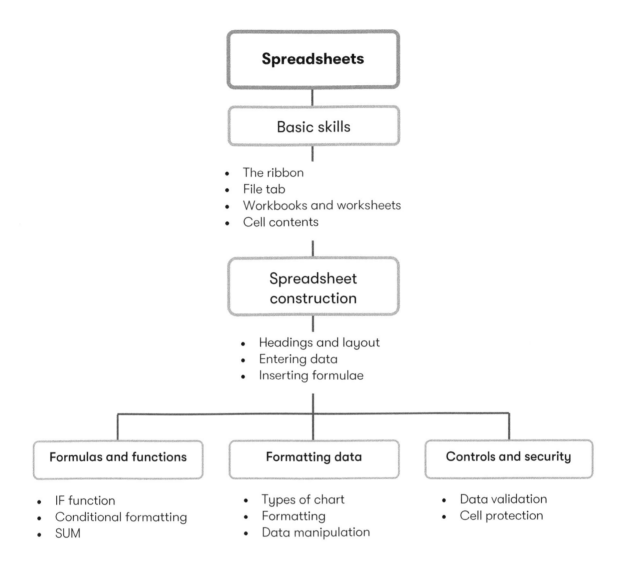

Spreadsheets

Basic skills

- The ribbon
- File tab
- Workbooks and worksheets
- Cell contents

Spreadsheet construction

- Headings and layout
- Entering data
- Inserting formulae

Formulas and functions

- IF function
- Conditional formatting
- SUM

Formatting data

- Types of chart
- Formatting
- Data manipulation

Controls and security

- Data validation
- Cell protection

Introduction

In this chapter we will look at spreadsheet techniques to provide management accounting information, with a focus on using spreadsheets for budgeting.

Uses of spreadsheets

Spreadsheets can be used for a wide range of tasks. Some common applications of spreadsheets are:

- Management accounts
- Cash flow analysis and forecasting
- Reconciliations
- Revenue analysis and comparison
- Cost analysis and comparison
- Budgets and forecasts

> Spreadsheet software also provides basic database capabilities, which allow simple records to be recorded, sorted and searched.

1 Organising and entering data

1.1 The ribbon

File tab

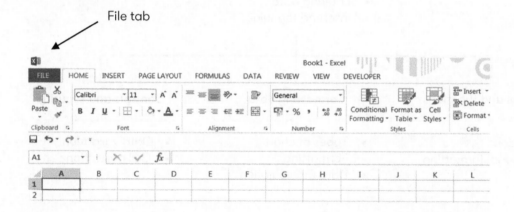

BPP
LEARNING
MEDIA

1.2 File tab

The **File tab** is a menu tab and provides access to several options.

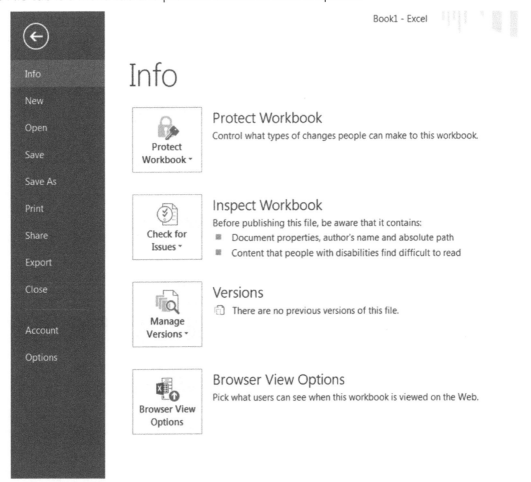

1.3 Workbooks and worksheets

At the bottom-left of the spreadsheet window you will see tabs which are known as **Worksheets**:

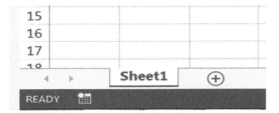

When **New** is selected from **File tab**, you will be given an option to choose from a number of templates. Choose **Blank workbook** to create a new blank **workbook**. The workbook consists of one or more **worksheets**. Think of worksheets as **pages** that make up the workbook.

Worksheets can provide a convenient way of organising information. For example, consider a business consisting of three branches. Worksheets 2–4 could hold budget information separately for each branch. When entering formulas into cells, it is possible to refer to cells in other worksheets within the workbook meaning that it would be possible for Worksheet 1 to act as a **summary sheet** linking the totals of the budget information for the whole business. Effectively, a 'three-dimensional' structure can be set up. We look at this in more detail later.

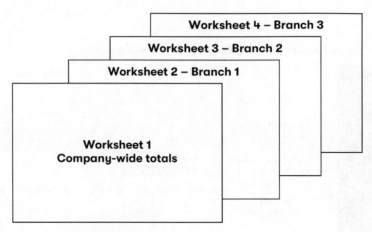

To add a worksheet, click on the plus button:

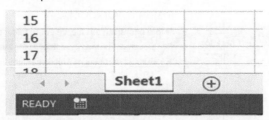

To change the name of the worksheet from 'Sheet 1', 'Sheet 2' etc, click on Sheet 1, then right click, select rename and type in an appropriate name such as 'Department 1' or 'Summary', then click elsewhere in the worksheet.

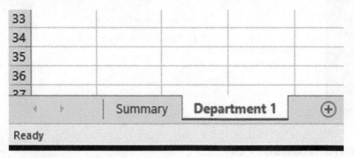

Opening an existing workbook

You can open an existing workbook file by using the menu commands **File button>Open** and then navigating to the location of the file (eg using 'Browse') and double-clicking on it.

If you open more than one workbook, each will open in a new window. To swap between open workbooks, click on the **File button** and choose the workbook you want from the **Recent documents** list.

Closing a workbook

There are two ways to close a spreadsheet file:

(1)   Click the **File button** and choose **Close** (fourth icon down)

(2)   Click on either the 'x' in the top right-hand corner of the window or the one just below it.

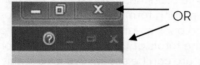

OR

In both cases, if you have made any changes to the spreadsheet you will be asked if you want to save them. Choose **Yes** to save any changes (this will overwrite the existing file), **No** to close the file without saving any changes, or **Cancel** to return to the spreadsheet.

1.4 Cell contents

The contents of any cell can be one of the following:

(a) **Text.** A text cell usually contains **words**. Numbers that do not represent numeric values for calculation purposes (eg a Part Number) may be entered in a way that tells Excel to treat the cell contents as text. To do this, enter an apostrophe before the number: '451, for example.

(b) **Values.** A value is a **number** that can be used in a calculation.

(c) **Formulas.** A formula **refers to other cells** in the spreadsheet, and performs some type of computation with them. For example, if cell C1 contains the formula =A1 – B1, cell C1 will display the result of the calculation, subtracting the contents of cell B1 from the contents of cell A1. In Excel, a formula always begins with an equals sign: = . This alerts the program that what follows is a formula and not text or a value. There is a wide range of formulas and functions available.

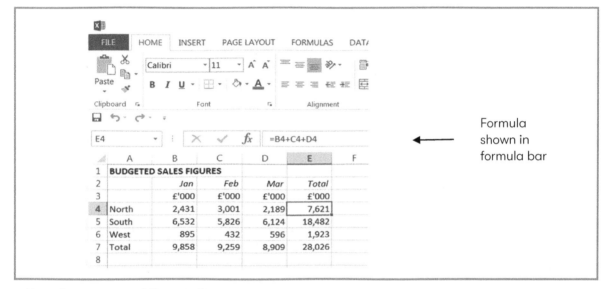

Formula shown in formula bar

Note the important difference between:

(1) What is shown in cell E4: 7,621.

(2) What is actually in cell E4: this is shown in the formula bar and it tells us that cell E4 is the result of adding together the contents of cells B4, C4 and D4.

The formula bar allows you to see and edit the contents of the active cell. The bar also shows, on the left side, the cell address of the active cell (E4 in the illustration above).

1.5 Entering data

It's important to remember that a spreadsheet is simply a tool used for summarising, analysing and presenting data. If the data input into the spreadsheet is unreliable, then any results from it are likely to be unreliable too. Manually keying in data is often essential but can be a source of errors. Data validation can help reduce inputting errors.

Data validation

Sometimes only a specific type or range of data is valid for a certain cell or cells. For example, if inputting hours worked in a week from a timesheet it could be known that no one should have worked more than 60 hours. It is possible to test data as it is input and to either prevent input completely or simply warn that the input value looks odd. This is known as 'data validation' or 'data restriction'. Errors or warnings can also be shown by circling invalid data in red.

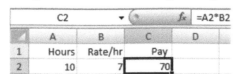

In this simple spreadsheet, C2 holds the only formula; A2 and B2 are cells into which data will be entered, but we want the data to conform to certain rules:

Hours <= 60. If greater than 60, a warning is to be issued.

Rate/hr >=8 and <=20. Data outside that range should be rejected.

Illustration 1: Data validation

(1)   Set up a new spreadsheet with the above data and make A2 the active cell. Go to **Data>Data Validation** (in **Data Tools** section).

(2)   Under the **Data Validation Settings** tab, **Allow Decimal**, select **less than or equal to** from the drop-down list and enter 60 as the **Maximum**.

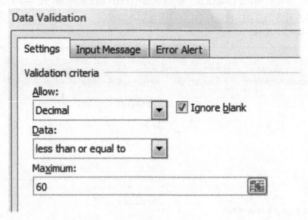

(3)   Under the **Input Message** tab enter 'Warning' as the title and 'Hours expected to be less than 60' as the input message.

(4)   Under the **Error Alert** tab, change the **Style** to **Warning**, enter 'Attention' as the title and 'Check hours: look too large' as the **Error message**.

(5)   Click **OK**.

(6)   Now try to enter 70 into A2. You will first see an information message explaining what data is expected, then a warning message and the option to continue.

(7)   Now try to set up cell B2 with appropriate messages and to prevent any value outside the range 8–20 from being entered at all.

Removing duplicates

If you wish to remove duplicate data from a worksheet this can be achieved by selecting the required data, then **Data>Remove Duplicates** (in **Data Tools** section). From here you can choose the columns to show the number of duplicate and unique data contained. This technique will help ensure that data has been entered accurately.

Linking data

Sometimes the source of data can be from another worksheet. Instead of re-typing the data, the worksheets can be linked with formulas.

For example, suppose a company has two departments, Stores and Production and each of them holds a number of inventory items. The company wants to know the total number of inventory items held.

Another way to enter data is to use the copy and paste function and the paste special function. We will look at this in Section 2.

2 Formulas and functions

2.1 The importance of formulas

Remember our spreadsheet of budgeted sales from Section 1.4.

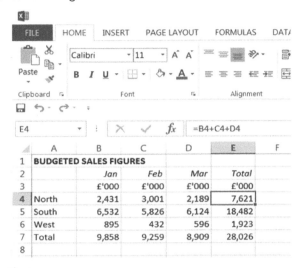

It is important to realise that:

- If a cell contains a value, such as sales for North in January, then that data is entered as a number

- If a cell shows the result of a calculation based on values in other cells, such as the total sales for January, then that cell contains a formula

This is vital, because now if North's January sales were changed to, say, 2,500, the total would be automatically updated to show 9,927. Also the total for North would change to 7,690.

 Illustration 2: Changing numbers and updating formulas

Open the workbook called 'ExcelExample1'. This is one of the files available for download from https://learningmedia.bpp.com/catalog?pagename=AAT_Spreadsheets. You can open a file by using the menu commands:

File button>Open

then navigating to, and double-clicking on, the file called 'ExcelExample1'.

Click on cell B4 to make it active, then typing 2,500, followed by the **Enter** key. You should see the total for North, the total for January and the total total change.

Now re-enter the original figure of 2,431 into cell B4

Similarly, if a number is used more than once, for example a tax rate, it will be much better if the number is input to one cell only. Any other calculations making use of that value should refer to that cell. That way, if the tax rate changes, you only have to change it in one place in the spreadsheet (where it was originally entered) and any calculations making use of it will automatically change.

Displaying spreadsheet formulas

It is sometimes useful to see all formulas held in your spreadsheet to enable you to see how the spreadsheet works. There are two ways of making Excel **display the formulas** held in a spreadsheet.

(a)   You can 'toggle' between the two types of display by pressing **Ctrl +`** (the latter is the key above the **Tab** key). Press **Ctrl +`** again to go back to the previous display.

(b)   You can also select the **File tab>Options>Advanced>Display options for this worksheet** and tick **Show formulas in cells instead of their calculated results**.

The formulas for the spreadsheet we viewed earlier are shown below.

	A	B	C	D	E
1	BUDGETED SA				
2		Jan	Feb	Mar	Total
3		£'000	£'000	£'000	£'000
4	North	2431	3001	2189	=B4+C4+D4
5	South	6532	5826	6124	=B5+C5+D5
6	West	895	432	596	=B6+C6+D6
7	Total	=B4+B5+B6	=C4+C5+C6	=D4+D5+D6	=E4+E5+E6
8					
9					
10					
11					

Examples of spreadsheet formulas

Formulas in Microsoft Excel follow a specific syntax. All Excel formulas start with the equals sign =, followed by the elements to be calculated (the operands) and the calculation operators (such as +, -, /, *). Each operand can be a:

*   Value that does not change (a constant value, such as the VAT rate)

*   Cell or range reference to a range of cells

*   Name (a named cell, such as 'VAT')

*   Worksheet function (such as 'AVERAGE', which will work out the average value of defined values)

Formulas can be used to perform a variety of calculations. Here are some examples:

(a)   =C4*5. This formula **multiplies** the value in C4 by 5. The result will appear in the cell holding the formula.

(b)   =C4*B10. This **multiplies** the value in C4 by the value in B10.

(c)   =C4/E5. This **divides** the value in C4 by the value in E5. (* means multiply and / means divide by.)

(d)   =C4*B10−D1. This **multiplies** the value in C4 by that in B10 and then **subtracts** (or minus) the value in D1 from the result. Note that generally Excel will perform multiplication and division before addition or subtraction. If in any doubt, use brackets (parentheses): =(C4*B10)−D1.

(e)   =C4*120%. This **adds** 20% to the value in C4. It could be used to calculate a price including 20% VAT.

(f)   =(C4+C5+C6)/3. Note that the **brackets** mean Excel would perform the addition first. Without the brackets, Excel would first divide the value in C6 by 3 and then add the result to the total of the values in C4 and C5.

(g)   = 2^2 gives you 2 **to the power** of 2, in other words 2 squared. Likewise = 2^3 gives you 2 cubed, and so on.

(h)   = 4^(1/2) gives you the **square root** of 4. Likewise 27^(1/3) gives you the cube root of 27, and so on.

Freezing rows and columns

When dealing with large worksheets it can be useful to **Freeze** rows or columns so that specified ranges of data (eg headings) remain 'frozen' while scrolling and navigating throughout a worksheet. To do this select the data you wish frozen and select your choice by going to View>Freeze Panes

2.2   SUM

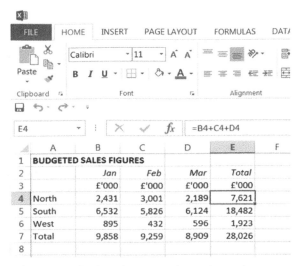

In the example above, totals were calculated using a formula such as:

=B4+C4+D4

That is fine provided there are not too many items to be included in the total. Imagine the difficulty if you had to find the total of 52 weeks for a year. Adding up rows or columns is made much easier by using the **SUM** function. Instead of the formula above, we could place the following calculation in cell E4:

= SUM (B4:D4)

This produces the sum of all the cells in the range B4 to D4. Now it is much easier to add up a very long row of figures (for example, SUM(F5:T5)) or a very long column of figures (for example, SUM(B10:B60)).

There are several ways in which the SUM function can be entered. One way is simply to type =SUM(B4:D4) when E4 is the active cell. Alternatively, you could try these ways and decide which you prefer:

Illustration 3: SUM function

Use the spreadsheet from the previous illustration.

Make E4 the active cell by moving the cursor to it, using the arrow keys or by clicking on it.

Type =**Sum(**
Click on cell B4
Type a colon :
Click on cell D4
Close the bracket by typing)
Press the **Enter** key

Or

Make E4 the active cell by moving the cursor to it, using the arrow keys or by clicking on it.

Click on the AutoSum button

Press the **Enter** key

BPP
LEARNING
MEDIA

If the AutoSum automatically selects the wrong set of numbers to add up, use the mouse to select the correct cells before pressing the enter key.

2.3 Percentages

Percentages can be calculated using a formula, or by using the percentage function. When using a formula always remember to multiply your answer by 100. For example, to calculate 40 out of 200 as a percentage value the formula would be = (40/200)*100

Alternatively, the percentage function can be used instead. Using the same figures as above simply enter =40/200 and this will show a decimal value.

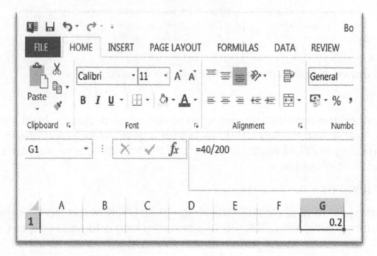

Then go to **Home, Number** and **Percentage.**

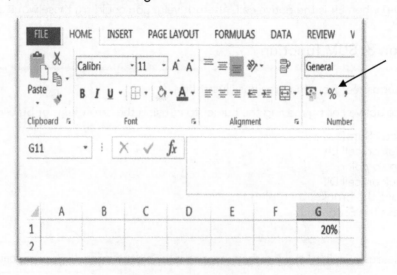

The decimal value will now be expressed as a percentage.

2.4 Copying and pasting formulas

You have already seen that formulas are extremely important in spreadsheet construction. In Excel it is very easy to define a formula once and then apply it to a wide range of cells. As it is applied to different cells the cell references in the formula are automatically updated. Say that, you wanted to multiply together each row of figures in columns A and B and to display the answer in the equivalent rows of column C.

 Illustration 4: Copy and Paste

Open a new worksheet and type the following figures into cells A1 to B5.

	A	B	C
1	400	582	
2	250	478	
3	359	264	
4	476	16	
5	97	125	

(1) Make C1 the active cell.

(2) Type =, then click on cell A1, then type * and click on cell B1.

(3) Press **Enter**.

The formula =A1*B1 should be shown in the formula bar, and the amount 232,800 should be shown in C1.

(4) Make C1 the active cell and obtain the black + by positioning the cursor at the bottom right of that cell.

(5) Hold down the mouse button and drag the cursor down to row 5.

(6) Release the mouse button.

Look at the formulas in column C. You will see that the cell references change as you move down the column, updating as you move from row to row.

| C3 | ▾ | ⋮ | ✕ | ✓ | *fx* | =A3*B3 |

	A	B	C	D
1	400	582	232800	
2	250	478	119500	
3	359	264	94776	
4	476	16	7616	
5	97	125	12125	

It is also possible to copy whole blocks of cells, with formulas being updated in a logical way.

(1) Make A1 the active cell and select the range A1:C5, for example, by dragging the cursor down and rightwards.

(2) Press **Ctrl+C** (the standard Windows Copy command) or click on the **Copy** symbol in the **Home** section of the ribbon.

Paste

Copy

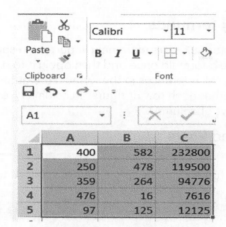

(3) Make E7 the active cell and press **Ctrl+V** or click on the **paste** button. E7 will become the top-right cell of the copied rectangle and will hold 400.

(4) Now, look at the formula shown in cell G7. It will show =E7*F7. So all cell references in the formulas have been updated relative to one another. This type of copying is called **relative copying**.

(5) **Delete** the range E7:G7. (Select the cells in E7:G7 and press the delete key.)

Sometimes you don't want to copy formulas and you only want to copy the displayed values. This can be done using **Paste special**.

 Illustration 5: Paste special

Open the spreadsheet called 'Paste special example' from the files available for download at

https://learningmedia.bpp.com/catalog?pagename=AAT_Spreadsheets.

You will see a simple inventory-type application listing quantities, prices and values.

The values are obtained by formulas multiplying together prices and quantities. Say that you just want to copy the values of cells D3:D8, without the underlying formulas.

(1) Select the range D3:D8.
(2) Press **Ctrl+C** or the copy icon in the **Clipboard** part of **Home** on the Ribbon.
(3) **Right-click** on cell C12 to make it active, and choose **Paste Special** from the list.
(4) Check the **Values** radio button.
(5) Click **OK**.

The list of figures will be pasted, but if you look in the formula bar, you will see that they are just figures; there are no formulas there.

Note. If you change a quantity or price in the original table, the figures you have just pasted will not change; they have become pure numbers and do not link back to their source.

Often you will need to insert or delete whole rows or columns in spreadsheets. This can easily be done and sometimes formulas are correctly updated – but they should always be checked.

2.5 Inserting and deleting

Illustration 6: Using insert and delete

Close the spreadsheet you have recently been working on and go back to the spreadsheet 'ExcelExample1'.

Let's now assume that we have a new region, East and that we want this to be in a row lying between North and South.

(1)   Select row 5, by clicking on the 5, then click the right mouse button (right-click) and select **Insert**. You will see rows 5, 6 and 7 move down.

(2)   Make B8 the active cell and you will see that the formula in the formula bar is =B4+B6+B7. If we were to put the figures for East into row 5 then those would not be correctly included in the total, though B5 has been updated to B6 etc.

(3)   Reverse the last step (**Ctrl+Z**).

(4)   Now, in cell B7 insert =SUM(B4:B6).

(5)   Copy B7 across columns C7 to E7 (black cross and drag across).

(6)   Insert a whole row above row 5 (select row 5>right-click>**Insert**).

(7)   Inspect the formulas in row 8, the new total row.

The formulas in the total row will now be showing =SUM(B4:B7), =SUM(C4:C7), etc. In this case the new row will be included in the total. Effectively, the range over which the totals are calculated has been 'stretched'. Depending how your copy of Excel is set up, you may notice little green triangles in row 8. If so, place your cursor on one and press the exclamation symbol. The triangles are warning that you have included empty cells in your total – not a problem here, but it might have been in some cases. Don't worry if the triangles aren't showing.

(8)   Finally, delete row 5. Select the whole row by clicking on the 5, then right-click and choose **Delete** from the menu.

The cells below Row 5 will move up and the SUM formulas are again updated.

New columns can also be added. Say that we now wanted to include April in the results.

(1)   Select column E, by clicking on the E, then click the right mouse button (right-click) and select **Insert**. You will see column E move to the right.

(2)   Inspect the formulas now in Column F, the new total column, to make sure that they include column F.

You will see that the formula in F7 still says = SUM(B7:D7). It has **not been updated** for the extra column.

So, if an extra row or column is inserted in the middle of a range, the formula is updated because the new row or column probably (but not always) becomes part of the range that has to be added up.

However, if the extra row or column is added at the end of a range (or the start) the formula will not be updated to include that. That's reasonably logical as new items at the very start or end have a greater chance of being headings or something not part of the range to be included in a calculation.

Assessment focus point

Whenever columns or rows are added or deleted always check that formulas affected remain correct.

2.6 Average, minimum, maximum and rounding

Subtotal formulas

Subtotals can also be calculated using formulas. Popular subtotal formulas include: average, maximum, minimum and a sum of values from a range of data.

Different calculations use an **'operation code'**. An operation code is a specific number inserted within a formula to request Excel to perform a particular operation, for example the number '1' denotes an average calculation. Other operation codes that can be used in a **subtotal** formula include:

Operation	Operation code
1	AVERAGE
4	MAXIMUM
5	MINIMUM
9	SUM

For example, a business has made the following weekly sales units:

	A	B
1		**Sales units**
2	Monday	240
3	Tuesday	300
4	Wednesday	320
5	Thursday	280
6	Friday	300
7	Saturday	440
8	Sunday	360
9		
10	**Average**	
11	**Maximum**	
12	**Minimum**	
13	**Sum**	

The business wishes to calculate the average, maximum, minimum and sum of the range of data using subtotals the following operational codes and formulas can be used:

	A	B
1		**Sales units**
2	Monday	240
3	Tuesday	300
4	Wednesday	320
5	Thursday	280
6	Friday	300
7	Saturday	440
8	Sunday	360
9		
10	**Average**	=SUBTOTAL(1,B2:B8)
11	**Maximum**	=SUBTOTAL(4,B2:B8)
12	**Minimum**	=SUBTOTAL(5,B2:B8)
13	**Sum**	=SUBTOTAL(9,B2:B8)

The calculated values are:

	A	B
1		**Sales units**
2	Monday	240
3	Tuesday	300
4	Wednesday	320
5	Thursday	280
6	Friday	300
7	Saturday	440
8	Sunday	360
9		
10	**Average**	320
11	**Maximum**	440
12	**Minimum**	240
13	**Sum**	2240

Rounding

The ability to display numbers in a variety of formats (eg to no decimal places) can result in a situation whereby totals that are correct may actually look incorrect.

Illustration 7: Rounding errors

The following illustration shows how apparent rounding errors can arise.

	A	B	C
1	*Petty cash*		
2	Week ending 31/12/20X6		
3			£
4	Opening balance		231.34
5	Receipts		32.99
6	Payments		-104.67
7	Closing balance		159.66

	A	B	C
1	*Petty cash*		
2	Week ending 31/12/20X6		
3			£
4	Opening balance		231
5	Receipts		33
6	Payments		-105
7	Closing balance		160

Cell C7 contains the formula =SUM(C4:C6). The spreadsheet on the left shows the correct total to two decimal places. The spreadsheet on the right seems to be saying that 231 + 33 – 105 is equal to 160, which is not true: it's 159 (check it). The **reason for the discrepancy** is that both spreadsheets actually contain the values shown in the spreadsheet on the **left**.

However, the spreadsheet on the right has been formatted to display numbers with **no decimal places**. So, individual numbers display as the nearest whole number, although the actual value held by the spreadsheet and used in calculations includes the decimals.

The round function

One solution, that will prevent the appearance of apparent errors, is to use the ROUND function. The ROUND function has the following structure: ROUND (value, places). 'Value' is the value to be rounded. 'Places' is the number of places to which the value is to be rounded.

The difference between using the ROUND function and formatting a value to a number of decimal places is that using the ROUND function actually **changes** the **value**, while formatting only changes the **appearance** of the value.

In the example above, the ROUND function could be used as follows. The following formulas could be inserted in cells D4 to D7:

D4 = ROUND(C4,0)
D5 = ROUND(C5,0)
D6 = ROUND(C6,0)
D7 = Round (SUM(D4:D6),0)

Column C could then be hidden by highlighting the whole column (clicking on the C at the top of the column), then right clicking anywhere on the column and selecting **Hide**. Try this for yourself, using the 'Rounding example' spreadsheet.

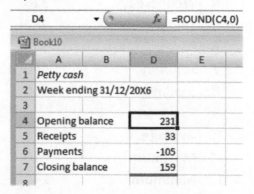

Note that using the ROUND function to eliminate decimals results in slightly inaccurate calculation totals (in our example 160 is actually 'more correct' than the 159 obtained using ROUND). For this reason, some people prefer not to use the function, and to make users of the spreadsheet aware that small apparent differences are due to rounding.

Roundup and Rounddown

The ROUND function can be adapted to round numbers to a required number of decimal places, either by rounding up, rounding down.

Roundup

For example, if a cost per unit was £100.828392 and management wished to express this value rounded up to 0, 1 and 2 decimal places then the following **Roundup** formulas could be used.

	A	B	C
1	Costs	Rounding required	Roundup
2	100.828392	0	=ROUNDUP(A2,B2)
3	100.828392	1	=ROUNDUP(A3,B3)
4	100.828392	2	=ROUNDUP(A4,B4)

Looking at the formula shown in cell C2 the A2 reference picks up the value to be rounded, and B2 is the number of decimal places to round up to. In C2 we are requesting Excel to round the value up to zero places, and so on.

The rounded up results would then be as follows.

	A	B	C
1	Costs	Rounding required	Roundup
2	£100.828392	0	£101.00
3	£100.828392	1	£100.90
4	£100.828392	2	£100.83

Using the same value £100.828392 and using the Rounddown formula, the formulas would be as follows.

	A	B	C
1	Costs	Rounding required	Rounddown
2	100.828392	0	=ROUNDDOWN(A2,B2)
3	100.828392	1	=ROUNDDOWN(A3,B3)
4	100.828392	2	=ROUNDDOWN(A4,B4)

The rounded down results would be:

	A	B	C
1	Costs	Rounding required	Rounddown
2	£100.828392	0	£100.00
3	£100.828392	1	£100.80
4	£100.828392	2	£100.82

2.7 Formulas with conditions ('IF' function)

A company lists its four sales people and compares their budgeted sales to their actual sales.

	A	B	C	D	E
1	Sales team comparison of actual vs budget				
2	Name	Sales (budget)	Sales (Actual)	Difference	
3		£	£	£	
4	Northington	275,000	284,000	9,000	
5	Souther	200,000	193,000	(7,000)	
6	Weston	10,000	12,000	2,000	

	A	B	C	D	E
7	Easterman	153,000	152,000	(1,000)	
8					

Suppose the company wants to award a bonus to people who exceed their target by more than £1,000. The spreadsheet could work out who is entitled to the bonus.

To do this we would enter the appropriate formula in cells E4 to E7. For salesperson Easterman, we would enter the following in cell E7:

=IF(D7>1000,"BONUS"," ")

We will now explain this IF function.

IF statements follow the following structure (or 'syntax').

=IF(logical_test, value_if_true, value_if_false)

The **logical_test** is any value or expression that can be evaluated to Yes or No. For example, D7>1000 is a logical expression; if the value in cell D7 is over 1,000, the expression evaluates to Yes. Otherwise, the expression evaluates to No.

Value_if_true is the value that is returned if the answer to the **logical_test** is Yes. For example, if the answer to D7>1000 is Yes, and the value_if_true is the text string "BONUS", then the cell containing the IF function will display the text "BONUS".

Value_if_false is the value that is returned if the answer to the logical_test is No. For example, if the **value_if_false** is two sets of quote marks " " this means display a blank cell if the answer to the **logical_test** is No. So in our example, if D7 is not over 1,000, then the cell containing the IF function will display a blank cell.

Note the following symbols which can be used in formulas with conditions:

<	less than
<=	less than or equal to
=	equal to
>=	greater than or equal to
>	greater than
<>	not equal to

Care is required to ensure **brackets** and **commas** are entered in the right places. If, when you try out this kind of formula, you get an error message, it may well be a simple mistake, such as leaving a comma out.

Illustration 8: The IF function

Using the IF function.

A company offers a discount of 5% to customers who order more than £10,000 worth of goods. A spreadsheet showing what customers will pay may look like:

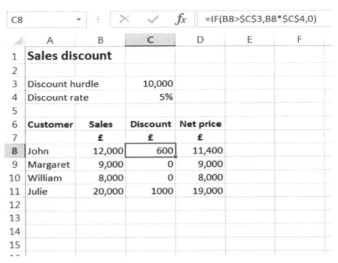

The formula in cell C8 is as shown: =IF(B8>C3, B8*C4, 0). This means, if the value in B8 is greater than £10,000 multiply it by the contents of C4, ie 5%, otherwise the discount will be zero. Cell D8 will calculate the amount net of discount, using the formula: =B8-C8. The same conditional formula with the cell references changed will be found in cells C9, C10 and C11.

Illustration 9: The IF function – exam results

Open the spreadsheet called 'Exam Results' (one of the spreadsheets downloaded from https://learningmedia.bpp.com/catalog?pagename=AAT_Spreadsheets).

There are ten candidates listed, together with their marks.

The pass mark has been set at 50%.

See if you can complete column C rows 6–15 so that it shows PASS if the candidate scores 50 or above, and FAIL if the candidate scores less than 50.

Once it's set up and working correctly, change the pass mark in cell B3 to 60 and ensure that the PASS/FAIL indications reflect the change.

The formulas you need will be based on the one for cell C6.

	C6		×	✓	*fx*	=IF(B6>=B3,"PASS","FAIL")

	A	B	C	D	E	F
1	**Exam results**					
2						
3	Pass mark	50				
4						
5	**Candidate**	**Mark**	**Pass/fail**			
6	Alf	51	PASS			
7	Beth	56	PASS			
8	Charles	82	PASS			
9	David	42	FAIL			
10	Edwina	68	PASS			
11	Frances	36	FAIL			
12	Gary	75	PASS			
13	Hugh	53	PASS			
14	Iris	72	PASS			
15	John	34	FAIL			

Conditional formatting

In addition to the condition determining whether PASS or FAIL appear, you can also conditionally format cell contents – for example, by altering the colour of a cell to highlight problems. This can be done by accessing the **Conditional Formatting** option in the **Styles** section of the **Home** tab of the Ribbon.

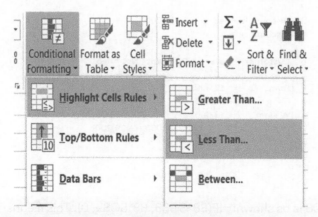

The marks which are less than the value in B3 have been highlighted by making the cell background red and the text white, as illustrated below:

	A	B	C
1	**Exam results**		
2			
3	Pass mark	50	
4			
5	**Candidate**	**Mark**	**Pass/fail**
6	Alf	51	PASS
7	Beth	56	PASS
8	Charles	82	PASS
9	David	42	FAIL
10	Edwina	68	PASS
11	Frances	36	FAIL
12	Gary	75	PASS
13	Hugh	53	PASS
14	Iris	72	PASS
15	John	34	FAIL

To produce the above result:

(1) Change the pass mark back to 50% if it is still at 60%.

(2) Highlight the numbers in column B.

(3) Click **Conditional formatting>Highlight cell rules>Less than.** You will see there are two white entry boxes.

(4) Click on cell B3. This will be entered automatically into the first box.

(5) Then click on the down arrow next to the second entry box. Click on **Custom format>Fill** and choose the red box. This changes the colour of the cell.

(6) Then click on **Font** and click the down arrow next to **Automatic**, under **Colour** and choose the white box.

(7) Click **OK**.

You can also use Conditional formatting to highlight the top three results, for example:

▲	A	B	C	D
1	**Exam results**			
2				
3	Pass mark	50		
4				
5	**Candidate**	**Mark**	**Pass/fail**	
6	Alf	51	PASS	
7	Beth	56	PASS	
8	Charles	82	PASS	
9	David	42	FAIL	
10	Edwina	68	PASS	
11	Frances	36	FAIL	
12	Gary	75	PASS	
13	Hugh	53	PASS	
14	Iris	72	PASS	
15	John	34	FAIL	
16				
17				
18				
19				
20				

To produce the above result:

> (1) Highlight the numbers in column B.
>
> (2) Click **Conditional formatting>Top/Bottom rules>Top 10 items**.
>
> (3) In the first entry box, change the number from 10 to 3.
>
> (4) In the second entry box, click on **Custom format>Fill** and choose the green box. This changes the colour of the cell.
>
> (5) Then click on **Font** and click the down arrow next to **Automatic,** under **Colour** and choose the white box.
>
> (6) Click **OK**.

Count

The count formula is used to count a range of cells containing numeric data.

The following count formula will give an answer of 5 because there are five cells containing numerical data.

	A
1	434
2	123
3	754
4	33
5	238
6	=COUNT(A1:A5)

Counta

The counta formula can be used to count the number of cells in a range that are not empty, and do not hold a value. Bear in mind that although a cell may appear blank technically it may not be empty as may contain a non-visible value.

The cells below in A1, A2 and A3 hold a non-visible value (apostrophes in this case) so there are three cells that are not empty.

The following **counta** formula will give the correct count of **3**.

	A
1	
2	
3	
4	=COUNTA(A1:A3)

Countif

The countif formula can be used to **count** how many cell values meet a specific criteria **if** a condition is met.

A business records its sales for four weeks and wishes to know how many times sales have exceeded £10,000.

The answer here is twice, or **2** as both £12,000 and £14,000 are over £10,000. The following countif formula would calculate **2** as the result.

	A	B
1		**Sales £**
2	**Week 1**	8000
3	**Week 2**	12000
4	**Week 3**	9000
5	**Week 4**	14000
6		**=COUNTIF(B2:B5,">10,000")**

Sumif

The sumif formula can be used to **sum** cell values that meet a specific criteria **if** a condition is met.

The following sumif formula will give an answer of £1,549 because the sum of the cells containing a number over 100 is 434 +123 + 754 + 238 = 1,549 (cells A1+A2+A3+A5).

	A
1	434
2	123
3	754
4	33
5	238
6	=SUMIF(A1:A5,">100)

Compound (nested) IF functions

IF functions can also have multiple conditions within a formula meaning that two or more conditions need to be met for the calculation.

For example, a business may wish to give a 5% discount to customers who have made a sales order between £500 and £1,000. Here the IF function used would need to include two conditions for '>500' and '<1,000' and also be able to calculate the value of the 5% discount.

The following customers have made the following orders:

	A	B	C
1	Customer	Order £	Discount £
2	Cerise plc	450	
3	Green Ltd	800	
4	Plum Partners	1060	
5	Violet Ltd	900	

To calculate the discounts in column C the following IF formulas can be used:

	A	B	C
1	Customer	Order £	Discount £
2	Cerise plc	450	=IF((B2>500),(B2<1000))*B2*0.05
3	Green Ltd	800	=IF((B3>500),(B3<1000))*B3*0.05
4	Plum Partners	1060	=IF((B4>500),(B4<1000))*B4*0.05
5	Violet Ltd	900	=IF((B5>500),(B5<1000))*B5*0.05

To give the following results:

	A	B	C
1	Customer	Order £	Discount £
2	Cerise plc	450	0
3	Green Ltd	800	40
4	Plum Partners	1060	0
5	Violet Ltd	900	45

Note how two conditions have been included in one formula and these have to be met before the discount of 5% applies.

2.8 VLOOKUP, HLOOKUP

The Look-up function allows you to find and use data that is held in a table.

VLOOKUP is used for finding data in vertical columns.

HLOOKUP is used for finding data in horizontal rows.

Here is a simple example:

	A	B	C	D	E	F	G	H	I
1	Salesman Ltd								
2	Part code	VATcode	Unit price		VAT rate	20.0%			
3			£						
4	129394	1	20.00						
5	129395	1	14.00		Invoice				
6	129396	0	12.00						
7	129397	0	14.00						
8	129398	1	37.00		Part code	Quantity	Unit price	VAT	£
9	129399	0	65.00		129396	10	12.00	0	120.00
10	129400	1	34.00					Net	120.00
11	129401	0	20.00					VAT	0.00
12	129402	1	10.00					Total	120.00
13	129403	0	34.00						
14	129404	0	25.00						
15	129405	1	35.00						
16									
17									

On the left is a price list. If a part has a VAT code of 1, then VAT will be charged at the rate as set in cell F2; if the VAT code is 0, then no VAT is chargeable.

To create this invoice, you would look down the part numbers column until you found 129396. You would then read across to find the unit price and VAT code and, together with the quantity sold, you could create the invoice.

This process has been automated in the spreadsheet 'Salesman Ltd'.

---

(1) Open the spreadsheet called 'Salesman Ltd'.
(2) Click on cell G9 to reveal the use of the VLOOKUP function.

Cell G9 holds the formula =VLOOKUP(E9,A4:C15,3, FALSE)

This means: look for the value held in cell E9, in the first row of the range A4:C15, and return the value in the third column of the range: it will return the price relating to the part number. **FALSE** (at the end of the statement) asks it to find an exact match so if a non-existent part code is entered in E9 you will get an error message (**#N/A**).

Similarly, cell H9 holds the formula =VLOOKUP(E9,A4:C15,2) and will return the VAT code relating to the part number.

Cell I11 holds a conditional (IF) function that will calculate VAT if the VAT code is 1 and insert 0 if the VAT code is 0.

Note that some cells have been formatted to show two decimal places and some to show no decimal places. Cell F2 is formatted as a percentage and, because VAT might need to be changed, VAT is held in only one location with other cells referring to it.

Try out different part codes and quantities in the invoice.

2.9 Days

The DAYS function shows the number of days between two dates.

Use =DAYS(A2,A1) to show the number of days between the dates in cells A1 and A2.

2.10 Goal seek

What if you already know the result you want from a formula but not the value the formula itself needs to calculate the result? In this case you should use the **Goal Seek** function, which is located in the **Forecast** section of the **Data** tab on the Ribbon within What-if analysis. Goal seek allows you to work backwards to find an input that would result in a particular output or goal.

 Illustration 10: Goal seek

Open the 'Mortgage' spreadsheet from the downloaded files. Let's assume that we have enough income to make a monthly mortgage payment of £300 and want to know how many years it will take to pay off the mortgage.

(1) Copy the data on Sheet 1 and paste it to Sheet 2.

(2) Click **Data>What-If Analysis>Goal Seek**.

(3) Enter D9 at **Set cell**, as this is the figure we know and enter -300 in the **To value** box (make sure that you enter a negative figure to match the figure already in D9).

(4) Enter C5 in the **By changing cell** box, as this is the figure we are looking for.

(5) Click **OK**.

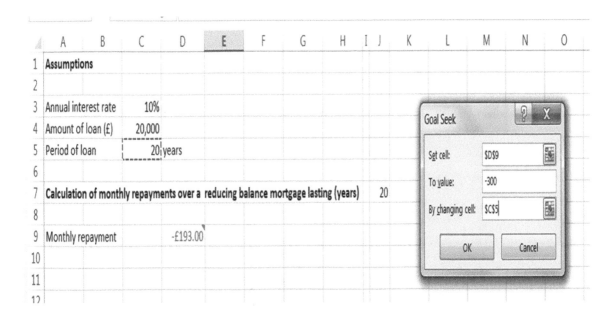

Goal seek will find the solution, 8.14 years, and insert it in cell C5.

2.11 Forecast

The forecast function can be used to predict a value based on existing values. For example, a business records its activity levels and costs for several months. It expects the activity level next month to be 10,100 units.

	A	B	C
1	Activity level (units)	Cost £	
2	10,500	52,750	
3	9,000	45,250	
4	11,000	55,250	
5	8,700	43,750	
6	6,900	34,750	
7	10,600	53,250	
8	11,250	56,500	
9	10,100		

The forecast function looks like this:

=FORECAST(x, known_y's,known x's) where x is value (such as an activity leve) that you want to make a forecast for, known ys is the range of dependent variables that you have collected data for and known xs is the range of independent variables that you have collected data for.

Therefore to forecast the cost for 10,100 units, the formula in cell B9 needs to be:

=FORECAST(A9,B2:B8,A2:A8)

Where A9 is the activity level the cost forecast relates to, B2:B8 is the range of costs that we have recorded and A2:A8 is the range of activity levels we have recorded.

B9	▼	⋮	✕	✓	*fx*	=FORECAST(A9,B2:B8,A2:A8)

◢	A	B	C	D	E
1	**Activity level (units)**	**Cost £**			
2	10,500	52,750			
3	9,000	45,250			
4	11,000	55,250			
5	8,700	43,750			
6	6,900	34,750			
7	10,600	53,250			
8	11,250	56,500			
9	10,100	50,750			

3 Tools to support data analysis

3.1 Data sort/data filter

Simple data manipulation

Illustration 11: Data manipulation

A database can be viewed simply as a collection of data. There is a simple database related to inventory, called 'Stockman Ltd' within the files downloaded from https://learningmedia.bpp.com/catalog?pagename=AAT_Spreadsheets. Open it now.

There are a number of features worth pointing out in this spreadsheet before we start data manipulation.

(1)   Each row from 4 to 15 holds an inventory record.

(2)   Column G makes use of the **IF** function to determine if the inventory needs to be reordered (when quantity < reorder level).

(3)   In row 2, the spreadsheet uses automatic word wrap within some cells. This can improve presentation if there are long descriptions. To use word wrap, select the cells you want it to apply to, then click the **Wrap Text** icon in the **Alignment** section of the **Home** tab. The height of the cells needs to be increased to accommodate more than one line of text. To do this, select the whole row, then double-click on the line between the row numbers 2 and 3; or, instead, select **AutoFit Row Height** in the **Cells** section of the **Home** tab.

The data is currently arranged in part number order.

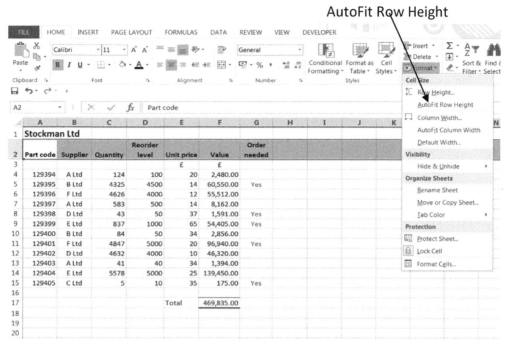

The horizontal rows are records: one record for each inventory type. The vertical columns are attributes (qualities) relating to each record.

Sorting the data

Let's say that we want to sort the data into descending value order.

(1) Select the data range A4:G15.

(2) Look for the **Sort & Filter** drop-down menu in the **Data** tab.

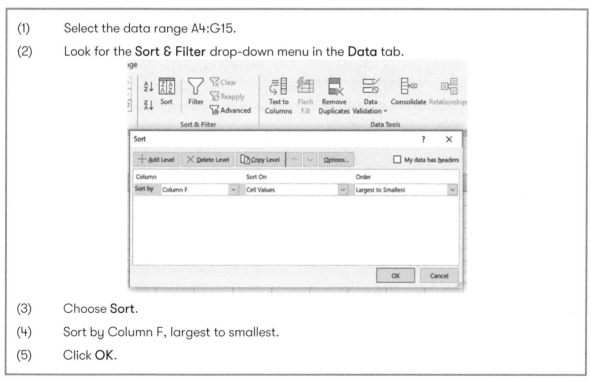

(3) Choose **Sort**.

(4) Sort by Column F, largest to smallest.

(5) Click **OK**.

You will see that the data has been sorted by value.

If you now **Sort by** Supplier (ie sort by **Column B, Order A–Z**) you will have the data arranged by supplier and, within that, by value.

Sorting with multiple criteria

You may wish to sort your data using two more criteria (rather than by one column in the illustration above).

To sort data using multiple criteria within **Sort** select **Add Level** to add additional sort criteria.

Filtering the data

Filtering data allows you to select and display just some of it in the table. This is useful if the table consists of many records but you only wish to view some of them. Data can be analysed by applying multiple filters, allowing various combinations of data to be analysed.

Illustration 12: Applying a filter to data

(1)   Let's continue with the 'Stockman Ltd' spreadsheet.

(2)   Let's say we just want to find inventory records relating to suppliers B and C.

(3)   Select the data range A2:G2 and then select **Filter** from the **Sort & Filter** drop-down menu.

(4)   Click on the drop-down arrow that has appeared at the top of the Supplier column.

(5)   Deselect (ie click on the box to remove the tick) **Select All**, then select B and C.

(6)   Click on **OK**.

Only the records relating to suppliers B and C are visible and these can be manipulated (eg sorted) as an independent subset of the whole table.

Note that the other records are still there and are included in the total value figure. It's simply that they have been hidden for presentation.

You will also see a little funnel symbol at the top of the Supplier column; this informs you that there is filtering in place.

Make all the records visible again by removing the filter:

(1)   Drop-down arrow in the Supplier column.
(2)   Select **Select All**.
(3)   Click on **OK**.
(4)   Sort the data back into Part code order if it's not already in that order.

To get rid of the little filter arrows, select the relevant cells and then click on the funnel symbol in the **Sort & Filter** area of the Ribbon to disengage it.

3.2 Pivot tables

Pivot tables are a very powerful way of analysing data. Look at the following simple example relating to sales by a music company.

	A	B	C
1	**Sales data**		
2			
3	**Customer**	**Source**	**Amount spent (£)**
4	Bill	CDs	50
5	Chris	Vinyl	10
6	Sandra	Merchandise	30
7	Graham	CDs	45
8	Chris	Merchandise	20
9	Chris	Vinyl	10
10	Chris	CDs	10
11	Caroline	Merchandise	30
12	Graham	Tickets	75
13	Fred	Vinyl	30
14	Bill	CDs	20
15	Graham	CDs	60
16	Chris	Vinyl	10
17	Sandra	Tickets	50
18	Bill	Tickets	26
19	Caroline	Vinyl	24
20			
21		Total	£500

The information has simply been listed and totalled on the spreadsheet. It would be useful to be able to show:

- Sales per customer
- Sales by source

Ideally, we would like to produce a table which displays sales by both source and by customer: this type of table is called a **pivot table**.

 ## Illustration 13: Creating a pivot table

(1) Open the spreadsheet file called 'Pivot Table Example' which contains the above data.

(2) Select the range A4:C19.

(3) On the Ribbon, select **Insert>PivotTable**.

(4) Select the **Existing Worksheet** radio button on the **Create PivotTable** option window.

(5) Enter E4 as the location.

(6) Click **OK**. The **PivotTable Field List** window opens.

(7) Check Customer, Source, Amount spent (£).

(8) You will see that Customer and Source go by default into **Row Labels**. The resulting table is quite useful, but not quite what we wanted.

Therefore:

(9) Drag Customer from **Row Labels** to **Column Labels**.

The pivot table is now transformed into the two-dimensional table we want.

(10) Tidy it up a little by selecting F5 to L5 and right-justifying these names by clicking on the appropriate **Home>Alignment** button on the Ribbon.

Note the two drop-down arrows on the pivot table that allow filtering of the data.

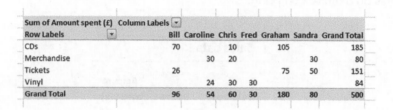

Sum of Amount spent (£)	Column Labels						
Row Labels	Bill	Caroline	Chris	Fred	Graham	Sandra	Grand Total
CDs	70		10		105		185
Merchandise		30	20			30	80
Tickets	26				75	50	151
Vinyl		24	30	30			84
Grand Total	96	54	60	30	180	80	500

Pivot charts

The information contained in a pivot table can be visually presented using a pivot chart.

> (1)   Click on any cell inside the pivot table.
>
> (2)   On the **Insert** tab, click **Pivot chart** and select one of the graph types. For example, 'clustered column'
>
> **Note.** Any changes you make to the pivot table will be immediately reflected in the pivot chart and vice versa.

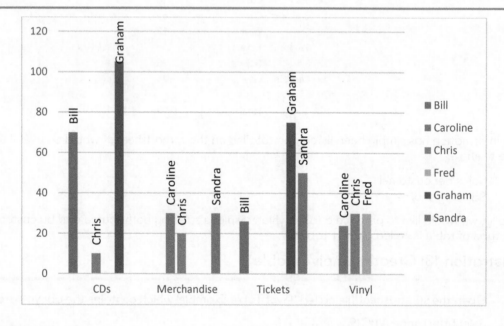

3.3   Comments

You may wish to add information to your spreadsheets by using **comment boxes** to annotate worksheets. Comment boxes can be added through **Review>New Comment.** You can 'show comments' through the **Review** tab if you prefer your annotations to be in sight.

4 Formatting data

4.1 Setting up a spreadsheet

Spreadsheets are often created by a single person but used by several different people, so an easy-to-follow layout is important. The following should be kept in separate identifiable areas of the spreadsheet:

(1)   An inputs and assumptions section, containing the variables (eg the amount of a loan and the interest rate, planned mark-ups, assumptions about growth rates).

(2)   A calculations section containing formulas.

(3)   The results section, showing the outcome of the calculations.

Sometimes it is convenient to combine (2) and (3).

It is also important to consider the following:

(1)   Document data sources. For example, where did the data come from? If you don't know that, how will you ever test the validity of that data and any results arising from it?

(2)   Explain calculation methods. This is particularly important if calculations are complex or have to be done in a specified way.

(3)   Explain the variables used in functions. Some functions require several input variables (arguments) and may not be familiar to other users.

(4)   Set out the spreadsheet clearly, using underlinings, colour, bold text etc to assist users.

 Illustration 14: Spreadsheet construction, formulas and formatting

Constructing a costing spreadsheet.

You want to set up a spreadsheet to record the time you and your colleagues spend on an assignment, and to cost it using your group's internal chargeout rates which are as follows:

Divisional chief accountant	£72.50
Assistant accountant	£38.00
Accounting technician (you)	£21.45
Secretary	£17.30

The spreadsheet needs to show the hours spent and costs per person, by week, for a three-week assignment. The time spent each week is shown below:

	Week 3	Week 2	Week 1
Divisional chief accountant	6 hrs 45 mins	4 hrs 30 mins	–
Assistant accountant	35 hrs	40 hrs	20 hrs
You	37 hrs 30 mins	40 hrs	32 hrs
Secretary	37 hrs 15 mins	32 hrs 15 mins	15 hrs

Setting up the assumptions area

As we will be referring to the chargeout rates for each week's costs, set these up in a separate area of the spreadsheet.

Headings and layout

Next we will enter the various **headings** required.

You want your spreadsheet to look like this:

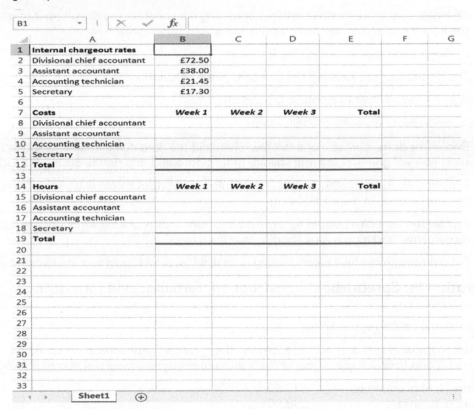

Note the following points.

(a) Column A is wider to allow longer items of text to be entered. Depending on how your copy of Excel is set up, this might happen automatically or you may have to **drag the line** between the A and B columns to the right.

(b) We have used a **simple style for headings**. Headings tell users what data relates to and what the spreadsheet 'does'. We have made some words **bold**.

(c) **Numbers** should be **right-aligned** in cells. This usually happens automatically when you enter a number into a cell.

(d) We have left **spaces** in certain rows (after blocks of related items) to make the spreadsheet **easier to use and read**.

(e) Totals have been highlighted by a single line above and a double line below. This can be done by highlighting the relevant cells, go to the **Font** area of the **Home** section and click on the drop-down arrow to access the list of **borders** available:

Entering data

Enter the time data in cells B15 to D18. Make sure you enter it correctly – the data is given to you in the order week 3 to week 1 but you would prefer it to be in the order week 1 to week 3. You will need to convert the time to decimal numbers.

	Hours	Week 1	Week 2	Week 3	Total
13					
14	**Hours**	**Week 1**	**Week 2**	**Week 3**	**Total**
15	Divisional chief accountant	0	4.5	6.75	
16	Assistant accountant	20	40	35	
17	Accounting technician	32	40	37.5	
18	Secretary	15	32.25	37.25	
19	**Total**				
20					
21					
22					
23					
24					

Inserting formulas

The next step is to enter the **formulas** required. For example, in cell B19 you want the total hours for Week 1. In cell B8 you want the total cost of time spent. You could enter this formula as =B15*B2, but you need to make sure that, as you copy the formula across for Weeks 2 and 3, you still refer to the chargeout rate in B2.

The quick way to insert a series of formulas is to type in the initial one and then to copy across a row or down a column. You may remember that cell references are cleverly updated as you move along the row or column. This was called **relative copying**. However, that will get us into trouble here. If cell B8 contains the formula =B15*B2 and that is copied one cell to the right, into column C, the formula will become =C15*C2.

The C15 reference is correct because we are progressing along the row, one month at a time, but the C2 reference is incorrect. The location of the chargeout rate does not move: it is **absolute**. To prevent a cell reference being updated during the copying process put a $ sign in front of the row and/or column reference.

A reference like $A1 will mean that column A is always referred to as you copy across the spreadsheet. If you were to copy down, the references would be updated to A2, A3, A4, etc.

A reference such as A$1 will mean that row 1 is always referred to as you copy down the spreadsheet. If you were to copy across, the references would be updated to B1, C1, D1, etc.

A reference like A1 will mean that cell A1 is always referred to, no matter what copying of the formula is carried out.

You should end up with the following figures:

B8			fx	=B15*B2		

	A	B	C	D	E	F	G
1	**Internal chargeout rates**						
2	Divisional chief accountant	£72.50					
3	Assistant accountant	£38.00					
4	Accounting technician	£21.45					
5	Secretary	£17.30					
6							
7	Costs	*Week 1*	*Week 2*	*Week 3*	Total		
8	Divisional chief accountant	0	326.25	489.375			
9	Assistant accountant	760	1,520	1,330			
10	Accounting technician	686.4	858	804.375			
11	Secretary	259.5	557.925	644.425			
12	Total						
13							
14	Hours	*Week 1*	*Week 2*	*Week 3*	Total		
15	Divisional chief accountant	0	4.5	6.75			
16	Assistant accountant	20	40	35			
17	Accounting technician	32	40	37.5			
18	Secretary	15	32.25	37.25			
19	Total						
20							
21							
22							
23							

Note that the formula in B8 refers to cell B15 (Week 1 hours) but to cell B2 – the absolute address of the chargeout rate.

The costs figures look untidy, for example, some have one decimal place, some two. To tidy this up we will use the **Number** section of the Ribbon to format these numbers as **Currency**, and for the required **Decimal places** (two decimal places in this example). It is good practice to also format our results using **1000 separators**.

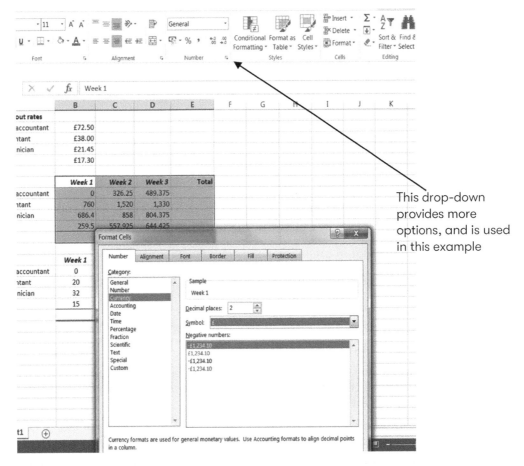

This drop-down provides more options, and is used in this example

(1) Select the range of cells B8:E12.

(2) Click in the small arrow just right of the word **'Number'** to open the **Format Cells** window.

(3) Select **Currency,** make sure the **Decimal places** reads 2 and that the £ symbol is showing.

You should see that all the figures in your spreadsheet are now in the same format.

(4) In cells E8 to E11 and B12 to E12, enter a formula to total the costs. Do the same to total the number of hours.

The spreadsheet should now be like this:

	A	B	C	D	E	F
	B8		fx	=B15*B2		
1	**Internal chargeout rates**					
2	Divisional chief accountant	£72.50				
3	Assistant accountant	£38.00				
4	Accounting technician	£21.45				
5	Secretary	£17.30				
6						
7	**Costs**	*Week 1*	*Week 2*	*Week 3*	*Total*	
8	Divisional chief accountant	£0.00	£326.25	£489.38	£815.63	
9	Assistant accountant	£760.00	£1,520.00	£1,330.00	£3,610.00	
10	Accounting technician	£686.40	£858.00	£804.38	£2,348.78	
11	Secretary	£259.50	£557.93	£644.43	£1,461.85	
12	**Total**	**£1,705.90**	**£3,262.18**	**£3,268.18**	**£8,236.25**	
13						
14	**Hours**	*Week 1*	*Week 2*	*Week 3*	Total	
15	Divisional chief accountant	0	4.5	6.75	11.25	
16	Assistant accountant	20	40	35	95	
17	Accounting technician	32	40	37.5	109.5	
18	Secretary	15	32.25	37.25	84.5	
19	**Total**	**67**	**116.75**	**116.5**	**300.25**	
20						
21						
22						

And the formulas behind the cell contents should be:

	Costs	Week 1	Week 2	Week 3	Total
6					
7	Costs	Week 1	Week 2	Week 3	Total
8	Divisional chief accountant	=B15*B2	=C15*B2	=D15*B2	=SUM(B8:D8)
9	Assistant accountant	=B16*B3	=C16*B3	=D16*B3	=SUM(B9:D9)
10	Accounting technician	=B17*B4	=C17*B4	=D17*B4	=SUM(B10:D10)
11	Secretary	=B18*B5	=C18*B5	=D18*B5	=SUM(B11:D11)
12	Total	=SUM(B8:B11)	=SUM(C8:C11)	=SUM(D8:D11)	=SUM(E8:E11)
13					
14	Hours	Week 1	Week 2	Week 3	Total
15	Divisional chief accountant	0	4.5	6.75	=SUM(B15:D15)
16	Assistant accountant	20	40	35	=SUM(B16:D16)
17	Accounting technician	32	40	37.5	=SUM(B17:D17)
18	Secretary	15	32.25	37.25	=SUM(B18:D18)
19	Total	=SUM(B15:B18)	=SUM(C15:C18)	=SUM(D15:D18)	=SUM(E15:E18)
20					
21					
22					

Before we continue the example, let's look at some other formatting.

Right click and **Format Cells** to reach these options.

(a)   **General format** is the format assumed unless another format is specified. In general format the number is displayed with no commas and with as many decimal places as entered or calculated that fit in the cell.

(b)   **Number format** displays the number in the cell rounded off to the number of decimal places you select.

(c)   **Currency format** displays the number with a '$' in front, with commas and a default of two decimal places, eg $10,540.23.

(d)   **Percentage format** multiplies the number in the display by 100 and follows it with a percentage sign. For example, the number 0.548 in a cell would be displayed as 54.8%.

(e)   **Accounting format** is similar to the currency format, but the decimal points will be aligned, the currency symbol and any minus sign are always displayed on the far left of the cell.

Note you can increase or decrease the number of decimal places using the icons in the Number tab in the Home ribbon.

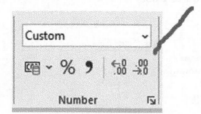

You can line up numbers using the icons in the Alignment tab in the Home ribbon.

Illustration 15: Spreadsheet construction, formulas and formatting ctd

After designing the spreadsheet, you find out that the Divisional Chief Accountant has worked for 6 hours in week 4. He also wants you to add in to your calculations the costs of using two laptop computers, which were charged out at £100 per week each, for the first 3 weeks. You have also found out that the secretarial chargeout rate was increased by 10% in week 3. You now need to amend the spreadsheet to reflect these changes.

(1)   Insert a column between columns D and E.

(2)   Label E7 and E14 as Week 4.

(3)   Enter the 6 hours in cell E15.

(4)   Enter a formula in cell E8 to calculate the cost of these hours.

(5)   Insert a row between rows 11 and 12.

(6)   Enter Laptops in cells A6 and A12.

(7)   In cell A22, enter Laptops and enter the number of laptops used each week.

(8)   In cell B6 enter the cost of each laptop per week.

(9)   Use a formula in cells B12 to D12 to calculate the cost of the laptops.

(10)   Insert two rows between row 6 and 7.

(11)   In cell B7, enter the percentage increase in the secretary's chargeout rate. Format this cell as percentage. Amend the formula in cell D13 accordingly.

(12)   You may have noticed that the total cost and total hours total have not altered. This is because we have inserted rows and columns which were outside the range of the original formula used to calculate the totals. Amend your formulas accordingly.

Tidy the spreadsheet

The presentation is reasonable as we have taken care of it as we have developed the spreadsheet. This is good practice. You can now apply different formatting techniques – changing font colour or cell colour, for example. To change font colour, font type (eg Arial) and size including **cell fill colour** or shading go to **Home>Font**. Save the spreadsheet as 'Costing Exercise-finished'.

The menu extract below indicates the **font type** is Calibri, and is in size 11. The **cell fill colour** icon is similar in appearance to a paint pot. The **font colour** can be changed by the drop down menu in the 'A' next to the cell fill colour icon. To make text into italics or bold, select the text you want to format and click on the B button or I button in Home.

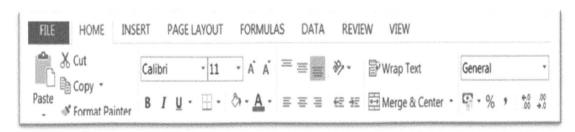

Once you have tidied up your spreadsheet save the spreadsheet as 'Costing Exercise-finished'.

The spreadsheet should now look like this before updating cell F22 to include the Divisional chief accountant's week 4 hours:

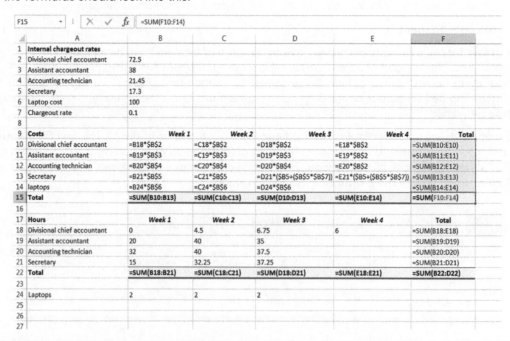

And the formulas should look like this:

Adverse or negative figures

Negative numbers can be entered using the minus sign but accountants often use brackets to indicate a cost or an adverse variance instead of a minus sign. You can format cells so that negative numbers appear with brackets

Click on the triangle left of the A cell to select the whole worksheet, then right click, format cells.

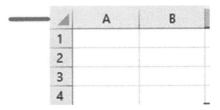

On the number tab, select Custom, then select a format, eg #,##0;-#,##0 and change the minus number into an open bracket and add a close bracket.

Then select OK. Now when you type a negative number, say -200, it will appear as (200).

4.2 Charts and graphs

Charts and graphs are useful and powerful ways of communicating trends and relative sizes of numerical data in various outputs to meet equality of opportunity for users. Excel makes the production of charts relatively easy through the use of the chart wizard.

We will use the 'Sales discount' spreadsheet (one of the spreadsheets downloaded from https://learningmedia.bpp.com/catalog?pagename=AAT_Spreadsheets) to generate a number of different charts.

	A	B	C	D
1	**Sales discount**			
2				
3	Discount hurdle		10,000	
4	Discount rate		5%	
5				
6	Customer	Sales	Discount	Net price
7		£	£	£
8	John	12,000	600	11,400
9	Margaret	9,000	0	9,000
10	William	8,000	0	8,000
11	Julie	20,000	1000	19,000

First, we will generate a simple pie chart showing the total sales figure, before discounts.

 ## Illustration 16: Pie charts

(1) Open the 'Sales discount' spreadsheet.

(2) Place your cursor on the word Customer, hold down the mouse button and drag the cursor downwards until you have selected the four names and four sales figures (A6:B11).

(3) Select the **Insert>Pie Chart icon** section from the Ribbon, then **3-D Pie**.

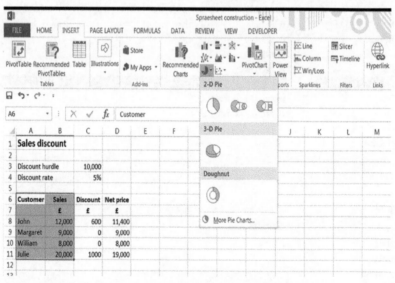

This will generate a pie chart that looks similar to this:

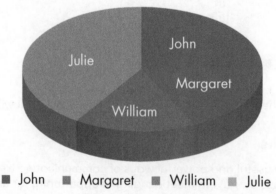

You will see that it already has a title, 'Sales £'. To make any changes to this, double-click the area where the title appears, then enter additional text or delete text you do not want. Below we have added 'for 20XX' and brackets around the pound sign.

Sales for 20XX (£)

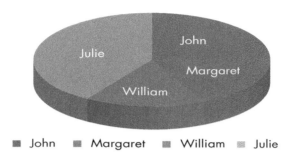

Changing the chart type

If you decide that a different chart may be more suitable for presenting your data you can easily change the chart type.

(1)   Click on your chart in the white area to the left of the purple segment. The chart options should become available at the top of the window.

(2)   Click **Change Chart Type** (or **Design>Change Chart Type**).

(3)   From here, pick some charts from the following chart types to see what they produce.

Bar charts

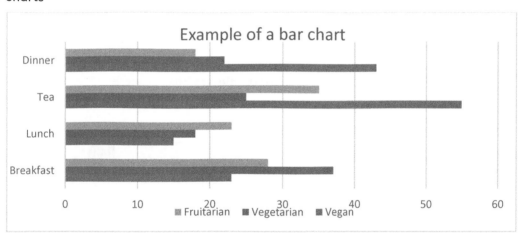

A pie chart is good for showing relative sizes of elements making up a total. However, sometimes you may want to be able to compare how two series of data are moving: sales and gross profit for example. In this case, bar charts (or line charts) are more suitable. Excel makes a distinction between bar charts that show vertical bars and those that show horizontal bars. **When the data is shown *vertically* Excel refers to the chart as a *column* chart, whereas if the data is shown *horizontally* it is a *bar* chart.**

Line chart

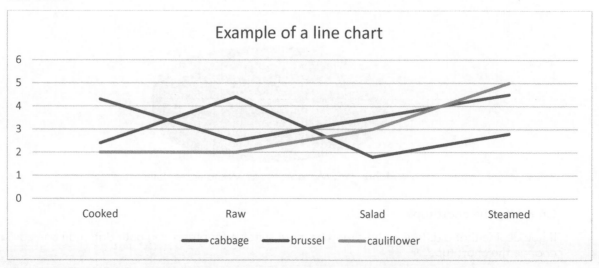

We are going to create a column chart showing the Sales and Net Price figure from the data on the 'Sales Discount' spreadsheet.

(1) Delete your chart by clicking on its outermost frame and pressing the **Delete** key.

(2) Place the cursor on the word Customer and drag the cursor down until all four names have been selected.

(3) Hold down the **Ctrl** key and select B6:B11. Still holding the **Ctrl** key down, select D6:D11.

(4) Release the mouse button and **Ctrl** key.

(5) On the Ribbon, choose **Insert>Column Chart icon>2D Column**.

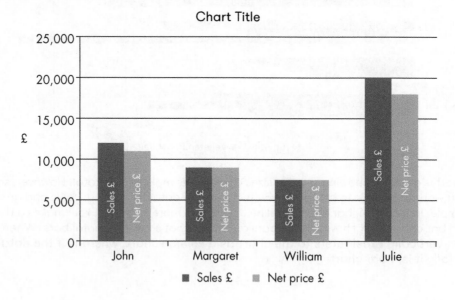

To change the chart title:

Click on the chart. At the top of the window you will see chart tools appear:

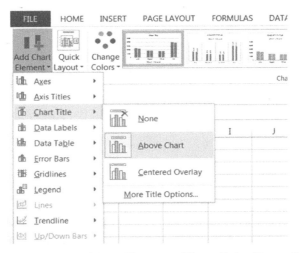

From the **Design** section, choose **Add Chart Element>Chart Title>Above Chart**. Type in 'Sales and Net Prices for 20XX (£)'.

To the bottom of the chart you will see a description for each column. This is called a Legend.

You should also label the horizontal axis and the vertical axis.

(1)   To label the horizontal axis, click **Design>Add Chart Element>Axis Titles>Primary Horizontal** (make sure you are clicked on the chart to see the **Chart Tools** tabs).

(2)   The words 'Axis Title' appear at the bottom of the chart. Click on this, then press **Ctrl + A** to select all the words and type in your axis title, in this case 'Customer'.

(3)   To label the other axis, this time choose **Primary Vertical** and type a pound sign.

You can change the direction of the titles using **Add Chart Elements>Axis Titles>More Axis Titles Options**. Try experimenting with that now.

Exploded charts

These are useful when you want to highlight key areas of data within the chart itself

Using the spreadsheet 'Sales discount'

(1)   Highlight the data to create a pie chart (cells A6:B11), click on **Insert>Charts** (you may have a **Recommended Charts** icon or a **pie chart icon**, either will work, you are aiming to create a pie chart initially)

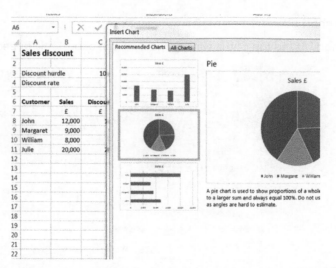

(2) Click OK to accept the pie chart option.

(3) Right click to see the options and select **Format Chart Area,** and the options will open on the right hand side of the screen. Click on **Chart Options** drop down box will offer a fresh set of options, including **Series Sales £.**

(4) There are three tab options available: Fill & Line, Effects and Series Options. You need to select Series Options:

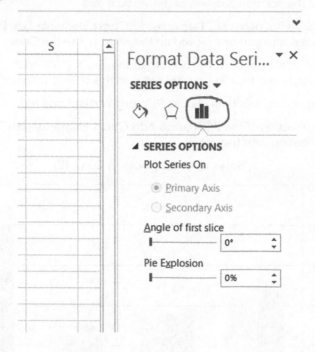

(5) Go to the option of Pie Explosion, and using the arrows, select 10% and the chart's pies will all explode out of alignment:

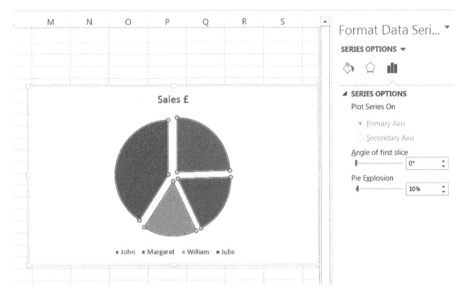

(6) If you want to select only one slice to explode, in order to highlight that particular piece of data, then you can simply click and slide the pie away from the others:

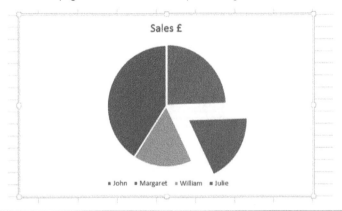

Formatting existing charts

Even after your chart is finished you can change it in a variety of ways.

(a) You can **resize it**, simply by selecting it and dragging out one of its corners.

(b) You can change the scale by dragging out the top, base or sides. To do so, hover your cursor over the dot in the middle of the relevant top, base or side until your cursor turns into a **double-ended arrow**. Click and it will turn into a large cross, then drag with the mouse button still held down.

(c) You can also select any item of text and alter the wording, size or font, or change the **colours** used, using the buttons on the **Font** section of the Home part of the ribbon. For example, practise increasing and decreasing the size of the font by clicking on the text you wish to change, then experimenting with the two different-sized capital A buttons:

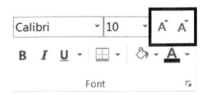

(d) There is also a variety of colour schemes available from the chart Ribbon.

4.3 Trace precedents

Tracing precedents and dependents

As spreadsheets are developed it can become difficult to be sure where figures come from and go to (despite being able to display formulas in all the cells). A useful technique is to make use of the 'trace precedents' and 'trace dependents' options. These are available on the **Formulas** section of the Ribbon.

Illustration 17: Auditing formulas

(1)   Open the 'Precedent example' spreadsheet from the downloaded files and make cell F4 active.

(2)   Choose the **Formulas** section of the Ribbon and click on **Trace Precedents** in the Formula Auditing group of icons.

You should see:

	A	B	C	D	E	F
1	BUDGETED SALES FIGURES					
2		Jan	Feb	Mar		Total
3		£'000	£'000	£'000		£'000
4	North	2,431	3,001	2,189		7,621
5	South	6,532	5,826	6,124		18,482
6	West	895	432	596		1,923
7	Total	9,858	9,259	8,909		28,026
8						
9						
10						
11						

Now it is very obvious that anything in column E, like April figures, will not be included in the total.

(3)   Click on **Remove Arrows** in the **Formula Auditing** group.

(4)   Make B4 the active cell.

(5)   Click on **Trace Dependents**. This will show what cells make use of this cell:

	A	B	C	D	E	F
1	BUDGETED SALES FIGURES					
2		Jan	Feb	Mar		Total
3		£'000	£'000	£'000		£'000
4	North	2,431	3,001	2,189		7,621
5	South	6,532	5,826	6,124		18,482
6	West	895	432	596		1,923
7	Total	9,858	9,259	8,909		28,026
8						

The ability to trace precedents and dependents is a valuable skill in being able to check your spreadsheet for any potential problems, and is particularly useful for checking that your formulas contain the correct set of figures.

5 Protecting and presenting information

5.1 Protection

Protection

(a) **Cell protection/cell locking.** This prevents the user from inadvertently changing cells that should not be changed. There are two ways of specifying which cells should be protected.

   (i) All cells are locked, except those specifically unlocked.

   This method is useful when you want most cells to be locked. When protection is implemented, all cells are locked unless they have previously been excluded from the protection process. You will also see here a similar mechanism for hiding data. In this way specified **ranges** of cells can be locked and unlocked. See Illustration 18.

   (ii) Most are unlocked, except those specified as being locked. See Illustration 19. This method is useful if only a few cells have to be locked.

Illustration 18: Protecting worksheets 1

(1) Open the spreadsheet 'Costing Exercise–Finished'.

(2) Highlight the range B2:B5. This contains some of the assumptions on which the cash flow forecast is based and this is the only range of cells that we want to be unlocked and available for alteration.

(3) In the **Home** section of the Ribbon, click on the small arrow beside **Fonts** and then choose **Protection**.

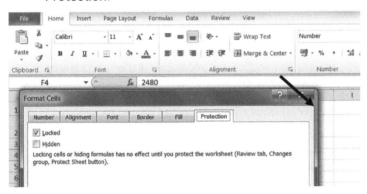

(4) Untick the **Locked** box.

(5) Click on **OK**.

(6) Now go to the **Review** group on the Ribbon.

(7) Click on **Protect Sheet**.

(8) Don't enter a password when prompted, simply click **OK**.

Now investigate what you can change on the spreadsheet. You should find that only cells B2:B5 can be changed. If you try to change anything else, a message comes up telling you that the cell is protected.

Click on **Unprotect Sheet** to make every cell accessible to change again.

Illustration 19: Protecting worksheets 2

(1) Open the spreadsheet 'Sales discount'.

(2) Assume that we want to lock only the 10,000 in cell C3 and the 5% figure in cell C4.

(3) Select the whole spreadsheet and, as we did above, click on the small arrow beside **Fonts**. Then choose **Protection** and untick the **Locked** and **Hidden** boxes. The cells can still be changed if you do not do this step.

(4) Select the range of cells C3:C4.

(5) In the **Home** section of the Ribbon go to the **Cells** group and click on **Format**.

(6) Click on **Lock Cell**.

(7) Click on **Protect Sheet** from the same **Format** menu. The cells remain editable if you do not do this step.

You are offered the chance to enter a password.

Now you will be prevented from changing just those two cells.

(8) **Hiding and showing formulas** – the same process can be used to hide or show formulas on a worksheet by selecting **Hidden** within **Protection** to hide formulas, and deselect **Hidden** to allow formulas to be seen by users.

(b) **Passwords.** There are two levels of password.

(i) All access to the spreadsheet can be protected and the spreadsheet encrypted. This can be done by:

> (1) **File button>Info>Protect Workbook>Encrypt with Password.**
>
> (2) You are then asked to enter, and verify, a password. Heed the warning: if you forget the password, there's no likelihood of recovery of the spreadsheet.
>
> (3) To remove the password protection use:
>
> **File button>Info>Protect Workbook>Encrypt with Password**
>
> (4) Then delete the asterisks in the password box and click OK.

(ii) The spreadsheet can be password-protected from amendment, but can be seen without a password. This can be done as follows:

> (1) **File tab>Info>Protect Workbook>Protect Current Sheet**
>
> (2) Select the level of access allowed to users.
>
> (3) In the **Password to modify** box type a password, then retype it to confirm and click **OK**.
>
> (4) Click **Save**.

Now, if you close the file and re-open it, you will be asked for a password to get full access; without the password you can open it in read-only mode, so that it can be seen but not changed.

 ### Assessment focus point

Task 6 in AAT's Practice Assessment 1 requires the worksheet to be protected, leaving the password blank. Make sure you practise doing this.

 BPP LEARNING MEDIA

5.2 Visual presentation

Preparing your spreadsheet for printing: Page set-up

The **Page Setup** area of the **Page Layout** tab on the Ribbon also allows you to specify certain details that affect how your spreadsheet looks when it prints out.

From here you can set the size of the **Margins** (the white spaces that print around the spreadsheet) and choose whether to print the spreadsheet in landscape **Orientation** (ie wider than tall) rather than the default portrait **Orientation** (taller than wide).

If you want to make sure that your spreadsheet will print onto one page, you can choose to **Fit to** 1 page wide by 1 page tall. This can be done by accessing the **Page Setup** options, by clicking on the little arrow in the bottom-right corner of the section on the ribbon.

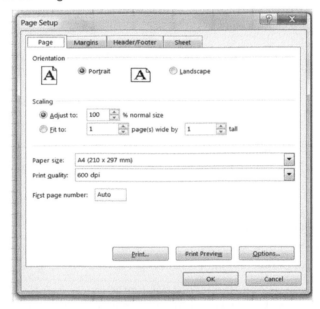

Print settings can also be accessed through the **File tab.**

Imagine you are printing out a spreadsheet that will cover several pages. It is important that certain information is present on each page. For example:

The spreadsheet title

The page number and total pages

The author

The row and column headings

This can be done by accessing the **Page Setup** options, in the way outlined above, or by clicking on the **Print Titles** icon.

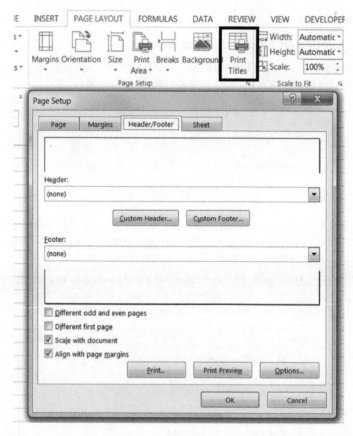

Headers appear at the top of each page. For example, a custom header could be:

Author   Budget for 2013   Date printed

Footers appear at the bottom of each page, for example:

Page   File name

Changing column width and row height

You may occasionally find that a cell is not wide enough to display its contents. When this occurs, the cell displays a series of hashes ######. There are several ways to deal with this problem:

- Column widths can be adjusted by positioning the mouse pointer at the head of the column, directly over the little line dividing two columns. The mouse **pointer** will change to a **cross** with a double-headed arrow through it. Hold down the left mouse button and, by moving your mouse, stretch or shrink the column until it is the right width. Alternatively, you can double-click when the double-headed arrow appears and the column will automatically adjust to the optimum width.

- Highlight the columns you want to adjust and choose **Home>Cells>Format>Column Width** from the menu and set the width manually. Alternatively, you can right-click the highlighted column(s) and choose **Column Width** from the menu.

- Highlight the columns you want to adjust and choose **Home>Format>Autofit Column Width** from the menu and set the width to fit the contents.

Setting row heights works similarly.

Columns and rows can also be hidden from view by making the selection and going to **Home>Format>Hide & Unhide**.

Chapter summary

- A **spreadsheet** is basically an electronic piece of paper divided into **rows** and **columns**. The intersection of a row and a column is known as a **cell**.

- Essential basic **skills** include how to **move around** within a spreadsheet, how to **enter** and **edit** data, how to **fill** cells, how to **insert** and **delete** columns and rows and how to improve the basic **layout** and **appearance** of a spreadsheet.

- **Relative** cell references (eg B3) change when you copy formulas to other locations or move data from one place to another. **Absolute** cell references (eg B3) stay the same.

- A wide range of **formulas** and functions are available within Excel. We looked at the use of conditional formulas that use an **IF** statement.

- A spreadsheet should be given a **title** which clearly defines its purpose. The contents of rows and columns should also be clearly **labelled**. **Formatting** should be used to make the data in the spreadsheet easy to read and interpret.

- **Numbers** can be **formatted** in several ways, for instance with commas, as percentages, as currency or with a certain number of decimal places.

- Excel includes the facility to produce a range of charts and graphs.

- **Goal seek** is a function that allows you to explore various results using different sets of values in one or more formulas.

- Excel offers sophisticated data handling, including **filtering, pivot tables** and **look-up tables**.

- It is important to **control the security** of spreadsheets through passwords, locking (protecting) cells against unauthorised or accidental changes, or data validation on input.

- Spreadsheets can be used in a variety of accounting contexts. You should practise using spreadsheets; **hands-on experience** is the key to spreadsheet proficiency.

Keywords

- **Absolute (reference):** A cell reference that does not change and is particularly useful when copying a formula across data

- **Bar chart:** A chart where data is grouped into 'bars', customarily used to show relative size between groups

- **Conditional formatting:** Allows users to format cells depending on specified conditions

- **Copying and pasting formulas:** A technique using an existing formula to quickly apply to different cell references within a spreadsheet

- **Data table:** A table that allows data results to change, based on changing assumptions

- **Data validation:** A function that can provide warning messages and other protection when invalid data is entered

- **Formulas:** Used in calculating a range of requested values

- **Goal seek:** Function that can identify the inputs required into a formula to arrive at a known outcome

- **IF function:** A logical function that calculates a value or outcome depending on specified conditions

- **Look-up tables:** A function that allows users to find and use data held in a table

- **Mean:** An average value calculated by adding up values and dividing by the number of values

- **Median:** The value that is the middle value when values are arranged in an ascending or descending sequence

- **Mode:** The most frequently occurring value within a sequence of values

- **Paste special:** Used when copying values instead of formulas

- **Passwords:** A data protection system that restricts user access by a unique sequence of characters

- **Pivot table:** A table that allows users to change its structure by selecting and choosing the style of how data is presented

- **Pie chart:** A circular chart displaying segments of data

- **Relative copying:** A cell reference that does change when copying a formula across data

- **Sort and filter:** A function that allows data to be sorted in a requested order, for example A-Z. A filter allows users to select and display part of the contents of a table of data

- **Trace precedents and dependents:** Error-detection methods that use tracer arrows to identify data used in formulas and relationships between active cells

- **Summary sheet:** A worksheet that links to other data or worksheets

- **Workbook:** A spreadsheet that consists of one or more worksheets

- **Worksheet:** Individual spreadsheet pages contained in a workbook

Test your learning

1   Jugf Ltd budgeted to produce 4,000 units of product but actually produced 6,000 units of product. It therefore wants to flex its budget.

	A	B	C	D	
1	Jugf Ltd Operating statement				
2					
3	Number of units:	4,000		6,000	
4		Original budget	Flexed budget	Actual results	Variances
5	Revenue				

(a) What formula could be entered into cell B2 to calculate the percentage by which to flex the original budget?

(b) How would cell B2 be formatted as a percentage?

2   How do you display formulas instead of the results of formulas in a spreadsheet?

3   List five possible changes that may improve the appearance of a spreadsheet.

4   What is the syntax (pattern) of an IF function in Excel?

5   The following spreadsheet shows sales of two products, the Ego and the Id, for the period July to September.

	A	B	C	D	E
1	Sigmund Ltd				
2	Sales analysis - quarter 3, 2010				
3		July	August	September	Total
4	Ego	3,000	4,000	2,000	9,000
5	Id	2,000	1,500	4,000	7,500
6	Total	5,000	5,500	6,000	16,500

Devise a suitable formula for each of the following cells.

(a) Cell B6
(b) Cell E5
(c) Cell E6

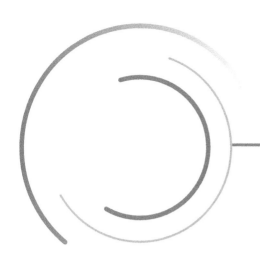

Activity answers

CHAPTER 1 Introduction to management accounting

Activity 1: Information for management

Management accountants may provide information for management on the following:

	✓
Cost of goods and services	✓
Actual costs compared to expected costs	✓
Expected profits and production plans	✓

CHAPTER 2 Cost classification and cost behaviour

Activity 1: Fixed cost per unit

(a) | £ | 20 |

Working £20,000/1,000 = £20

(b) | £ | 2 |

Working £20,000/10,000 = £2

(c) | £ | 1 |

Working £20,000/20,000 = £1

(d) | £ | 0.20 |

Working £20,000/100,000 = £0.20

As the number of units increase, the fixed cost per unit decreases.

Activity 2: Fixed and variable elements of cost

The fixed element of the overhead cost is £580,000 × 55% = | £ | 319,000 |

The variable element of the overhead cost is £580,000 × (100% – 55%) = | £ | 261,000 |

Activity 3: High–low method – manufacturing business

| £ | 110,500 |

Workings

	Units		£
High output	8,000	Total cost	115,000
Low output	6,000	Total cost	97,000
Difference	2,000		18,000

Variable cost per unit £18,000/2,000 = £9

Substituting in high volume:

	£
Total cost	115,000
Variable cost (8,000 × £9)	(72,000)
Fixed costs (balance)	43,000

At output of 7,500 units:

	£
Fixed costs	43,000
Variable costs (7,500 × £9)	67,500
Estimated total cost	110,500

BPP
LEARNING
MEDIA

Activity 4: High–low method – service business

£	210

Workings

	Units		£
High output	3,000	Total cost	220
Low output	2,100	Total cost	184
Difference	900		36

Variable cost per unit £36/900 = £0.04

Substituting in high volume:

	£
Total cost	220
Variable cost (3,000 × £0.04)	(120)
Fixed costs (balance)	100

	£
Total cost in June	
Fixed costs	100
Variable cost (2,750 × £0.04)	110
	210

Activity 5: Changing activity levels – costs

Cost	Stay the same	Increase	Decrease
Variable cost per unit	✓		
Fixed cost per unit			✓
Semi-variable cost per unit			✓
Total cost per unit			✓

Activity 6: Changing activity levels – revenue, cost and profit

	Statement	True	False
(1)	As levels of output decrease, the amount of revenue per unit will decrease		✓
(2)	As levels of output decrease, the amount of fixed cost per unit will stay the same		✓
(3)	As levels of output increase, the amount of total cost per unit will increase		✓
(4)	As levels of output increase, the amount of profit per unit will increase	✓	

(1)   is false because the revenue per unit is unaffected by activity levels.

(2)   is false because as output decreases, there are fewer units to spread the fixed costs over, therefore the fixed cost per unit increases.

(3)   is false because as output increases, the variable element of cost per unit will remain the same, but the fixed element of the cost will decrease per unit. Therefore total cost per unit will decrease.

(4)   is true because as output increases, the total cost per unit decreases and therefore the profit per unit increases.

CHAPTER 3 Materials and labour costs

Activity 1: Control accounts – Bodger & Co

Payables control account

	£		£
		Inventory materials	5,000

Inventory control account

	£		£
Payables	5,000		

Activity 2: Issuing materials – Bodger & Co

Inventory control account

	£		£
Payables	5,000	Production	5,000

Production control account

	£		£
Inventory	5,000		

Activity 3: Holding inventory

	✓
To avoid production stoppages due to a shortage of materials	✓
To take advantage of quantity discounts	✓
To avoid the detrimental effect of price fluctuations	✓
To provide a buffer or fail-safe in times of general shortage or heavy demand	✓

Activity 4: Inventory control levels

(a) Reorder level = (Average usage × Average lead time) + Inventory buffer

= (350 parts × 13 days) + 1,750

= 6,300 parts

(b) Minimum inventory reorder quantity = Average usage per day × Average lead time

= (350 parts × 13 days)

= 4,550 parts

(c) Maximum inventory reorder quantity = Maximum inventory level - inventory buffer

= 10,820 parts – 1,750 parts

= 9,070 parts

Activity 5: EOQ

$$EOQ = \sqrt{\frac{2 \times 32 \times 150 \times 12}{25 \times 0.18}} = \sqrt{\frac{115,200}{4.5}} = \sqrt{25,600} = \boxed{160 \text{ parts}}$$

Activity 6: CCS Ltd

(a) The highest reported profit would be arrived at by using FIFO. This is because the earliest inventory with the lower costs are assumed to be issued first. This results in a lower cost of sales and therefore a higher profit.

(b) Inventory record card for potatoes

Date	Receipts Quantity tonnes	Cost per tonne £	Total cost £	Issues Quantity tonnes	Cost per tonne £	Total cost £	Balance Quantity tonnes	Total cost £
Balance as at: 1 June							72	10,512
2 June	70	150.00	10,500				142	21,012
3 June				90	72 at £146.00 18 at £150.00	13,212	52	7,800
4 June	50	152.00	7,600				102	15,400
5 June				70	52 at £150.00 18 at £152.00	10,536	32	4,864

Activity 7: Closing work in progress

Cost per EU £ 15

Closing WIP £ 8,100

Total production cost = £30,000 + £20,000 + £10,000 = £60,000.

WIP equivalent units = 900 units × 60% = 540 units

Cost per equivalent unit = £60,000 / (3,460 + 540) = £15

The closing WIP value = 540 × £15 = £8,100

Activity 8: Overtime premium

Basic pay   £   120.00

Overtime premium   £   7.50

Mark's total wage   £   127.50   for the day

			£	
Basic pay	=	8 hours @ £15	120.00	(direct cost)
Overtime premium	=	1 hour @ ½ × £15	7.50	(indirect cost)
			127.50	

Activity 9: Job 146

Basic pay   £   315,000

Overtime premium   £   57,750

Direct labour cost of Job 146 is   £   372,750

		£
Basic pay	= 45,000 hours @ £7	315,000
Overtime premium	= 33,000 hours @ 25% × £7	57,750
Total direct labour cost		372,750

Activity 10: Component C

Cost at normal rate:	5,000 hours @ £10	=	£50,000
	2,000 hours @ £10	=	£20,000
	1,000 hours @ £10	=	£10,000
			£80,000
Cost at time and a half:	2,000 hours @ £10 × 0.5	=	£10,000
Cost at double time:	1,000 hours @ £10 × 1	=	£10,000
(a) **Total cost of direct labour**		=	£100,000

(b)   **Cost per unit** = $\dfrac{£100,000}{500,000\,\text{units}}$ = 20p per unit

CHAPTER 4 Allocation and apportionment

Activity 1: Allocation

Cost	
Wages of the supervisor of department A	Allocate to department A
Wages of the supervisor of department B	Allocate to department B
Indirect materials consumed in department A	Allocate to department A
Rent of the factory shared by departments A and B	Cannot be allocated

Both the wages of the supervisor of department A and the materials consumed by department A can be charged to the cost centre department A because they relate to that cost centre only.

The wages of the supervisor of department B can be charged to the cost centre department B because they relate to that cost centre only.

The cost of rent relates to both of the cost centres so it would be unfair to charge the cost to one of the cost centres only. Instead we need to charge a fair share of the cost of rent to both cost centres. This is called apportionment.

Activity 2: Apportionment bases

Cost	Basis of apportionment
Rent, rates and insurance	Floor space (square metres)
Light, heat and power	Floor space (square metres)
Depreciation charge of machinery	Carrying amount
Canteen costs	Number of employees

Activity 3: Allocation and apportionment basis

Overhead	Basis of apportionment
Rent/rates	Floor area
Depreciation	NBV or cost of equipment
Staff canteen costs	Number of employees
Heat, light	Volume of space occupied/floor area
Insurance of equipment	Value of equipment insured
Stores costs	Allocate to stores cost centre

Activity 4: Overhead apportionment

Allocation and apportionment

	Total £	Processing dept £	Packing dept £	Canteen £
Canteen	18,000	–	–	18,000
Processing dept supervisor	15,000	15,000	–	–
Packing dept supervisor	10,000	–	10,000	–

	Total £	Processing dept £	Packing dept £	Canteen £
Rent (50:25:5)	20,000	12,500	6,250	1,250
Heat (50:25:5)	5,040	3,150	1,575	315
Depreciation (3:3:1)	7,000	3,000	3,000	1,000
Welfare (5:4:1)	5,000	2,500	2,000	500
Total	80,040	36,150	22,825	21,065

Activity 5: Overhead reapportionment – direct method

Reapportionment – inter-service centre work is ignored here.

Direct method

	Production depts		Service centres		
	X £	Y £	Stores £	Maintenance £	General admin overheads £
Overheads	70,000	30,000	20,000	15,000	6,000
Reapportion Stores (62.5% and 37.5%)	12,500	7,500	(20,000)		
Reapportion Maintenance (8,000/15,000) and (7,000 / 15,000)	8,000	7,000		(15,000)	
Reapportion General admin overheads (50:50)	3,000	3,000			(6,000)
Total	93,500	47,500			

Activity 6: Overhead reapportionment – step down method

Step-down method – inter-service work is taken into account in the first step only.

	Production Depts		Service Centre	
	X £	Y £	Stores £	Canteen £
Allocated overhead	70,000	30,000	20,000	15,000
Apportion stores (50:30:20)	10,000	6,000	(20,000)	4,000
			–	19,000
Apportion canteen (45:50)	9,000	10,000	–	(19,000)
Total	89,000	46,000	–	–

CHAPTER 5 Absorption costing

Activity 1: Overhead absorption bases

	Mixing	Stirring
Direct labour hours	20,000	5,000
Direct machine hours	2,000	60,000

Mixing department: OAR should be based on | Budgeted direct labour hours |

Stirring department: OAR should be based on | Budgeted direct machine hours |

As we can see from the table, the mixing department has a higher proportion of labour hours than machine hours meaning it is labour intensive and therefore labour hours would be an appropriate basis for absorption. The stirring department has a higher proportion of machine hours compared to labour hours meaning it is machine intensive and therefore machine hours would be an appropriate basis for absorption.

Activity 2: Overhead absorption rates (OAR) 1

Budgeted OAR = Budgeted overheads / budgeted machine hours

Budgeted OAR = £40,000 / 2,000 = £20 per machine hour

Activity 3: Overhead absorption rates (OAR) 2

As units are not identical the units basis of absorption is not appropriate.

The Mixing department is labour intensive, therefore a suitable

$$OAR = \frac{£10,000}{20,000 \text{ labour hours}} = 50p \text{ per labour hour}$$

The Stirring department is machine intensive, therefore a suitable

$$OAR = \frac{£15,000}{60,000 \text{ machine hours}} = 25p \text{ per machine hour}$$

Activity 4: Overhead absorption rates in the service sector

OAR = £130,000/325,000 miles = 40p per mile

Activity 5: Overhead absorption rates (OAR) 3

(a) $$OAR = \frac{Budgeted overheads}{Budgeted direct labour hours} = \frac{£400,000}{3,200 \text{ hours}}$$

$$= £125 \text{ per labour hour}$$

(b) $$OAR = \frac{Budgeted overheads}{Budgeted machine hours} = \frac{£400,000}{10,000 \text{ hours}}$$

$$= £40 \text{ per machine hour}$$

(c) As the painting division is machine intensive a machine hour based OAR is more appropriate for calculations (£40 per machine hour).

(d) Absorbed overheads = £40 × 12,562 machine hours

$$= £502,480$$

Overheads actually incurred   = £521,262

Therefore, overheads were under-absorbed by £521,362 – £502,480 = £18,782.

Activity 6: Over- and under-absorption

(a)   Fixed overheads absorbed in Assembly department

775 actual machine hours × £10 = overheads absorbed of £7,750

(b)   Fixed overheads absorbed in Finishing department

1,250 direct labour hours × £7.50 = overheads absorbed of £9,375

(c)   (i)   Under-absorption in Assembly department

Overheads absorbed   <   Actual overheads
£7,750   £8,110

There is an under-absorption of (£8,110 – £7,750) = £360

(ii)   Over-absorption in Finishing department

Overheads absorbed   >   Actual overheads
£9,375   £9,000

There is an over-absorption of £375.

Activity 7: Mars Ltd

	£	£
Direct costs		
Materials		5.00
Labour		
Mixing (2.0 × £8.60)		17.20
Stirring (0.5 × £8.60)		4.30
Total direct costs		26.50
Overheads		
Mixing department (2.0 × £0.50)	1.00	
Stirring department (6.0 × £0.25)	1.50	
Total overheads		2.50
Total cost		29.00

Activity 8: Recording production overheads – Bodger & Co

Payables control account

	£		£
		Inventory materials	5,000
		Production overheads	6,000

Production overheads control account

	£		£
Payables	6,000	Overheads absorbed:	
		Manufacturing dept	4,000
		Finishing dept	600
		Quality control	500
		Statement of profit or loss	900
	6,000		6,000

Production control

	£		£
Inventory materials	5,000		
Production overheads absorbed (mfg, finishing & quality control)	5,100		

Activity 9: Activity-based costing

(a)

$\dfrac{\text{Set - up costs}}{\text{Number of production runs}}$	$\dfrac{£5,250}{21}$	=	£250	per production run
$\dfrac{\text{Stores receiving}}{\text{Number of requistions raised}}$	$\dfrac{£3,600}{80}$	=	£45	per requisition raised
$\dfrac{\text{Inspection / quality control}}{\text{Number of production runs}}$	$\dfrac{£2,100}{21}$	=	£100	per production run
$\dfrac{\text{Materials handling and despatch}}{\text{Number of orders executed}}$	$\dfrac{£4,620}{42}$	=	£110	per order executed

(b)

	P1	P2	P3	P4
Number of production runs	6	5	4	6
Cost per production run	£250	£250	£250	£250
Set-up costs per product	£1,500	£1,250	£1,000	£1,500

	P1	P2	P3	P4
Number of requisitions raised	20	20	20	20
Cost per requisition raised	£45	£45	£45	£45
Stores receiving costs per product	£900	£900	£900	£900

	P1	P2	P3	P4
Number of production runs	6	5	4	6
Cost per production run	£100	£100	£100	£100
Inspection/quality control costs per product	£600	£500	£400	£600

	P1	P2	P3	P4
Number of orders executed	12	10	8	12
Cost per order executed	£110	£110	£110	£110
Materials handling and despatch per product	£1,320	£1,100	£880	£1,320

(c)

	P1 £	P2 £	P3 £	P4 £
Direct material	4,800	5,000	2,400	7,200
Direct labour	3,360	2,100	1,120	2,520
Production overhead				
Set-up costs	1,500	1,250	1,000	1,500
Stores receiving	900	900	900	900
Inspection/quality control	600	500	400	600
Material handling and despatch	1,320	1,100	880	1,320
Total cost	12,480	10,850	6,700	14,040
Unit costs	(÷ 120) £104	(÷ 100) £108.50	(÷ 80) £83.75	(÷ 120) £117

CHAPTER 6 Job, batch and service costing

Activity 1: Job 4321

			Job 4321	
			£	£
Direct materials: department	A		4,000	
	B		1,000	
	C		1,500	
				6,500
Direct labour: department	A		1,800	
	B		1,600	
	C		2,000	
				5,400
Fixed production overhead:	900 hrs × £5			4,500
Total production cost				16,400
Fixed administration overhead: 80% × £16,400				13,120
Total cost				29,520
	Profit 20% × £29,520			5,904
Selling price				35,424

Activity 2: Splodge Ltd

Job 08/10/04 No 111	Workings	£
Materials – bricks		
– Issued	40 kg @ £5.00	200.00
– Issued for rework	10 kg @ £5.00	50.00
Labour		
• Louis		
– Basic hours	4 hrs @ £8.00	32.00
– Overtime premium	2 hrs @ £16.00	32.00
• Ben		
– Basic hours	3 hrs @ £8.50	25.50
– Reworked hours	3 hrs @ £8.50	25.50
Total direct cost		365.00
Overheads (£200 per job)		200.00
Total job cost		565.00

Activity 3: Waste

	Kgs
Normal loss	400
Abnormal loss	100
Cost per kg	£0.25

Normal loss = 2,000 kg × 20% = 400 kg

Actual loss = 2,000 kg - 1,500 kg = 500 kg

Therefore abnormal loss = 500 kg – 400 kg = 100 kg

$$\text{Cost per 'good' kg} = \frac{\text{Total costs - scrap proceeds from normal loss}}{\text{Unit input - normal loss units}}$$

= (£400 – £0) / (2,000 kg – 400 kg) = £0.25

CHAPTER 7 Standard costing and budgeting

Activity 1: Latt

Unit	Quantity	Cost per unit	Total unit cost
Material	3 kg	5.00	15.00
Labour	2 hours	7.00	14.00
Fixed overheads*			10.00
Total			39.00

*£50,000 / 5,000 units = £10 per unit

Activity 2: Production budget

The correct answer is: 3,504 units

Workings

	Units
Sales	3,500
Less opening inventories of finished goods	(800)
Add closing inventories of finished goods	600
Production quantity	3,300
Anticipated defective units 3,300 × 5/95	174
Required production	3,504

Activity 3: Material usage budget

The correct answer is: 85,556 kg

		Kg
Kg required for production	5 × 15,400	77,000
Additional for wastage	77,000 × 10/90	8,556
Required usage	15,400 × 5 × 100/90	85,556

Activity 4: Materials purchases budget

The correct answer is: £ 327,860

	Litres
Materials usage	124,000
Less opening inventory	(14,000)
Add closing inventory 14,000 × 1.15	16,100
Materials purchases	126,100
Cost of purchases 126,100 × £2.60 = £327,680	

BPP
LEARNING
MEDIA

Activity 5: Country soups

Cans made		350,000 £	400,000 £	450,000 £
Cost element	Cost			
Direct materials	10p per can	35,000	40,000	45,000
Direct labour	8p per can	28,000	32,000	36,000
Canning costs	2p per can	7,000	8,000	9,000
Depreciation	£16,000	16,000	16,000	16,000
Rent and rates	£28,000	28,000	28,000	28,000
Other overheads	£36,000	36,000	36,000	36,000
Total cost (£)		150,000	160,000	170,000
Cost per can (£)		0.429	0.400	0.378

Activity 6: Charter flights

Likely miles	5,000 £000	6,000 £000	7,000 £000
Sales revenue	2,500	2,950	3,400
Variable/semi-variable costs:			
Aviation fuel	400	480	560
Landing and servicing fees	850	900	950
Other variable overheads	135	162	189
Fixed costs:			
Wages and salaries	420	420	420
Other fixed overheads	625	625	625
Total cost	2,430	2,587	2,744
Total profit	70	363	656
	£	£	£
Profit per mile flown	14.00	60.50	93.71

Workings

Sales revenues £2,500 + (0.45 × 1,000 miles) = £2,950;

£2,500 + (0.45 × 2,000 miles) = £3,400

Landing & servicing fees = £600 + (0.05 × 6,000 miles) = £900;

£600 + (0.05 × 7,000 miles) = £950

Activity 7: TV dinners

Batches made and sold	5,000 £	6,000 £	7,000 £
Sales revenue	30,000	36,000	42,000
Costs:			
Direct materials	1,250	1,500	1,750
Direct labour	3,000	3,600	4,200
Overheads			
Variable element	7,500	9,000	10,500
Fixed element	8,800	8,800	8,800
Total Cost	20,550	22,900	25,250
Total profit	9,450	13,100	16,750
Profit per batch	1.890	2.183	2.393

Workings

Variable cost per unit = $\dfrac{£20,800 - £16,300}{8,000 - 5,000\,\text{units}}$ = £1.50 per unit

Fixed cost = £20,800 − (£1.50 × 8,000 units) = £8,800

CHAPTER 8 Variance analysis

Activity 1: Protec Ltd

	Flexed budget	Actual	Variance	Favourable F or Adverse A
Volume sold	100,000	100,000	–	
	£000	**£000**	**£000**	
Sales revenue	3,000	5,400	2,400	F
Less costs:				
Direct materials	525	795	270	A
Direct labour	600	720	120	A
Fixed overheads	1,470	1,842	372	A
Operating profit	405	2,043	1,638	F

The flexed budget is the same as original budget because the volume produced and sold is the same for budget and actual.

Activity 2: Zetec Ltd

	Flexed budget	Actual	Variance	Favourable F or Adverse A
Volume sold	12,350	12,350	–	
	£	**£**	**£**	
Sales revenue	370,500	407,550	37,050	F
Less costs:				
Direct materials	61,750	53,000	8,750	F
Direct labour	49,400	49,000	400	F
Overheads	110,000	178,000	68,000	A
Operating profit	149,350	127,550	21,800	A

Workings

Sales revenue

Budgeted sales price per unit = £300,000/10,000 units = £30 per unit

So, 12,350 units of revenue should have been 12,350 × £30 = £370,500

Direct materials

Budgeted material cost per unit = £50,000/10,000 = £5 per unit

So, 12,350 units of material should have cost 12,350 × £5 = £61,750

Direct labour

Budgeted labour cost per unit = £40,000/10,000 = £4 per unit

So, 12,350 units of material should have cost 12,350 × £4 = £49,400

Fixed overheads

Fixed overheads do not change as volume/activity changes. But actual fixed overheads have changed to £110,000.

Operating profit

Operating profit = £370,500 – £61,750 – £49,400 – £110,000 = £149,350

CHAPTER 9 Marginal costing

Activity 1: Contribution

	J	K	L
Sales price	10.00	5.00	3.00
Less: all variable costs:			
Materials	(3.00)	(2.50)	(0.50)
Labour	(1.00)	(1.50)	(1.25)
Sales	(0.25)	(0.15)	(0.30)
Overheads	(0.75)	(0.10)	(0.25)
Contribution/unit	5.00	0.75	0.70

Activity 2: Unit cost

(a)

Absorption costing – unit cost	£
Direct material	3.40
Direct labour	6.80
Variable overhead	1.20
Prime cost	11.40
Fixed overhead ((£340,000/100,000) × 2)	6.80
Absorption cost	18.20

(b)

Marginal costing – unit cost	£
Direct material	3.40
Direct labour	6.80
Variable overhead	1.20
Marginal cost	11.40

Activity 3: MC vs AC cost per unit

(a)

Marginal costing	£
Direct materials	£12.00
Direct labour	£13.50
Variable overheads per unit =	
£88,000/11,000 units	£8.00
Total variable (marginal cost)	£33.50

(b)

Full absorption costing	£
Total variable cost	£33.50
Add: Overhead absorption rate	
£110,000/11,000 units	£10.00
Full product cost	£43.50

Activity 4: Marginal costing profit statement

	Standard £	Vegetarian £	Total £
Selling price per meal	$\dfrac{£1,040,000}{130,000} = £8.00$	$\dfrac{£1,500,000}{200,000} = £7.50$	
Less: variable costs per meal			
Direct materials	$\dfrac{£468,000}{130,000} = £3.60$	$\dfrac{£600,000}{200,000} = £3.00$	
Direct labour	£2.00	£2.00	
Variable overheads	£2.00	£1.50	
Contribution per unit	£0.40	£1.00	
Sales volume (units)	130,000	200,000	
Total contribution	£52,000	£200,000	£252,000
Less: fixed costs			£212,000
Budgeted profit or loss			£40,000

Activity 5: MC v AC

(a)

	£
Selling price/unit	12
Prime cost/unit	4
Variable production cost/unit	3
Marginal cost (MC)/unit	7
= Contribution/unit	5

(b)

	£
Selling price/unit	12
Marginal cost/unit	7
Fixed production cost/unit (30,000/15,000 units)	2
FAC cost/unit	9
= Profit/unit	3

(c)

	£	£
Sales (12,000 units at £12)		144,000
Opening inventory (2,000 units at £7)	14,000	
Variable production costs (15,000 units at £7)	105,000	
Closing inventory (5,000 units at £7)	(35,000)	
Cost of sales (MC basis)		(84,000)
Contribution		60,000
Fixed costs		(30,000)
Profit		30,000

(d)

	£	£
Sales (12,000 units at £12)		144,000
Less: cost of sales		
Opening inventory (2,000 units at £9)	18,000	
Production costs (15,000 units at £9)	135,000	
Closing inventory (5,000 units at £9)	(45,000)	
Cost of sales (FAC basis)		(108,000)
Profit		36,000

(e) The two profit figures differ by **£6,000** because under FAC the **increase** in the valuation of inventory during the month is **higher** than the **increase** under MC.

This is because fixed overhead cost has been carried forward in the statement of financial position in the inventory valuation as an asset under FAC principles, but written off against profit under MC principles.

CHAPTER 10 Short-term decision making

Activity 1: Breakeven units

Breakeven point $= \dfrac{£360,000}{£28 - £19}$

$= \boxed{40,000}$ units

Activity 2: Breakeven revenue

BEP in units $= \boxed{3,800}$ units

Breakeven revenue $= \boxed{£ \quad 30,400}$

$$BEP = \frac{Fixed\,costs}{Unit\,contribution}$$

First we need to find the fixed and variable costs and the unit contribution

	Output Units	Total costs £
High	8,000	57,700
Low	6,000	44,700
Difference	2,000	13,000

Variable cost per unit = £13,000/2,000

$= £6.50$

Substituting in high volume

	£
Total cost	57,700
Variable cost (8,000 × £6.50)	52,000
Fixed costs (balance)	5,700

Unit contribution = Selling price − Variable cost = £8.00 − £6.50

$= £1.50$

$$BEP = \frac{Fixed\,costs}{Unit\,contribution}$$

$= \dfrac{£5,700}{£1.50} = \underline{3,800\ units}$

Breakeven revenue = BEP × selling price

= 3,800 × £8

= £30,400

Activity 3: Profit volume ratio

$$\text{PV ratio} = \frac{\text{Contribution}}{\text{Sales}} = \frac{£1.50}{£8} = 0.1875 = \boxed{18.75} \%$$

$$\text{BE Revenue} = \frac{\text{Fixed costs}}{\text{PV ratio}} = \frac{£5,700}{0.1875} = £ \boxed{30,400}$$

Unit contribution = Selling price − Variable cost = £10.00 − £6.50

$$= £3.50$$

$$\text{PV ratio} = \frac{\text{Contribution}}{\text{Sales}} = \frac{£3.50}{£10.00} = 0.35 = \boxed{35} \%$$

✓ Revised selling price and fixed cost

The revised selling price and fixed cost has a higher PV ratio

Activity 4: Margin of safety

Margin of safety in units = Budgeted sales volume − Breakeven sales volume

$$= 5,000 \text{ units} - 3,800 \text{ units} = \boxed{1,200} \text{ units}$$

$$\text{Margin of safety} = \frac{\text{Budgeted sales volume} - \text{BE sales volume}}{\text{Budgeted sales volume}} \times 100\%$$

$$= \frac{5,000 - 3,800}{5,000} \times 100\%$$

$$= \boxed{24} \%$$

In other words, sales could fall by up to 24% compared to budget before we would start to make a loss.

Activity 5: Target profit level

$$\text{Sales volume to achieve target profit} = \frac{\text{Fixed costs} + \text{Required profit}}{\text{Unit contribution}}$$

$$= \frac{£5,700 + £10,000}{£1.50}$$

$$= \boxed{10,467} \text{ units}$$

CHAPTER 11 Cash management

Activity 1: Differences between cash flow and profit

(a) **Bank overdraft.** Cash may be obtained from a transaction which has nothing to do with profit or loss. For example, an increase in bank overdraft provides a source of cash for payments, but it is not reported in the statement of profit or loss.

(b) **Purchase of new non-current asset.** Cash may be paid for the purchase of non-current assets, but the charge in the statement of profit or loss is depreciation which is only part of an asset's cost.

(c) **Goods sold on credit.** The statement of profit or loss reports the total value of sales in a year. If goods are sold on credit, the cash receipts will differ from the value of sales.

(d) **Materials bought on credit.** Similarly, the statement of profit or loss reports the cost of goods sold during the year. However, if materials are bought on credit, the cash payments to suppliers will be different from the value of materials purchased.

You were only asked for four differences but another difference that you may have thought of, is that cash may be paid for something which has nothing to do with profit or loss. For example, the repayment of the capital element of a loan will affect cash only. It is the interest element of a repayment that will affect the profit (as well as cash).

Activity 2: Reconciling profit to cash

Profit	Add ✓	Deduct ✓
Drawings by owner		✓
Receipt for the sale of a non-current asset	✓	
Depreciation	✓	
Loan repayment		✓
Receipt of a loan	✓	

Activity 3: Lagged receipts

	January £	February £	March £
Cash received from invoices issued in:			
January	0	75% × 125,000 = 93,750	125,000 – 93,750 = 31,250
February	0	0	75% × 150,000 = 112,500
March	0	0	0
Total receipts from sales	0	93,750	143,750

Activity 4: Lagged payments

	January £	February £	March £
Payments for purchases	45,000	0	65,000

Activity 5: Cash on disposal of non-current assets

	✓
£21,500	
£56,500	
£70,000	
£91,500	✓

Working

Original cost	£105,000
Accumulated depreciation	– £48,500
Carrying value	£56,500
Profit on disposal	+ £35,000
Cash received on disposal of building	= £91,500

Activity 6: A simple cash budget

	October £	November £	December £
Cash receipts			
Loan		10,000	
Receivables	0	3,000	6,000
Total receipts	0	13,000	6,000
Cash payments			
Non-current asset	(8,000)		
Payables	(5,000)	(2,000)	(4,000)
Running expenses	(1,600)	(1,600)	(1,600)
Loan repayment			(250)
Drawings	(1,000)	(1,000)	(1,000)
Total payments	(15,600)	(4,600)	(6,850)
Net payments	(15,600)	8,400	(850)
Opening balance	15,000	(600)	7,800
Closing balance	(600)	7,800	6,950

Activity 7: Liquid and non-liquid assets

	Liquid assets	Non-liquid assets
Notes and coins	✓	
Receivables	✓	
Property		✓
Inventory		✓
Bank balance	✓	

The liquidity of receivables and inventory is variable; they cannot always be converted quickly to cash.

Activity 8: Working capital cycle

Average collection period	$\dfrac{172,800}{864,000}$	× 365	= 73.0 days
Inventory days	$\dfrac{270,000}{756,000}$	× 365	= 130.4 days
Average payables period	$\dfrac{86,400}{518,400}$	× 365	= 60.8 days

Cash operating cycle = 142.6 days

Activity 9: Reducing the working capital cycle

	Increase ✓	Decrease ✓
Inventory turnover		✓
Receivables' days		✓
Payables' days	✓	

Activity 10: Working capital cycle changes

(i)

	Increase ✓	Decrease ✓
Will this increase or decrease the working capital cycle of the business?	✓	

The changes will lengthen the cash operating cycle by two days. (The positive effect of the three days' reduction in inventory holding period is outweighed by the need to pay the suppliers five days earlier to obtain the discount.)

(ii)

	Days
Inventory holding period	27
Trade receivables collection period	46
Trade payables payment period	(35)
Working capital cycle	38

(iii)

	Days
Inventory holding period	24
Trade receivables collection period	46
Trade payables payment period	(30)
Working capital cycle	40

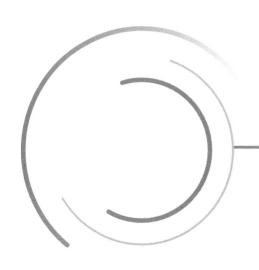

Test your learning:
Answers

CHAPTER 1 Introduction to management accounting

1 ☑ A unit of product or service in relation to which costs are ascertained

This is the definition of a cost unit.

The hour of operation and the unit of electricity are both examples of cost units for which costs have been ascertained.

A measure of work output in a standard hour is an example of a particular cost unit which may be used for control purposes. It is not a definition of the term 'cost unit'.

2 ☑ It is used as part of the planning process and represents what the organisation wants to achieve.

☑ It is used as a control mechanism by highlighting departures from budgeted figures.

The purpose of budgeting is to help with planning and control. A budget provides a quantified plan of action, and aids control when actual results are compared with the budget.

3 The three main functions of management are planning, control and decision making.

CHAPTER 2 Cost classification and cost behaviour

1

	Capital	Revenue
A new telephone system. This will be used within the business for several accounting periods. All the associated costs of installation can be capitalised.	✓	
Depreciation of vehicles. Depreciation can be thought of as the way in which part of a capital cost is converted to a revenue expense.		✓
Salesperson's car. A company car is used by the salesperson to obtain benefits for the business in the form of sales.	✓	
Road fund licence for delivery van. Although the van is a capital item, the road fund licence is a revenue expense of running the van.		✓
Telephone bill. The bill for rental and calls on the telephone system is a revenue expense.		✓
Computer software costing £10,000. Another example of something that is used by the business to bring benefits. The software might be used for the main business activity, such as in design of buildings by an architect, or in the processing of information necessary to administer the business.	✓	
Repairs to the Managing Director's company car after an accident. This will not improve the earnings capacity of the car; it just restores it to what it was before.		✓

2

		Cost behaviour	
		Does fit the graph shape	Does NOT fit the graph shape
(a)	Plastic used in the manufacture of moulded plastic furniture. A bulk-buying discount is given at point A on the graph.		✓
(b)	Straight-line depreciation of a freehold factory. A new factory is bought at point A.	✓	
(c)	Rent of a warehouse. A further warehouse is rented at point A.	✓	
(d)	Electricity costs that have a standing charge and a cost per unit of power used. At point A the level of production reaches the point where a night shift is required, which uses electricity at a cheaper rate.		✓

Explanation

(a) This is a variable cost. The bulk purchase discount would give a one-off kink in the graph at point A. The graph would appear as shown below.

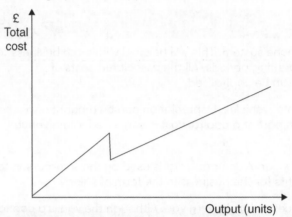

(b) and (c) are both stepped costs and will fit the graph shape.

(d) This is a semi-variable cost. At point A, where the cheaper rate of electricity kicks in, the graph will flatten as each unit of product will cost slightly less in electricity. This is illustrated in the graph below.

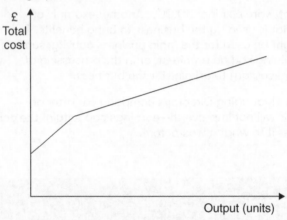

3   Total cost at 12,000 units   £   28,500

Workings

Output	Units	Total cost £
Highest	13,500	31,500
Lowest	6,500	17,500
High–low	7,000	14,000

$$\text{Variable cost per unit} = \frac{\text{High cost - Low cost}}{\text{High output - Low output}}$$

$$= \frac{£14,000}{7,000}$$

$$= £2$$

At 6,500 units

	£
Total cost	17,500
Less variable cost (6,500 × £2)	13,000
= fixed cost	4,500

Using the fixed cost of £4,500, and the variable cost of £2 per unit, we can now estimate the total cost at 12,000 units:

	£
Fixed cost	4,500
Add variable cost (12,000 × £2)	24,000
Total cost	28,500

4

Cost card: Filing cabinet	£
Direct materials (3.80 + 1.80 + 0.90)	6.50
Direct labour	6.70
Prime cost	13.20
Production overheads (0.30 + 0.20)	0.50
Production cost	13.70
Non-production overheads	
– Selling and distribution	3.00
Total cost	16.70

5 ☑ Be constant per unit of output

Variable costs are conventionally deemed to increase or decrease in direct proportion to changes in output. Therefore the correct answer is 'be constant per unit of output'. 'Vary per unit of output as production volume changes' and 'vary, in total, from period to period when production is constant' imply a changing unit rate, which does not comply with this convention. 'Be constant in total when production volume changes' relates to a fixed cost.

6 ☑ Electricity bills made up of a standing charge and a variable charge

The depicted cost has a basic fixed element which is payable even at zero activity. A variable element is then added at a constant rate as activity increases. Therefore the correct answer is 'Electricity bills made up of a standing charge and a variable charge'.

Graphs for the other options would look like this.

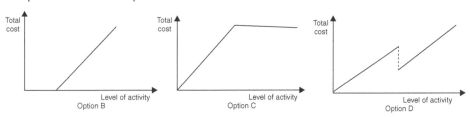

7 ☑ Graph 2

The cost described consists of a fixed amount up to a certain level of activity. This will be represented by a straight, horizontal line. At a certain point a variable element is added and the cost line will slope upwards at a constant rate. Graph 2 demonstrates this pattern, therefore the correct answer is Graph 2.

If you selected Graph 4, you had the right idea for the second part of the graph. However, Graph 4 depicts zero cost up to a certain level, which is not correct.

8 ☑ Graph 1

The cost described will increase in steps, remaining fixed at each step until another supervisor is required. Graph 1 depicts a step cost.

9 ☑ Graph 3

The cost described begins as a linear variable cost, increasing at a constant rate in line with activity. At a certain point the cost becomes fixed regardless of the level of activity. Graph 3 demonstrates this behaviour pattern.

10 ☑ A semi-variable cost

The salary is part fixed (£650 per month) and part variable (5 pence per unit). Therefore it is a semi-variable cost.

If you chose a variable cost or a fixed cost you were considering only part of the cost.

The option 'a stepped cost' involves a cost which remains constant up to a certain level and then increases to a new, higher, constant fixed cost.

11 ☑ The total of direct costs

Prime cost is the total of direct materials, direct labour and direct expenses.

All costs incurred in manufacturing a product describes total production cost. The material cost of a product is only a part of prime cost. The cost of operating a department is an overhead or indirect cost.

12 ☑ Cost of transporting raw materials from the supplier's premises

Cost of transporting raw materials from the supplier's premises is a part of the cost of direct materials.

Wages of factory workers engaged in machine maintenance and cost of indirect production materials are production overheads. Depreciation of lorries used for deliveries to customers is a selling and distribution expense.

13 ☑ The cost of special designs, drawing or layouts

☑ The hire of tools or equipment for a particular job

Special designs and the hire of tools for a particular job can be traced to a specific cost unit. Therefore they are direct expenses.

Salesperson's wages is a selling and distribution overhead and rent, rates and insurance of a factory describes production overheads.

CHAPTER 3 Materials and labour costs

1   (a)   FIFO

	Inventory record card							
	Purchases			**Requisitions**			**Balance**	
Date	**Quantity kg**	**Cost £**	**Total cost £**	**Quantity kg**	**Cost £**	**Total cost £**	**Quantity kg**	**Total cost £**
3 Jan							100	880
16 Jan	400	9.00	3,600				500	4,480
27 Jan				100	8.80	880		
				150	9.00	1,350		
				250		2,230	250	2,250
5 Feb				180	9.00	1,620	70	630
9 Feb	400	9.30	3,720				470	4,350
17 Feb				70	9.00	630		
				350	9.30	3,255		
				420		3,885	50	465
25 Feb	500	9.35	4,675				550	5,140

Cost of material issues = £2,230 + £1,620 + £3,885
                         = £7,735

Value of closing inventory   = £5,140

   (b)   AVCO

	Inventory record card							
	Purchases			**Requisitions**			**Balance**	
Date	**Quantity kg**	**Cost £**	**Total cost £**	**Quantity kg**	**Cost £**	**Total cost £**	**Quantity kg**	**Total cost £**
3 Jan							100	880.00
16 Jan	400	9.00	3,600				500	4,480.00
27 Jan				250	8.96	2,240	250	2,240.00
5 Feb				180	8.96	1,612.80	70	627.20
9 Feb	400	9.30	3,720				470	4,347.20
17 Feb				420	9.25	3,885	50	462.20
25 Feb	500	9.35	4,675				550	5,137.20

Cost of material issues = £2,240.00 + £1,612.80 + £3,885.00
                         = £7,737.80

Value of closing inventory = £5,137.20

2   Inventory control account

		£			£
1 Mar	Opening balance	12,400	31 Mar	Production	160,400
31 Mar	Bank/payables	167,200	31 Mar	Production o/h control	8,300
			31 Mar	Closing balance	10,900
		179,600			179,600

Production control account

		£			£
31 Mar	Inventory control	160,400			

Production overhead control account

		£			£
31 Mar	Inventory control	8,300			

3    $EOQ = \sqrt{\dfrac{2C_oD}{C_H}}$

$$= \sqrt{\dfrac{2 \times £50 \times (15 \times 52)}{£19.65}}$$

$$= \sqrt{3,969}$$

$$= 63 \text{ rolls}$$

4   Reorder level = (average usage × average lead time) + buffer inventory
                         = (175 litres per day × 6 days) + 550
                         = 1,600 litres

5   Using the FIFO method, the total value of the issues on 30 April is

£	2,765

Date	Receipts Units	Issues Units	Balance	£
1 April			275 @ £3.20	880
8 April	600		600 @ £3.00	1,800
15 April	400		400 @ £3.40	1,360
				4,040
30 April		900		£
		275 @ £3.20	=	880
		600 @ £3.00	=	1,800
		25 @ £3.40	=	85
				2,765

6   Using the weighted average price method of inventory valuation, the total value of the components remaining in inventory on 23 March was £ | 20,790

Average price of inventory on 23 March:

Units		£
2,400	× £6.00	14,400
4,000	× £6.20	24,800
2,000	× £6.86	13,720
8,400		52,920

Average price per component   = £52,920/8,400 = £6.30

Value of inventory on 23 March = (8,400 – 5,100) × £6.30

                                = £ | 20,790

7   Using the FIFO method of inventory valuation, the total value of the components issued on 23 March was £ | 37,140 | (to the nearest £)

The FIFO method uses the price of the oldest batches first:

		£
2,400	× £6.00	14,400
2,700	× £6.20	16,740
5,100		31,140

8   Direct labour cost = 40 hrs × £10 per hr = £400

Indirect labour cost = 5 hrs × £4 per hr = £20

Alternatively:
Direct cost   £
Basic pay (35 hrs × £10 per hr)   350
Overtime: at basic rate (5 hrs × £10 per hr)   50
                                                                          400

Indirect cost
Overtime: premium (5 hrs × £4 per hr)   20

9

✓	DEBIT	Production control account	£70,800	
	DEBIT	Production overhead control account	£2,000	
	CREDIT	Wages control account		£72,800

The overtime was not worked on any specific job and is therefore an indirect wages cost to be 'collected' in the overhead control account. The direct wages of £70,800 are debited to the production control account and the total wages cost is credited to the wages control account.

CHAPTER 4 Allocation and apportionment

1 ☑ Spread common costs over cost centres

Overhead apportionment involves sharing overhead costs as fairly as possible over a number of cost centres. Apportionment is used when it is not possible to allocate the whole cost to a single cost centre.

2 (a) Basis of apportionment

	Total £	Machine shop £	Assembly £	Painting £	Services £
Factory rent, rates and insurance (floor area) 5:2:3:2	9,000	3,750	1,500	2,250	1,500
Depreciation of machinery (value of machinery) 12:4:3:1	4,000	2,400	800	600	200
Supervisor's salary (number of employees) 8:9:5:2	8,000*	2,667	3,000	1,667	667
Heat and light (floor area) 5:2:3:2	2,000*	833	333	500	333
Apportionment to all departments	23,000	9,650	5,633	5,017	2,700

* there is a slight rounding difference here

(b) Reapportionment

	Total £	Machine shop £	Assembly £	Painting £	Services £
Reapportionment of services (40:30:30)	–	1,080	810	810	(2,700)
Total after reapportionment	23,000	10,730	6,443	5,827	Nil

3   (a)   Basis of apportionment

	Total £	V £	W £	S1 £	S2 £
Indirect materials	310,000	160,000	120,000	10,000	20,000
Indirect labour	1,125,000	400,000	650,000	40,000	35,000
Buildings depreciation and insurance (volume occupied) 60:30:8:2	100,000	60,000	30,000	8,000	2,000
Cleaning (volume occupied) 60:30:8:2	25,000	15,000	7,500	2,000	500
Machinery depreciation and insurance (value of machinery) 380:600:0:20	1,500,000	570,000	900,000	–	30,000
Supervision of production (supervisor hours) 15:20:0:0	70,000	30,000	40,000		
Power (% of power usage) 25:45:20:10	250,000	62,500	112,500	50,000	25,000
Heat and light (volume occupied) 60:30:8:2	20,000	12,000	6,000	1,600	400
Total after allocation and apportionment	3,400,000	1,309,500	1,866,000	111,600	112,900

(b)   Reapportionment

	Total £	V £	W £	S1 £	S2 £
(step-down					
method) S2 first					
40:50:10		45,160	56,450	11,290	(112,900)
				122,890	
S1 next 40:60		49,156	73,734	(122,890)	
Total after					
reapportionment	3,400,000	1,403,816	1,996,184	nil	nil

CHAPTER 5 Absorption costing

1   A   Overhead absorption rates are determined in advance for each period, usually based on budgeted data. Therefore statement (i) is correct and statement (iii) is incorrect. Overhead absorption rates are used in the final stage of overhead analysis, to absorb overheads into product costs. Therefore statement (ii) is correct. Statement (iv) is not correct because overheads are controlled using budgets and other management information. Therefore the correct answer is A.

2   A   Description B could lead to under-absorbed overheads if actual overheads far exceeded both budgeted overheads and the overhead absorbed. Description C could lead to under-absorbed overheads if budgeted overhead absorbed does not increase in line with actual overhead incurred. Description D could also lead to under-absorption if actual overhead does not decrease in line with absorbed overheads.

3   A   Budgeted overhead absorption rate $= \dfrac{£258,750}{11,250}$

= £23 per machine hour

	£
Overhead absorbed = £23 × 10,980 hours	252,540
Overhead incurred	254,692
Under-absorbed overhead	2,152

If you selected option B or C you calculated the difference between the budgeted and actual overheads and interpreted the result as an under- or over-absorption.

If you selected option D your calculations were correct but you misinterpreted the result as over-absorbed.

4   B   Overhead absorption rate $= \dfrac{\text{budgeted overheads}}{\text{budgeted labour hours}} = \dfrac{£148,750}{8,500}$

= £17.50 per hr

If you selected option A you divided the actual overheads by the budgeted labour hours. Option C is based on the actual overheads and actual labour hours. If you selected option D you divided the budgeted overheads by the actual hours.

5   D

	£
Overhead absorbed = £17.50 × 7,928	138,740
Overhead incurred	146,200
Under-absorbed overhead	7,460

If you selected options A or B you calculated the difference between the budgeted and actual overheads and interpreted it as an under- or over-absorption. If you selected option C you performed the calculations correctly but misinterpreted the result as an over-absorption.

CHAPTER 6 Job, batch and service costing

1

£	16,346.88

	£
Job costing schedule	
Materials	12,500.00
Direct labour – fitting 23 hours @ £8.60	197.80
– decorating 5 hours @ £6.50	32.50
Overheads 28 hours @ £12.40	347.20
Total costs	13,077.50
Profit 25% × 13,077.50	3,269.38
Cost to the customer	16,346.88

2

74.5	pence

	£
Ingredients	840.00
Labour 7 hours @ £6.50	45.50
Overheads 7 hours @ £1.20	8.40
	893.90

$$\text{Cost per pie} = \frac{£893.90}{1,200}$$
$$= 74.5 \text{ pence}$$

3 ✓ (i) and (iii) only

Cost per tonne–kilometre (i) is appropriate for cost control purposes because it combines the distance travelled and the load carried, both of which affect cost.

The fixed cost per kilometre (ii) is not particularly useful for control purposes because it varies with the number of kilometres travelled.

The maintenance cost of each vehicle per kilometre (iii) can be useful for control purposes because it focuses on a particular aspect of the cost of operating each vehicle.

The correct answer is therefore (i) and (iii) only.

4 ✓ An engineering company

All of the activities identified would use service costing, except the engineering company which will be providing products not services.

CHAPTER 7 Standard costing and budgeting

1

(a)

	Budget 4,000 units £	Actual 3,600 units £	Variance
Sales	96,000	90,000	6,000 Adv
Materials	18,000	15,120	2,880 Fav
Labour	27,200	25,200	2,000 Fav
Production overhead	5,700	5,900	200 Adv
Gross profit	45,100	43,780	1,320 Adv
General expenses	35,200	32,880	2,320 Fav
Operating profit	9,900	10,900	1,000 Fav

(b)

	Flexed budget 3,600 units £	Actual 3,600 units £	Variance
Sales 3,600 × £24.00	86,400	90,000	3,600 Fav
Materials 3,600 × £4.50	16,200	15,120	1,080 Fav
Labour 3,600 × £6.80	24,480	25,200	720 Adv
Production overhead	5,700	5,900	200 Adv
Gross profit	40,020	43,780	3,760 Fav
General expenses	35,200	32,880	2,320 Fav
Operating profit	4,820	10,900	6,080 Fav

2

	Flexed budget	Actual	Variance	Favourable F or Adverse A
Volume sold	72,000	72,000		
	£000	£000	£000	
Sales revenue	1,440	1,800	360	F
Less costs:				
Direct materials	252	265	13	A
Direct labour	288	240	48	F
Overheads	350	630	280	A
Operating profit	550	665	115	F

CHAPTER 8 Variance analysis

1

	Budget 200 units £	Budget per unit £	Flexed budget 230 units £	Actual 230 units £	Variance £ (A)/(F)
Sales	71,400	357	82,110	69,000	13,110 (A)
Variable costs					
Labour	31,600	158	36,340	27,000	9,340 (F)
Material	12,600	63	14,490	24,000	9,510 (A)
Fixed costs	18,900		18,900	10,000	8,900 (F)
Profit	8,300		12,380	8,000	4,380 (A)

CHAPTER 9 Marginal costing

1   (a)   Absorption costing – unit cost

	£
Direct materials	12.50
Direct labour assembly (4 × £8.40)	33.60
Finishing	6.60
Assembly overheads (£336,000/(60,000 × 4) × 4)	5.60
Finishing overheads (£84,000/60,000)	1.40
	59.70

   (b)   Marginal costing – unit cost

	£
Direct materials	12.50
Direct labour assembly (4 × £8.40)	33.60
Finishing	6.60
Assembly overheads $\dfrac{£336,000 \times 60\%}{240,000} \times 4$	3.36
Finishing overheads $\dfrac{£84,000 \times 75\%}{60,000}$	1.05
	57.11

CHAPTER 10 Short-term decision making

1   Breakeven point   = $\dfrac{£360,000}{£57 - £45}$

                                  = | 30,000 | units

      Margin of safety   = $\dfrac{38,000 - 30,000}{38,000} \times 100$

                                    = | 21% |

2   Target profit sales   = $\dfrac{£910,000 + £500,000}{£24 - £17}$

                                    = | 201,429 | units

3   Profit/volume ratio   = $\dfrac{£(40 - 32)}{£40} \times 100$

                                    =   20%

      Target profit sales revenue   = $\dfrac{£100,000 + £200,000}{0.20}$

                                    = | £ | 1,500,000 |

Alternatively (100,000 + 200,000)/8 = 37,500 units

37,500 units × £40 = £1,500,000

CHAPTER 11 Cash management

1   Although it is important for a business to **make a profit**, it can be argued that it is even more important for a business to **have a healthy cash balance** in order to be able to pay amounts when they are due.

2

	✓
Prepayment of rent	✓
Purchase of a non-current asset	✓
Purchases of inventory for cash	
Depreciation	✓
Cash sales	

3

	✓
30 days	
40 days	
54 days	✓
124 days	

Workings

Inventory holding period	=	$\dfrac{£68,000}{£593,000} \times 365$	=	42 days
Trade receivables' collection	=	$\dfrac{£102,000}{£790,000} \times 365$	=	47 days
Trade payables' payment	=	$\dfrac{£57,000}{£593,000} \times 365$	=	(35 days)
Cash operating cycle			=	54 days

4

	✓
25 days	
39 days	
46 days	✓
56 days	

Workings

	Days
Inventory holding period	21
Plus trade receivables' collection period	60
Less trade payables' payment period	(X)
Cash operating cycle	35

The trade payables' payment period in days is: 21+ 60 – 35 = 46 days.

5
- Cash in hand
- Bank current account
- Bank deposit account

6 Longer inventory holding period will result in more capital tied up in inventory and the business taking longer to convert inventory into cash.

CHAPTER 12   Spreadsheets

1 (a)   =D3/B3

  (b)   Click on the percentage icon

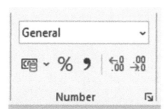

2   Select **Formulas** on the Ribbon then click **Show Formulas**.

3   Adding shading, adding borders, using different fonts and font sizes, presenting numbers as percentages or currency or to a certain number of decimal places.

4   =IF(logical test, value if true, value if false)

5 (a)   =Sum(B4:B5) or =B4+B5

  (b)   =Sum(B5:D5)

  (c)   =Sum(E4:E5) or =Sum(B6:D6) or, best of all, to check for errors:

         =IF(SUM(E4:E5)= Sum(B6:D6), Sum(B6:D6),"Error")

Glossary of terms

It is useful to be familiar with interchangeable terminology including IFRS and UK GAAP (generally accepted accounting principles).

Below is a short list of the most important terms you are likely to use or come across, together with their international and UK equivalents.

UK term	International term
Profit and loss account	Statement of profit or loss (or statement of profit or loss and other comprehensive income)
Turnover or Sales	Revenue or Sales revenue
Operating profit	Profit from operations
Reducing balance depreciation	Diminishing balance depreciation
Depreciation / depreciation expense(s)	Depreciation charge(s)
Balance sheet	Statement of financial position
Fixed assets	Non-current assets
Net book value	Carrying amount
Tangible assets	Property, plant and equipment
Stocks	Inventories
Trade debtors or Debtors	Trade receivables
Prepayments	Other receivables
Debtors and prepayments	Trade and other receivables
Cash at bank and in hand	Cash and cash equivalents
Long-term liabilities	Non-current liabilities
Trade creditors or creditors	Trade payables
Accruals	Other payables
Creditors and accruals	Trade and other payables
Capital and reserves	Equity (limited companies)
Profit and loss balance	Retained earnings
Cash flow statement	Statement of cash flows

Accountants often have a tendency to use several phrases to describe the same thing! Some of these are listed below:

Different terms for the same thing
Nominal ledger, main ledger or general ledger
Subsidiary ledgers, memorandum ledgers
Subsidiary (sales) ledger, sales ledger
Subsidiary (purchases) ledger, purchases ledger

Bibliography

International Accounting Standards Board. (2003) IAS 2 Inventories. In *International Financial Reporting Standards* (2003). Available from: http://eifrs.ifrs.org [Accessed 24 August 2021]

Index